STUDIEN
ZUR GERMANISTIK, ANGLISTIK UND KOMPARATISTIK
HERAUSGEGEBEN VON ARMIN ARNOLD
BAND 5

YVAN GOLL

AN ICONOGRAPHICAL STUDY OF HIS POETRY

VON VIVIEN PERKINS

1970

H. BOUVIER u. CO. VERLAG · BONN

ACKNOWLEDGEMENTS

I would like to express my sincere thanks to my Supervisor, Professor H. S. Reiss of the German Department, University of Bristol, for his advice and encouragement during the past two years. I would also like to express my gratitude to Mme. Claire Goll, widow of Yvan Goll, for her generosity in allowing me access to unpublished manuscripts and rare editions of her husband's works.

Finally my thanks are due to the Publications Committee of Bristol University for generous assistance towards the publication of this work.

ISBN 3 416 00674 7

YVAN GOLL

AN ICONOGRAPHICAL STUDY OF HIS POETRY

RX7Sd

IV

CONTENTS

PREFATORY NOTE

Whenever a cycle of poems bears the same title as an individual poem within the cycle, the little of the cycle is marked with an asterisk to avoid confusion.

SYNOPSIS

The aim of this thesis is to study the iconography of Yvan Goll's later poetry and to consider the implications of his use of esotericism. If, as frequently happens, esotericism creates barriers between the poet and the majority of his readers, it creates even more difficulties for the critic who is required to "break down" those barriers. Such a process is in itself complex, as noted in the Introduction, for not only must the critic be capable of characterising the original symbols, he must also be aware of possible modifications determined by the particular experiences of the poet in question.

Chapter I begins with a brief survey of Goll's esoteric sources, a basic knowledge of which is essential for a primary identification of his imagery. The deeper levels of enquiry necessary for an iconographical study of Goll's poetry form the basis of the second part of Chapter I, and of Chapters II—IV, in which an analysis of six cycles of poems is undertaken.

Since it is generally felt that esotericism in literature requires, for its justification, specific attitudes and motives on the part of the author using it, further discussion along these lines is necessary. In Chapter V an assessment of Goll's general attitude towards his material is attempted by a comparative method of enquiry. There follows an investigation of Goll's statements of theory related to his use of esoteric imagery. Finally an attempt is made to suggest possible reasons for Goll's interest in, and use of esoteric doctrines.

The Conclusion constitutes a brief recapitulation of the main points which emerge from the investigation.

INTRODUCTION

Iconographical analysis ... dealing with images, stories and allegories ... presupposes, of course, much more than that familiarity with objects and events which we acquire by practical experience. It presupposes a familiarity with specific themes or concepts as transmitted through literary sources, whether acquired by purposeful reading or by oral tradition. Our Australian bushman would be unable to recognize the subject of a Last Supper; to him, it would only convey the idea of an excited dinner party. To understand the iconographical meaning of the picture he would have to familiarize himself with the content of the Gospels. When it comes to representations of themes other than biblical stories or scenes from history and mythology which happen to be known to the average 'educated person', all of us are Australian bushmen. In such cases, we, too, must try to familiarize ourselves with what the authors of those representations had read or otherwise knew [1].

Although these words were written with specific reference to the problems confronting art historians, their relevance to the study of much literature of the twentieth century is becoming increasingly apparent. Some critics — F. R. Leavis, for example — view the use of obscure subject-matter in modern poetry as one facet of the modern tendency towards specialisation. "For not only poetry, but literature and art in general, are becoming more specialised: the process is implicit in the process of modern civilisation. The important works of today, unlike those of the past, tend to appeal only at the highest level of response, which only a tiny minority can reach, instead of at a number of levels" [2].

To those acquainted with the poetry of Yvan Goll, the relevance of such a statement will be obvious. Most of the poetry studied in this thesis is poetry of a highly specialized nature, requiring specialized knowledge of esoteric doctrines and specific knowledge of autobiographical circumstances. Indeed, Goll's use of obscure material, together with

In these notes and those of the following chapters, abbreviations used after the initial citation of a work are given in parentheses.

[1] ERWIN PANOFSKY, *Studies in Iconology*, 2nd ed., New York and Evanston 1962, pp. 11—12.
[2] F. R. LEAVIS, *New Bearings in English Poetry*, London 1932, p. 213.

additional problems raised by his bilingualism [3], undoubtedly accounts for the neglect his work has suffered. Léon-Gabriel Gros refers to Goll as "un poète trop négligé, bien qu'il soit un des meilleurs de sa génération ..." [4]. In common with much twentieth century poetry, Goll's poems require a definitive statement of meaning, without which they cannot be justly evaluated, nor Goll's stature as a poet fully assessed. This study is an attempt to explain that "meaning" by elucidating as far as possible the obscure allusions.

Naturally an estimation of Goll's rank as a poet cannot be based solely on an iconographical study. The limitations and dangers of such an approach, but also its necessity, are summarized by Wilhelm Emrich:

> Die Unmöglichkeit, Bilder zu deuten, ohne ihren Bildcharakter zu zerstören, eine Wesensbestimmung zu erreichen, ohne ihr Wesen als Bild selbst aufzuheben, gilt nicht nur für einzelne Bilder und Symbole im engeren Sinne, sondern erstreckt sich auf die Dichtung überhaupt. Aus keinem anderen Grunde gleicht jede Interpretation von Dichtung, wie sie auch immer geartet sein möge, in einem sehr ernsten Sinne der Arbeit des Sisyphos ... Die Dichtung selbst fordert immer wieder dazu auf, erschlossen, enthüllt, zulänglich gedeutet zu werden. Aber jede Erschliessung bedeutet nicht nur Gewinn, sondern auch Verlust. Sie öffnet ein Phänomen − ein psychologisches, soziologisches, gehaltliches, formales usw. − und wird zwangsläufig blind für ein anderes, ja verdeckt es. Denn die wissenschaftliche Wesensbestimmung eines Phänomens macht dieses Phänomen verständlich und einsichtig, aber bewegt sich zugleich, mag sie auch noch so treu an der Dichtung sich orientieren, aus der Dichtung heraus in ein generelles kategoriales Deutungssystem, das die anderen Phänomene der Dichtung überdeckt und unsichtbar macht, die Besonderheit der Dichtung aufhebt [5].

In the case of Goll, such a study can help towards a more complete understanding of his work by focussing attention on that aspect of his poetry which hitherto has been virtually disregarded. Moreover, a detailed investigation of Goll's subject-matter would be essential if Goll − "dont la notoriété se réduisait jusqu'à ce jour à des cercles

---

[3] Goll was bilingual in French and German, but also wrote poetry in other languages, including English.

[4] LÉON-GABRIEL GROS, from an article entitled "La Parole est à la Matière" in *Cahiers du Sud*, no. 298, Marseilles 1949, p. 485.

[5] WILHELM EMRICH, from "Das Problem der Symbolinterpretation im Hinblick auf Goethes *Wanderjahre*" in W. E., *Protest und Verheissung, Studien zur klassischen und modernen Dichtung*, 2nd. ed., Frankfurt am Main and Bonn 1963, p. 49 (EMRICH)

assez restreints de connaisseurs"[6] — were ever to be brought to the attention of a wider public and consequently find the place in twentieth century literature that he deserves.

It is unfortunate that the success of a poet's works is largely determined by the extent of critical acclaim he receives, since many critics view with suspicion any form of esotericism in poetry. Such critics are unable or unwilling to free themselves from the Romantic belief that poetry should appeal primarily to the emotions, and consequently find themselves at a loss when confronted with poetry that does not conform to their view.

In general the critics' view of the nature of poetry determines their view of the nature of literary criticism. Thus the concept of lyric poetry as essentially emotive must deny the poet the use of esoteric allusions or imagery, since this would preclude the instant communication that these critics demand. In their eyes a poet using such material is therefore frustrating his own ends. In addition, this view must deny the critic any investigation of "meaning" which is not immediately apparent, condemning it as external both to the nature of poetry and of criticism.

Moreover, by insisting that what the poet believes or professes to believe can be the object of an aesthetic judgement, these same critics are denying the validity of iconographical studies. Such an attitude, precluding any rational approach to "obscure" poetry, constitutes a negation of the function of iconography, which is the reconstruction of the ideas and associations underlying the work of art. Iconography is not concerned with what can be subjectively read out of the poem, that is, with the analysis of the reader's reaction to it (which is neither consistent nor necessarily related to what the poet was thinking), but rather it is concerned as far as possible with the interpretation of each image in its full depth.

A study of the intentional meaning of Goll's poetry is therefore to a large extent a study of the intellectual substructure of his work. In his case, much of the source material, by its very nature, acts as a deterrent to the development of iconographical studies. Alchemy, cabbalism, etc., have always been likened in most people's minds to unhealthy pseudo-scientific cults. Little distinction is made between these doctrines and the practices of

---

[6] Léon-Gabriel Gros, from a further article entitled "Yvan Goll, l'alchimiste fraternel" in *Cahiers du Sud*, no. 337, Marseilles 1956, p. 427.

3

theosophists, mediums, and so forth. Consequently the body of theory is inseparably linked with frauds and charlatanry, and the modern mind is both bewildered and repelled by it. It is not the purpose of this study to vindicate such doctrines, but to elucidate their basic principles as they become relevant to an understanding of Goll's poetry.

An investigation of Goll's imagery is a complex procedure necessitating various levels of enquiry: (i) a primary identification of the image is necessary. In other words, the sphere of reference from which it has been taken must be identified, a procedure dependent for its success upon the reader's personal knowledge and experience; (ii) the traditional meanings (material and spiritual) of the image within the context of its particular sphere of reference must be established; this requires consultation of specialized works; (iii) the deeper symbolic value of the image (i. e. its iconographical significance) must be considered. In this case, history, in the sense of biographical data, contacts, reading-matter, is of paramount importance, since an interpretation on this level relies for its accuracy on such information.

The choice of poetry for investigation in this thesis was governed by two main factors. Firstly, the selected cycles constitute a major part of Goll's lyric poetry and, spanning the last decade of his life, are therefore representative of his mature outlook and technique. Secondly, because of their "obscurity" these particular cycles have rarely — in some cases never — been the object of critical investigation.

Chapter 1

GOLL'S ESOTERIC SOURCES: A BRIEF SURVEY

It is difficult to state with certainty exactly when Goll first became interested in esoteric doctrines; there are vague indications of it as early as 1915 in his Expressionist poem *Noëmi:*

In Schrift und Zeichnung und Kabbala
Erörtertest du kalt
Den Prozess des Himmels [1]

It is possible that Goll's interest may have been further stimulated by his contact in Ascona (during the years 1917 and 1918) with the Eranos group, whose members formed the centre of an occultist movement [2]. However, it was not until well over two decades later that Goll made systematic use of esotericism in his poetry, principally in *Le Char Triomphal de l'Antimoine, Les Cercles Magiques* *, *Le Mythe de la Roche Percée*, the English cycle *Fruit from Saturn*, and also to a certain extent in other cycles such as *Masques de Cendre, Neila, Multiple Femme* *, and *Traumkraut*.

That Goll was intensely interested in esoteric and mystical literature is attested by Mme. Goll. The critic F. J. Carmody quotes her as saying: "La poésie ésotérique, hermétique et occulte l'a toujours préoccupé car Yvan est un mystique, un initié, qui étudiait sans cesse le Tarot, le Talmud, Paracelse, les Noces Mystiques de Christian Rosencreutz, l'Alchimie du moyen âge, la magie, lectures préférées également de Gérard de Nerval" [3].

The reference to Gérard de Nerval merits attention, for the republication of his works in 1936 coincided with Goll's renewed and more

---

[1] YVAN GOLL, *Dichtungen*, Darmstadt 1960, p. 49. (*Dicht*)
[2] It is worthy of note that two lectures by C. G. Jung on the subject of alchemy appeared in the *Eranos-Jahrbuch* in 1935 and 1936 respectively. They were entitled "Traumsymbole des Individuationsprozesses" and "Die Erlösungsvorstellungen in der Alchemie". It is possible, although not certain, that Goll read these.
[3] Cf. F. J. CARMODY, *The Poetry of Yvan Goll*, Paris 1956, p. 128. (CARMODY)

intensive interest in occultisms. Goll was well acquainted with Nerval's works and may possibly have found in them images or themes which appealed to him as potential material for his own poetry. The most immediate example that comes to mind is the image of the eye, which was to preoccupy Goll to a great extent in later years. However, this was also an image common to other poets, including Alfred de Vigny and Victor Hugo, and it is therefore equally possible that Goll's reading of their works provided the initial stimulus.

During his years of exile in the United States of America (1939—1947), Goll had frequent contact with poets and writers who were also interested in the Occult Sciences, among them André Breton and Denis de Rougemont. His contact with the former and with other members of the Surrealist movement may have helped to stimulate his growing interest in esoteric doctrines in general, although Goll's attitude towards such matters differed essentially from that of the Surrealists [4].

A survey of Goll's known source material reveals that it is primarily semitic; this does not come as a surprise in the light of his own claims to the Jewish faith. Judaism undoubtedly played a highly significant role in determining his choice of reading-matter. Goll utilizes material from the Bible, cabbalistic literature and various unidentified semitic legends. His interest in Zoroastrianism, Gnosticism, Manicheism and Hinduism is substantiated in various unpublished notes [5]. In *Fruit from Saturn* he makes specific allusions to occult works, so it is surely reasonable to assume that he was personally acquainted with them. He mentions Maimonides' *Guide for the Perplexed* [6], and Abulafia's *Book of Signs* [7]; he mentions Ibn Arabi, the hermetic philosopher

---

[4] This difference in attitude between Goll and the Surrealists is briefly discussed in CARMODY, pp. 130—131.

[5] Goll was apparently in the habit of making notes such as the following: "Gnosticisme: Philosophie des Mages. Le gnosticisme se rapproche à la fois du platonisme et du manichéisme. *Manès*, né en Perse vers 220 et mort en 277. Il fonda une religion où la lumière et la beauté, personifiant Dieu, sont en conflit avec le mal et le chaos. Il attribuait, comme Zoroastre, la création à deux principes, l'un essentiellement mauvais — et l'autre essentiellement bon. On a, par la suite, étendu le nom du manichéisme à toute doctrine fondée sur les deux principes opposés du bien et du mal. *Zoroastre* ou *Zarathustra*, fondateur mythique de la religion des Mages: le mazdéisme".

[6] MAIMONIDES, *Guide for the Perplexed*, trans. M. Friedländer, London 1919.

[7] According to the *Jewish Encyclopedia*, New York and London 1901, ABULAFIA's *Book of Signs* has been printed in the *Grätzjubelschrift*, Hebrew part, p. 65. I could find no reference to further publications of his work.

Giordano Bruno, the alchemist Zosimus, and elsewhere, Paracelsus and Heraclitus. The title of Goll's cycle of poems *Le Char Triomphal de l'Antimoine* is in fact the title of an alchemical work attributed to Basil Valentine. For his cycle of poems *Le Mythe de la Roche Percée*, Goll has taken a motto from Marbode, Bishop of Rennes — "lapides inesse vires" — whose lapidary described sixty gems, enumerating both their scientific and their magical properties. Material gleaned from two source books, namely *Das Buch Bahir* [8] (Illustrious Book) and Joshua Trachtenberg's *Jewish Magic and Superstition* [9] is particularly apparent in some parts of *Jean sans Terre* and to a lesser extent in *Le Char Triomphal de l'Antimoine* and *Les Cercles Magiques* *. Further reference books used by Goll will be indicated where relevant.

Having dealt very briefly with Goll's interest in esotericism, and certain of his verifiable sources, a discussion of the various types of esotericism — alchemy, cabbalism, the Tarot — is necessary in order to clarify many of his poems. Since an extensive consideration of these types lies beyond the scope of the present thesis, a discussion of them will be confined as far as possible to points relevant to Goll's poems. A similar procedure is adopted in the final chapter in which alchemy and cabbalism are reconsidered in their capacity as symbolic systems. However, Goll's practice of freely adapting his source material to suit his own ends frequently increases the difficulty of establishing direct links between the original material and the finished poem.

Since material pertaining to alchemy constitutes a high proportion of the subject-matter in *Le Char Triomphal de l'Antimoine* and to a lesser extent in *Les Cercles Magiques* * and other cycles, a brief general review of the aims of alchemy is indispensable [10]. The essential purpose of

---

[8] *Das Buch Bahir*, trans. and ed. Scholem, Leipzig 1923. (*Bahir*)

[9] JOSHUA TRACHTENBERG, *Jewish Magic and Superstition*, New York 1939. (TRACHTENBERG)

[10] The following books were consulted in connection with alchemy:

MARCELLIN BERTHELOT, *Les Origines de l'Alchimie*, Paris 1885. (BERTHELOT)

RONALD GRAY, *Goethe the Alchemist*, Cambridge 1952. (GRAY)

E. T. HOLMYARD, *Makers of Chemistry*, Oxford 1931.

E. T. HOLMYARD, *Alchemy*, Penguin Books, London 1957.

C. G. JUNG, *Psychology and Alchemy*, trans. R. F. C. Hull, Vol. 12 of the Collected Works, London 1953 (JUNG)

W. PAGEL, *Paracelsus*, Basel 1958.

GERSHOM G. SCHOLEM, *Alchemie und Kabbala*, Berlin 1927. (SCHOLEM)

KURT SELIGMANN, *The Mirror of Magic*, New York 1948. (SELIGMANN)

A. E. WAITE, *The Occult Sciences*, London 1891. (WAITE: O. S.)

alchemy was the perfection of matter and the understanding of it in terms of a spiritual world. The former might be termed the exoteric, the latter the esoteric aspect of alchemy. The Great Work of alchemy promised the prospect of transmutation and the attainment of the "Philosophers' Stone", itself a somewhat obscure and ambiguous concept, but synonymous with the fabrication of gold on an alchemical level, and with the comprehension of the ultimate nature of the universe on a spiritual level. The fabrication of the former was regarded as being secondary to the attainment of the latter, for the exterior manipulations of minerals were but the quasi-sacramental means by which the alchemist aimed to achieve an interior metamorphosis. Alchemists were in a sense both magicians and mystics, and alchemy, particularly during the "admirable 14e siècle" [11], was bound up with the entire religious and philosophical background of the times.

Alchemy was based upon the analogy between the macrocosm and the microcosm, and upon the belief that both were permeated by a universal spirit. Thus the alchemists were able to conceive of the similarity between the various stages of alchemic transmutation and the spiritual development of man himself. This process of transmutation was viewed as a cyclic one. The alchemists believed that in order for regeneration (Sublimation) to take place, "death" i.e. a return to primal matter or chaos (Putrefaction) was essential. This cyclic process of death and rebirth was symbolized by the self-devouring serpent (Ourobouros), and closely connected with this symbol was the concept of rotation [12]. This will be discussed in greater detail elsewhere.

Many of the difficulties facing the would-be interpreter of alchemical literature arise from the ambiguity of alchemical symbolism itself, symbolism which was for the most part allegorical and attempted to convey the philosophy of the subject in an esoteric way. By the frequent use of cover-names the Adepts hoped to guard their secrets from the profane. In Goll's poetry, the difficulties of thematic interpretation are increased by his tendency to modify an entire alchemical process almost beyond recognition, while at the same time retaining the commonplace

[11] ANDRÉ BRETON, Les Manifestes du Surréalisme, Paris 1947, p. 163.

[12] For a possible link with Gnosticism cf. SELIGMANN, p. 134: "Some sects of Gnosticism, it may be recalled, worshipped the serpent of paradise who had planted in man's heart the yearning for knowledge. This snake, the Ouroboros, became an alchemical emblem".

and widely accepted alchemical symbols within the framework of the whole.

An extremely common emblem of the Philosophers' Stone was that of the androgyne [13], a being uniting both male and female principles, and represented as holding in its hands the philosophic egg from which the universe was believed to have been hatched. The androgyne, symbolising as it did the union of opposites, the "coniunctio oppositorum", played an important part in the magical theory of the universe, for in order to gain mastery over all things man had to experience and reconcile opposites in his search for unity within diversity. The androgyne was frequently represented with wings, thus denoting intuition or spiritual potentiality. Goll was obviously fascinated by this hermaphroditic creature, for it appears in many of his poems under various guises, at times as a purely alchemical symbol and at others as a symbol of his "demon", the dualism of his own personality [14]. Goll's acute awareness of this "demon" precipitated the crisis that gave rise to the *Jean sans Terre* poems during the New York period.

Material taken from cabbalistic writings forms the basis of many of Goll's poems, particularly in *Le Char Triomphal de l'Antimoine* and also in *Fruit from Saturn*. Various definitions of cabbalism can be found among the poet's unpublished notes, for example: "Kabbala: a mysterious interpretation of the Old Testament, founded on tradition, or communicated by angels"; "Kabbala: the history of the celestial Chariot (or Car) mentioned in the vision of Ezekiel"; and finally: "Another theory: the Kabbala — a chemical science which resorts to incantations, but also includes a philosophic system, wherein angels hold a strong position" [15].

---

[13] Of particular interest in connection with the idea of the androgyne are the following books:
Mircea Eliade, *Méphistophélès et l'Androgyne*, Paris 1962.
Gray, pp. 221—249, where the author discusses Goethe's use of the symbol of the hermaphrodite; and also pp. 34—35, where he mentions the identification of the alchemical androgyne with the Philosophers' Stone.
Denis Saurat, *Literature and Occult Tradition*, trans. D. Bolton, London 1930, pp. 94 f., where the author discusses the androgyne's connection with the sexual law of the cabbala. (Saurat)
Seligmann, pp. 143—145.

[14] Cf. *Jean l'hermaphrodite* in Yvan Goll, *Jean sans Terre*, critical edition by Carmody, Berkeley and Los Angeles 1962, pp. 48—50. (*Jean sans Terre*)

[15] These unpublished notes are in the possession of Mme. Goll.

Cabbalism [16] was in fact a metaphysical or mystical system by which the elect aspired to know God and the universe. It is clear, therefore, that its aims in this respect were similar to those of alchemy. Further points of comparison between the two are discussed by Gershom Scholem in his book *Alchemie und Kabbala*. The task for the initiate was to solve the hidden meaning of the universe through methods handed down by tradition. (The word cabbalism comes from the Hebrew root signifying "to receive", since the knowledge embodied in cabbalistic literature is claimed to have been transmitted orally from generation to generation). In this task the Hebrew letters in which the sacred texts were written were of great importance, for they did not merely record thoughts and events, but were considered to be reservoirs of divine power. In cabbalistic writings Adam was said to have received a cabbalistic book from the angel Raziel, the guardian of divine secrets, and through the wisdom he gained from this book, was able to overcome the grief of his fall. Raziel figures predominantly in many of Goll's poems, and according to the definition used by Goll, "Raziel is the angel of mysteries, assigned to Adam after his banishment from paradise" [17].

The oldest cabbalistic book is the *Sepher Yetzirah* (Formation) [18], but it is the *Zohar* (Light or Splendour) [19] which is regarded as the holy book, the pillar of cabbalistic wisdom. It contains the fundamental idea that the universe can be understood to a very large extent through pure speculation. Yet another cabbalistic idea employed by Goll is that of the Sephiroth, the manifestations of God's existence in Creation. They are akin to the Neo-Platonic Intelligences, intermediaries between the in-

---

[16] The following books were consulted in connection with cabbalism:
J. ABELSON, *Jewish Mysticism*, London 1913. (ABELSON)
Bahir
A. FRANCK, *La Kabbale ou la Philosophie Religieuse des Hébreux*, 3rd. ed., Paris 1892. (FRANCK)
SAURAT
SCHOLEM
SELIGMANN
A. E. WAITE, *The Doctrine and Literature of the Kabalah*, London 1902. (WAITE: D. L. K.)
Zohar: Basic Readings from the Kabbalah, ed. Scholem, New York 1966, 3rd. ed. (*Zohar: Basic Readings*)
[17] Unpublished note in the possession of Mme. Goll.
[18] *Sepher Yetzirah*: for further information see WAITE: *D. L. K.*, pp. 167 f.
[19] For additional information on the *Zohar*, see WAITE: *D. L. K.*, pp. 187 f.

telligible world and the material world [20]. The ten Sephiroth are contained in Adam Kadmon, the archetypal man to whom Paul perhaps alludes: "The first man Adam was made a living soul; the last Adam was a quickening spirit" [21]. En Soph is the name given to the incomprehensible, limitless godhead from whom the Sephiroth sprang by emanation [22].

One of the most important laws in the cabbala was the relationship between the macrocosm and the microcosm, for "all that is on the earth is formed in the likeness of the world above; and there is not the smallest object in this world which has not its equivalent in the world above which governs it . . ." [23].

Many of Goll's poems are centred round the figure of the demon Lilith. Apart from her particular significance for Goll (to be discussed in due course), she is represented in the Bible and in various mythologies as a winged female, temptress of men and murderess of children. According to some legends Lilith was originally a wind-spirit, but during Talmudic times her name became confused with the Hebrew word "laylah" (night), which consequently led to the depiction of her as a night-demon [24]. Lilith was also supposed to have been Adam's first wife, but in none of his poems does Goll appear to allude to this particular version of the legend. Nevertheless, a version depicting Lilith as a hermaphrodite obviously did have significance for him.

In *Le Char Triomphal de l'Antimoine* Goll utilizes various ideas from the Tarot [25], a pack of playing cards founded on a system of occult symbols. The Tarot is linked with the cabbala by virtue of the fact

[20] The particular relationship between cabbalism, Platonism, and neo-Platonism is discussed in FRANCK, pp. 195 f.

[21] I Corinthians 15., v. 45.

[22] The doctrine of emanation is a neo-Platonic concept, that of the Sephiroth is probably Jewish.

[23] Quoted in SAURAT, p. 87.

[24] For further information, see W. O. E. OESTERLEY and T. H. ROBINSON, *Hebrew Religion — its Origin and Development*, London 1933, 3rd. ed., pp. 70—71. (OESTERLEY)

[25] The following books and articles were consulted in connection with the Tarot:
P. F. CASE, *The Tarot, a Key to the Wisdom of the Ages*, New York 1947.
JEAN CHABOSEAU, *Le Tarot — essai d'interprétation selon les principes de l'hermétisme*, Paris 1946. (CHABOSEAU)
DENIS DE ROUGEMONT, article entitled "Présentation du Tarot" in Goll's magazine *Hémisphères*, Spring ed., vol. 2, no. 5, New York 1945, pp. 31—43. (ROUGEMONT)
SELIGMANN, pp. 409—434.
WAITE: *D. L. K.*, pp. 479—483.

that each of its major trump-cards corresponds to one of the twenty-two letters of the Hebrew alphabet. In 1945 Denis de Rougemont contributed an article to Goll's magazine *Hémisphères* entitled "Présentation du Tarot" [26] in which he stated that each of the major arcana of the Tarot could be identified with (1) a planet; (2) a sign of the Zodiac; (3) a letter of the Hebrew alphabet; (4) a number (interpreted by the cabbala); (5) an alchemical element; (6) a colour; (7) a note of music; (8) a name. To these the occultist Lenain has added (9) a day; (10) an hour; (11) a degree; (12) a spirit; (13) a verse of the Psalm of David. To these, Denis de Rougemont maintains, modern psychoanalysts have added: (14) one of the four faculties (thought, intuition, emotion, sensation); (15) one of the archetypes of the collective unconscious! This does appear to be taking matters to extremes, and is all the more suspect in the light of a reputable critic's dismissal of the Tarot as "an obscure sheaf of hieroglyphs"! [27]. Despite these differences of opinion, however, the Tarot undoubtedly provides the occultist with a subject of meditation and with a series of exercises designed to lead to illumination. "Ses lames seraient en vérité autant de thèmes de méditations prolongées — la cure ou 'yoga' durait plusieurs années — et marqueraient les étapes d'une 'voie hermétique' aboutissant à la réalisation intime du Grand Oeuvre des alchimistes" [28]. A general renewal of interest in the Tarot round about 1945 and 1946 may have inspired Goll to make use of its symbolism in his own poetry, although he had been acquainted with the Tarot for many years and did in fact own a set. According to an entry in one of his note-books, Goll had read Jean Chaboseau's *Le Tarot* (1946) in connection with this subject [29]. At the same time, it is hardly surprising to find André Breton referring to the Tarot in one of his poems:

> La lame merveilleuse . . .
> Dans le reflet du 14e siècle de notre ère
> L'exprimera seule
> Par une des figures animées du tarot des jours à venir [30]

The entire magic theory of the Tarot rests upon the belief that in nature there is no accident, that every occurrence in the universe is caused by some

---

[26] This particular edition of the magazine was devoted to "Magie et Poésie". For details of Rougemont's article, see note 25.

[27] Cf. Waite: *D. L. K.*, p. 439.

[28] Rougemont, p. 36.

[29] For details of Chaboseau's book, see note 25.

[30] Quoted in Carmody, pp. 130—131.

pre-established law, even the most insignificant event being subject to this fundamental rule. Cards mixed at random produce results which are in effect the working of unalterable laws. The Tarot also proposes a method for predicting future events and man's character.

The preceding survey will serve to facilitate a primary identification of Goll's imagery. The deeper levels of enquiry necessary for an iconographical study of his poetry will form the main body of this thesis.

LE CHAR TRIOMPHAL DE L'ANTIMOINE

This cycle of fifteen sonnets was first published in 1949. Although the year 1945 has generally been accepted as the year of their composition, they were in fact composed just prior to publication, between January 14, 1949 and May 7, 1949 [31].

Since *Le Char Triomphal* represents Goll's most formal experiment with esotericism and reveals the full extent of his preoccupation with such topics, it will be dealt with before *Les Cercles Magiques* * which is by no means such a highly integrated cycle, being much more personal in content than *Le Char Triomphal*. The absence of extraneous and emotive elements in this cycle was alluded to by Émilie Noulet, who considered the poetry of *Le Char Triomphal* to be "Poésie dépouillée de toute grâce et même de tout envol et dont le chant est pure articulation" [32]. Such poetry, however, does present difficulties and disadvantages — a point raised by Léon-Gabriel Gros in an article entitled "La Parole est à la Matière":

[31] This information appears in Goll's unpublished notes. In any case, the later date would seem to be substantiated by Goll's reading-list:
New York, 4. 5. 47: Bachofen, Nietzsche, Franz Boas, Raimundus Lullus, Thomas von Aquin.
Paris, August 1947: La Kabbale, Le Zohar.
Paris, 20. 6. 48: Gershom G. Scholem, Major Trends in Jewish Mysticism, Jerusalem 1941.
Strassburg, 23. 11. 48: Karl von Bülow, Geologie für Jedermann.
Paris, 28. 2. 49: Basile Valentin, Les 12 clefs.
Paris, 8. 3. 49: Le Tarot de Jean Chaboseau; Basile Valentin, Le Char Triomphal.
Paris, 9. 3. 49: La Cabbale de Papus.
Paris, 31. 3. 49: Le Grand Livre de la Nature ou l'Apocalypse Hermétique, par O. Wirth, Paris 1910.
Paris, 15. 4. 49: Charles Werner, Philosophie Grèque.
[32] Cf. ÉMILIE NOULET, "Le Char Triomphal d'Yvan Goll", in *Synthèses*, Brussels, February 1951.

"Je crois d'ailleurs que c'est ce culte des mots rares, inévitable sans doute dans un ouvrage quasi-didactique comme "Le Char Triomphal de l'Antimoine", mais qui ne s'imposait pas dans les autres recueils, qui constitute le défaut capital de Goll et qui le 'date' fâcheusement". Moreover, Gros continues, Goll's "lyrisme n'est accessible qu'aux seuls initiés ... Elle (Goll's poetry) marque, en effet, une certaine tendance au didactisme, j'entends par là qu'elle ne fait pas seulement appel à l'inconscient de la sensibilité, mais à celui de l'intelligence" [33]. In this respect Goll's poetry is "scientific" (that is, dealing with knowledge) rather than "emotive".

As stated previously, the title of the cycle imitates that of the *Currus triumphalii antimonii* [34] attributed to the alchemist Basil Valentine, who was, like Goll himself, a native of Alsace. Except for the title and one or two images, however, Goll's cycle appears to have little in common with Valentine's work, which dealt with the preparation of the drug antimony. Goll's notes on Valentine are to be found in the unpublished *Triptyque de la Pierre*, together with the statement that "Le Char Triomphal de Valentin est consacré à l'histoire de l'antimoine, métal considéré comme une des merveilles du monde, créé pour purifier les hommes" [35]. Nevertheless, Goll's primary sources of inspiration in this cycle were undoubtedly the *Zohar*, the cabbala, the works of Paracelsus and possibly those of other alchemists.

As one critic has already pointed out, the sequence of the sonnets in *Le Char Triomphal* seems quite arbitrary and their arrangement has not so far been explained satisfactorily [36]. The thematic link proves somewhat difficult to trace at times, despite Goll's classification of these poems as

[33] Cf. Léon-Gabriel Gros, "La Parole est à la Matière", in *Cahiers du Sud*, no. 298, Marseilles 1949, pp. 482—483.

[34] Basil Valentine, *The Triumphal Chariot of Antimony*, trans. A. E. Waite, London 1893.

[35] Further notes on antimony are to be found among Goll's unpublished papers — for example: "Antimony: anti-monos — metal which has never been found in a pure state. A bluish-white metal with a silvery look, neither ductile nor malleable, and very brittle. Certain authorities put it in the category of half-metals — it resembles arsenic closely".

In a letter to the authoress dated November 13, 1967, Mme. Goll gave Goll's explanation of antimony: "Le nom latin de l'antimoine est stibium, d'où la formule Sb. Le supérieur d'un couvent, ayant remarqué l'embonpoint d'un troupeau de cochons qui paisaient aux environs d'une mine de sulfure d'antimoine, imagina de mêler ce corps aux aliments de ses moines. Les malheureux moururent, ce qui fit donner à cette substance le nom de l'antimoine!"

[36] Carmody, pp. 132—133.

"un recueil de sonnets hermétiques, en quête de la Pierre Philosophale" [37]. Indeed, were it not for this statement on the part of the poet himself, it would be tempting to reject a small number of these poems as having nothing at all, or at least very little in common with the subject of alchemy. None the less, the formal link between the poems is indisputable and certainly appears to indicate that Goll conceived the cycle as an integrated unit, and desired it to be considered as such, although each sonnet retains its integrity as an independent poem. Goll might have been influenced to a certain extent by the growing popularity of the sonnet form, which, after a period of general decline in Europe, had been revived in France and used to great effect by such poets as Hérédia, Lecomte de Lisle, Valéry, Mallarmé and Rimbaud. If one accepts the validity of Goll's classification of this cycle, his main aim was undoubtedly to use the sonnet sequence in order to amplify the limited scope of the single sonnet, and thus to reflect various aspects of one theme as an integrated whole.

Several themes and images new to Goll's poetry appear from about 1944 or 1945 onwards. The search for knowledge and a desire to dissociate himself from personal problems lead to the use of images from alchemy, cabbalism, geology and so forth. It is virtually impossible to deal with any of these themes or images in isolation since they are all so closely interrelated. For this reason it may not always be possible to discuss the material without a certain amount of reiteration. In the shorter cycles, the poems will be considered in the order in which they appear, since any attempt to consider them under "headings" would prove far too complicated and necessitate an excessive amount of cross-references. This latter approach has in fact been attempted by F. J. Carmody [38], but in order to arrive at neat classifications of the various themes, he has been obliged to omit those poems for which he can find no suitable pigeonhole [39].

As its title Le Grand Oeuvre [40] implies, the first sonnet deals with the main undertaking of alchemy; but on a symbolic level it has to do with the transmutation of man himself from an impure to a pure state. Marcel

[37] This appears in an unpublished group of notes entitled Triptyque de la Pierre.
[38] CARMODY, pp. 132—151.
[39] This is not intended as an adverse criticism of this approach, but is merely an indication of its limitations.
[40] Dicht., p. 406. Both the original French poems of Le Char Triomphal de l'Antimoine, and the German translations by Friedhelm Kemp are published in Dicht., pp. 405—435. Page references will indicate only the French poems.

Brion maintains that "C'est une poésie initiatique, au sens le plus haut du terme, en ce qu'elle nous conduit jusqu'à l'âme ardente et secrète des métaux qui brûlent dans le feu de la terre; le creuset de l'alchimiste, ici, l'athanor, est en même temps l'image de l'homme qui transmue dans son âme toutes les passions, dans le feu de l'amour" [41].

The poem opens with a description of the manipulation of mercury, the "prima materia", with strong emphasis placed on the "depersonalisation" of the experimenter during the Great Work:

> A manipuler le mercure
> Mes doigts inhumains devenus
> Transparents et chastement nus . . .

The renunciation of individuality in the case of man, or a reduction to first matter in the case of metals, was a necessary process of transmutation. It was a means of assuring the eradication or the destruction of imperfections. The image of the green lion which appears in the second verse is a standard alchemical term representing the devouring corrosive acid in the alchemical experiment, the mercurial fluid, which is the "prima materia" of the Stone:

> Le lion vert est ma monture
> Et pourquoi me bouderais-tu
> Sel démasquant toute vertu
> De ceux que la chair défigure

It is interesting to note in connection with this image that Key 8 of the Tarot pack, "Strength" or "Force", features a woman holding open the mouth of a green lion. It is possible that Goll took the image of "Sel démasquant toute vertu" from the *Currus* itself, although references to this could have been found in almost any alchemical treatise, since salt was generally considered to be anti-demonic and to possess, among other things, great powers of preservation and purification. Man's spiritual qualities, represented by "vertu", are distorted by his physical nature, represented by "chair", and it is only by ridding himself of the latter that he can hope to recover the former. In this poem the poet is seeking for a personal transmutation, for knowledge on a personal, rather than poetic level. A similar idea is expressed in Chant X of *Le Mythe de la Roche Percée*:

---

[41] From an article by MARCEL BRION in *Yvan Goll — Quatres Études*, in the series Poètes d'aujourd'hui, Paris 1956, p. 18. (*Quatre Études*)

Verse à nos alembics tes magnésies
A nos coeurs tes connaissances
Aide-nous à vendanger le vin de grenats
A jardiner les champs de sidérose [42]

Goll refers next to the alchemical "Matrices", the wombs in which objects are generated and from which they receive their ultimate destination:

Ma main dans la gueule du feu
Et sur les balances de l'eau
Mon coeur mordu par l'élément

The mere chemical components of an object are not as important as their immanent soul-like force, and these substances are but covers disguising a pattern of spiritual forces (in the same way as man's physical nature disguises his spiritual nature). It is in these three substances — fire, water and air, *inter alia*, that this pattern is least disguised and comparatively easy to recognise. So it is undoubtedly by means of these "spiritual" substances that the poet hopes to achieve what is, after all, a spiritual transmutation. The poet is no longer the mere experimenter in this alchemical procedure; in some mysterious way he has become the substance, the basis of the experiment:

Je me dissous alertement . . .

The concluding line of the poem shows the poet reflecting on those imperfections in man which must be eradicated before spiritual regeneration can be achieved:

Naître et n'être qu'insulte à Dieu

The long and arduous nature of the Great Work is stressed by Chaboseau in his discussion of the Tarot and its application to alchemy: ". . . le Tarot propose à la fois une direction éthique et une dogmatique métaphysique ou théodicée, et un processus alchimique proprement dit. L'Or, la matière la plus précieuse, est le symbole fondamental: il est enfoui dans la Terre, dans la Pierre, et sa recherche est pénible, dure et longue. Cet Or symbolise celui qui est en nous, l'être que nous devons projeter au dehors, et qui

---

[42] YVAN GOLL, *Der Mythus vom durchbrochenen Felsen*, Darmstadt 1956, p. 30. References indicate the original French poems and not the German translations by Mme. Goll which also appear in this book. In the text this cycle is always referred to by its original French title *Le Mythe de la Roche Percée*, but since the edition used has a German title, the abbreviated form (*Der Mythus*) is used in the notes.

deviendra l'Homme nouveau destiné à naître de nous-mêmes, le 'Nouvel Homme' de Saint Martin" [43].

In *Le Grand Oeuvre*, however, progress towards the goal of regeneration appears not to have passed beyond the stage of Putrefaction [44]. The process is not carried to any conclusion.

In the second sonnet Goll once again employs "recognisable" alchemical imagery [45]. The title *Azoth* refers once more to mercury or the "water of paradise" mentioned by Paracelsus. Goll may have taken the idea from Paracelsus' *Liber Azoth* or from the treatise on the same subject supposedly written by Valentine. Azoth is regarded as the universal solvent, an alkahest in Paracelsian terms, and considered to possess great occult power. To the alchemical material which forms the basis of this sonnet, Goll has added further images pertaining to the Tarot; he also refers briefly to circles, a dominant concept in *Les Cercles Magiques* *.

The opening lines of the sonnet are a reference to the Hanged Man, Key 12 of the Tarot [46]. His inverted position indicates the dependence of human personality upon cosmic life. Goll also alludes to the egg of Saturn, here a symbol of the underlying causes of reality — hence its ability to break through the circles. In this instance the circles denote freedom from every limitation, or infinity, and are thus analogous to the concept of the Zero card of the Tarot:

> Dans l'arbre où chante le pendu
> L'œuf de Saturne choit du nid
> Et roule jusqu'à l'infini
> Brisant les cercles défendus

[43] Chaboseau, p. 29.

[44] Cf. Gray, p. 13: "The expression 'Putrefaction' is meant to apply not only to the material but also to the spiritual world. It implies that man must 'die' in the sense that he must abandon worldly goods, detach himself from his personal desires, in order to be 'reborn' in the harmony of the Kingdom of Heaven. This symbolism of death and rebirth plays an important part in all alchemical writings ...".

[45] *Dicht.*, p. 408.

[46] Interestingly enough, this particular card of the Tarot is referred to by T. S. Eliot in *The Waste Land*, London 1965, Faber ed., pp. 28—29:
> "Here is the man with three stares, and here the Wheel
> And here is the one-eyed merchant, and this card,
> Which is blank is something he carries on his back
> Which I am forbidden to see. I do not find
> The Hanged Man. Fear death by water."

The second quatrain reveals that the poet is at the mercy of the substance he is attempting to manipulate. The metal is a "Tyran" and "un grand dément" at this stage of the procedure. According to Ronald Gray, the alchemists believed that metals "could only be transmuted into gold by first reducing them to a formless, indeterminate mass, that is, by melting them down. In this state, representing the primeval chaos, they were capable of being determined to any form the alchemist might choose, provided that the correct methods were known to him" [47]. In this instance, the alchemist/poet is unable to foresee the outcome of his attempts at liberation. It appears doubtful whether or not he knows the "correct methods" and he therefore runs the risk of being beaten at his own game:

> Je le libère imprudemment
> Qui de nous deviendra le serf?

The alchemical symbolism of the sestet, however, indicates that the experiment is working out successfully. The image "la rose naît du minerai" admits of two interpretations: firstly, as the flower-like crystals appearing on the side of the vessel in which the elements have been heated, and secondly, as the symbol of the alchemical work itself. In many alchemical writings the fish appears to symbolize the soul or spirit — thus the significance of the line "Du Poisson s'élève l'esprit" is unmistakable; the spirit has been liberated from matter. The ideas contained in the lines,

> O démiurge sans abri
> Le feu d'Égypte me nourrit

may have been suggested to Goll by Chaboseau's statement, "Avant la mise de cet oeuf (the philosophic egg) dans l'Athanor, l'adepte doit sceller avec art ce vaisseau, car il va subir le *Feu d'Égypte*, et il risque de s'y briser, la température allant doubler, tripler ..." [48]. Presumably on account of its potential danger to the adept, the "Feu d'Égypte" is called by Goll a "démiurge sans abri". Sublimation is symbolized in this sonnet by the emergence of the King dressed in red, "Et le roi rouge m'apparaît", red being the colour usually associated with the final stages of the Great Work, and the colour most frequently attributed to the Philosophers' Stone. Significant, too, is the optimistic tone of this second sonnet in contrast to the pessimism of the first.

---

[47] GRAY, p. 13—14.
[48] CHABOSEAU, p. 34.

The quest for illumination is once again expressed in symbolic terms in the third sonnet of the cycle, *L'Arbre Séphirot* [49]. This sonnet introduces material taken from the *Zohar*. In this instance, man's quest for knowledge is sought through communication with the Sephiroth, the primary emanations from God or the Divine Soul. The poem opens with a description of the cabbalistic tree; tree symbolism occurs frequently in the Bible, in pre-cabbalistic and cabbalistic texts, as a fundamental and ancient motif of cosmogony:

> Dix sont les fruits aux bras de l'arbre Séphirot

This is followed by the application of its symbolism in alchemical terms; first in the material world, secondly in the spiritual:

> Dix les métaux du corps recélant la splendeur
> Dix les sels de l'esprit nourriciers de la fleur
> Qui prépare mon âme aux puissances d'Azoth

Of great significance is the emphasis placed on the number ten in the opening lines, for the ten was revered by the ancients as the symbol of the Absolute and consequently was the number of perfection. This is particularly apparent in the *Sepher Yetzirah* which is pervaded with the mystical significance of numbers.

Such preparations as these are designed to help the adept in his search for spiritual illumination. They have their parallels in the reactions taking place within him:

> La pomme du pouvoir rondit en mon cerveau
> Et le vin de mon coeur inspire l'infini
> Les yeux de l'émeraude aux yeux de chair unis
> Allumeront en moi les fibres du flambeau

Each reaction in these lines has its equivalent in the corresponding line of the first verse: for example, "la pomme du pouvoir" (the fruit of the tree of knowledge) refers back to the "fruits ... de l'arbre Séphirot" of the opening line, and so on. In his desire for knowledge and illumination, the adept/poet desires to penetrate beyond the material world, "le vin de mon coeur inspire l'infini". The union of the "yeux de l'émeraude" and the "yeux de chair" constitutes, according to Goll's symbolism, a kind of alchemical "coniunctio" in which matter ("chair") is penetrated by spirit (symbolized by the emerald). The reference to the emerald is particularly

---

[49] *Dicht.*, p. 410.

apt in this context, since the occult property of the gem is the ability to bestow wisdom on its bearer. It is possible, but by no means certain, that Goll was aware of this attribute. Above and beyond this, the emerald embodies spirituality, and this spirituality is reflected in the translucent brilliance of the stone. The "fibres du flambeau" represent the rising flames of the spirit, the product of the "coniunctio". Thus the poet expresses the desire for deeper insight into the underlying causes of reality. In the final lines, with their analogy between the cabbalistic tree and the human body, Goll entreats the Sephiroth to descend:

> Descendez Séraphins l'escalier vertébral
> Où la nèfle du foie et le soufre natal
> S'oxyderont un jour pour créer la beauté

These lines appear to refer to the "green stage" of the alchemical process. Jung describes this stage in the following manner: "In the alchemical view rust, like verdigris, is the metal's sickness. But at the same time this leprosy is the 'vera prima materia', the basis for the preparation of the philosophical gold"[50]. Thus it is possible for the beauty of the Philosophers' Stone to be engendered from the oxidisation of the "nèfle du foie et le soufre natal". In personal terms this symbolism indicates the necessity of suffering if man is ever to achieve spiritual regeneration. Finally the adept or poet experiences a feeling of intoxication coursing through his veins as his body is pervaded with a new vitalising force:

> Cèdre de ma rigueur de royauté
> Par tes racines monte un alcool jamais bu
> Ta couronne me ceint du suprême attribut

The tree (significantly represented here by the evergreen cedar) is the symbol of Hermetic philosophy itself, and has the power to crown man accordingly with the "suprême attribut" of illumination. The Great Work is accomplished.

Sonnet IV, *Le Fou* [51], deals exclusively with the Fool, the Zero (i. e. the first) but also the last arcanum of the Tarot pack. The poet entreats man not to taunt the Fool, for he is merely feigning stupidity in order to deceive the uninitiated:

> Ne narguez pas le Fou
> Qui tourne dans vos têtes

[50] JUNG, p. 152.
[51] *Dicht.*, p. 412.

In occult terms he represents the primary aspect of universal consciousness; he symbolizes a state of preparation before conscience and individuation. As such he is inexperienced or, as Goll calls him, "l'aveugle". As the last card of the deck, however, the Fool is a representative of the Perfect Intelligence: he is "le voyant" and "l'obscur sage". According to Chaboseau, the Fool is "l'Illuminé qui met par son mutisme son secret à l'abri des vaines curiosités, mais c'est aussi le Sage errant, celui qui a quelque chose à transmettre, et qui le transmet au hasard, sans vouloir connaître celui à qui il s'adresse ... Rien ne le fait reconnaître extérieurement, si ce n'est que, lorsqu'il ouvre la bouche, tout le monde s'esclaffe, et qu'on le tient pour un fou ..." [52]. The Fool represents simplicity and total indifference to wordly goods and glory: "Cet arcane figure l'Adepte parfait, le véritable Sage, parvenu à la Suprême Compréhension, étranger au monde devenu pour lui une abstraction, une illusion. Les foules stupides peuvent hurler après lui ... lui, serein, méprise l'appréciation du vulgaire, voire même il la recherche, préférant son humble veste éffrangée et ses braies en loques aux plus beaux vêtements qui le feraient respecter. Il connaît le secret immémorial, qui fait de lui un être capable d'opérer toutes les transmutations" [53]. This latter statement serves to explain the paradoxical allusions:

> Ami du soufre blanc ...
> Fait fondre le soleil
>
> L'obscur sage dissout
> En plomb le pur vermeil

The Fool's dog, who has been changed by the processes of nature into a helper and companion of man, is "le fondement de la matière universelle, fidèle à l'artisan qui l'emploie selon son Art" [53]. The dog represents a more advanced stage of development than the wolf in whom man himself is caricatured:

> Son chien chasse le loup
> Malheureux que vous êtes

Goll's reference to the "âne à musique" may have been suggested to him by yet another of Chaboseau's statements: "On se souviendra de l'importance du symbolisme musical dans les figurations des hiéroglyphes hermétiques, notamment l'âne portant une lyre à Chartres ..." [53]. In this particular

---

[52] CHABOSEAU, p. 43.
[53] Ibid., p. 42.

sonnet Goll has adhered closely to the essence and interpretation of the Zero arcanum of the Tarot, and has successfully captured something of the paradoxical nature of the Fool.

Sonnet V, entitled *Raziel* [54], deals with cabbalistic material; in this poem Goll explores the letter system of the cabbala. As explained by Goll himself in connection with the poem bearing the same title in *Les Cercles Magiques**, "Raziel ist das Pseudonym, das der Kabbalist Abraham Abulafia gewählt hatte ..." [55]. In various unpublished notes Goll extends his explanation of Raziel and his work, for example: "Raziel se retira dans sa chambre d'études et pendant 20 ans s'obstina à trouver le nom de Dieu, par le mélange et la fabrication de mots émanés de l'alphabet hébreu. Il réussit, paraît-il, à créer 72 noms de Dieu". Elsewhere he states that "à l'âge de 31 ans (Raziel) se fixa à Barcelone pour se consacrer aux recherches cabalistiques, qui devaient lui révéler Dieu dans les noms émanés de l'alphabet hébreu" [56]. The poem itself reveals how Raziel created the "Word", the essence of God, by his manipulation and combination of the twenty-two letters of the Hebrew alphabet. These letters were in fact a mnemonic device which enabled the initiate to read occult messages. The profane were not even permitted to utter the name of God, but according to the cabbala, the secret names of God would be revealed to initiates by a study of the initial letters of consecutive words in the sacred books:

> Sur les vingt-deux piliers de l'alphabet hébreu
> Raziel construit de verbe une immense officine ...
>
> "El" fait-il "ELOHIM" peinant avec la hache
> Avec la fraise avec le diable avec la clé ...

According to the *Sepher Yetzirah* it was "By means of the twenty-two letters, by giving them a form and a shape, by mixing them and combining them in different ways, God made the soul of all that which has been created and of all that which will be. It is upon these same letters that the Holy One (blessed be He) has founded His high and holy name ... In short, the harmony of the cosmos is due to the Divine Wisdom underlying the manipulations of the twenty-two letters" [57].

---

[54] *Dicht.*, p. 414.
[55] Ibid., p. 553.
[56] From an unpublished note in the possession of Mme. Goll.
[57] Quoted from the *Sepher Yetzirah*, in ABELSON, p. 104.

In Goll's poem, the whole process is analogous to that of an alchemical experiment, as illustrated, for example, in the lines:

Où le mercure chante et l'oiseau se calcine
Exorcisant la pierre apprivoisant le feu

In the same way as alchemical substances are placed together in the hermetic vessel, so the words are placed by Raziel in a vast melting-furnace, "une immense officine", which probably symbolizes his mind. There they will be combined and transformed until they finally yield the "lapis" — in this case the seventy-two names of God. Thus from an act of apparent destruction, symbolized by the self-cremation of the phoenix, new life and spirit will arise:

Soixante-douze noms de l'innomable dieu
Au langage arrachés: par le quartz qui fulmine
De voyelles un prisme et l'oeil de cornaline

Raziel is aided by the fiery clarity of the precious stones, "quartz" and "cornaline", which in this case represent the words themselves which must be fashioned in the manner of precious stones. The emphasis on brightness and clarity indicates the spiritual nature of the undertaking. The allusion to "Moine de l'antimoine et magicien du blé" later in the poem appears to explain the title of the series of sonnets: it is Raziel-Abulafia who is the "monk of antimony". The immense effort and sacrifice involved in Raziel's work are indicated in the final lines of the poem:

Raziel le séducteur flattant ce qui se cache
Il assigne il épèle il chante de sa tour
Soixante-douze noms et devra mourir sourd

In his loneliness and isolation Raziel bears a striking resemblance to the figure whose emblem appears on the ninth Key of the Tarot — the Hermit.

The sixth sonnet Le Semeur d'Hexagones [58] is one of the most complex in this cycle as far as an identification of its imagery is concerned. The title appears to indicate that Goll had a specific source in mind, that he was thinking of a particular figure, but the source remains unknown. His reading of Joshua Trachtenberg could have suggested the idea of the hexagon to him initially [59]. The hexagon, on the other hand, is an extremely

---

[58] Dicht., p. 416.
[59] In Jean sans Terre p. 177, the editor Carmody quotes entries from Goll's notebook in support of this.

24

widespread mystical symbol, considered sacred by many nations since God created the world in six days. Six is of course the numerical equivalent of the hexagon and Goll was undoubtedly aware of the occult significance of the number six, having read such books as the *Sepher Yetzirah* in which numerology played such an important role. The fact that the poem has been placed sixth in the cycle is probably also significant in this respect.

The general significance of the number six in occult literature is discussed by A. E. Abbot in *The Secrets of Numbers* [60]: He states that it represents the number of balance and harmony, and the intermingling of matter and spirit. It is symbolized by the six-pointed star — this might well explain the line "L'étoile aux six yeux me toise". Friedhelm Kemp, who has translated these poems into German, offers the following explanation: "An sechster Stelle das Geheimnis der Sechszahl, der Verhärtung des Lichtes zu stofflicher Schöpfung" [61]. Chaboseau, in his discussion of the "sixes" of the Tarot pack, offers further interpretations: "Le travail lent et minutieux de la classification des principes par sériation progressive qui, se combinant entre eux, passent par des métamorphoses et des mutations, qui sont les effets de l'initiative et de l'harmonie. Les deux triangles en apparence opposés, qui doivent être réunis pour former l'Hexagramme parfait. C'est un autre aspect des luttes entre les influences contraires" [62].

Clearly, in the case of Goll's poem, the imagery indicates that a transmutation is taking place both within the universe and within man himself. This is given symbolic expression in the opening lines:

Le tambour du soleil sonne
A mon front de Lucifer ...

The macrocosm and the microcosm are undoubtedly the contending opposites, the "deux triangles opposés", or in other terms spirit and matter, God and man. Their union, being that of opposites, is necessary for the creation of ultimate harmony according to occult teaching. This harmony is symbolized by the hexagon or hexagram.

The imagery indicates that Goll was thinking of the cabbalistic idea of the sun as the emblem of unity between God and man. Moreover,

---

[60] A. E. Abbot, *The Secrets of Numbers*, London 1963, pp. 35—36.
[61] See *Dicht.*, p. 417 for Kemp's translation.
[62] Cf. Chaboseau, pp. 86—87.

cabbalism maintains that when man, either through his own efforts or through the exercise of magical powers, has become a son of Light ("Lucifer"), his natural ability is greatly increased and he becomes at times an independent creator like God Himself:

> Paysan de l'hexagone
> Aux semailles de l'hiver
> Neige miel ou belladone
> Je cultive l'univers

In this respect man is the means by which God's influence can permeate to the lower regions of creation. Goll's reference above to "Neige miel ou belladone" is undoubtedly an allusion to alchemical mercury, itself a symbol of the union of opposites, and as such a variant of the Philosophers' Stone. Mercury was thought by the alchemists to be metallic and liquid, matter and spirit, poison and antidote. Further alchemical ideas appear in the concept of the seasons — not, however, to be understood as seasons in the ordinary calendar sense. In alchemy the four seasons are spent in the hermetic vessel and constitute the period necessary for the production of philosophic gold. The alchemical year begins with "winter" and with the sowing of the "seed" of gold (cf. Goll's "Aux semailles de l'hiver"), and culminates in the "autumn". As the highest point of the alchemical year, autumn symbolizes the perfection of the Elixir.

Turning to the sonnet, it is clear from the sestet that the highest point of the year has been reached, although Goll gives no indication of the intervening seasons of "spring" and "summer". Man himself is penetrated by spirit ("L'étoile aux six yeux") and experiences a new life-force flowing through him, the purifying effect of which is emphasized by "eau" and "cristal". The paradoxical nature of alchemical symbolism is apparent in the image of "l'eau qui brûle dans les rhombes", but fire and water were considered by the alchemists to be one and the same thing, both capable of effecting a catharsis.

Whatever Goll's intentions in this sonnet, it is obvious that the images he uses are capable of a wide range of interpretations. No single esoteric doctrine suffices to explain all the "nuances". This being so, it is extremely difficult to provide a logical and satisfactory explanation of the poem in all its details. The general "idea" behind the poem is easier to assess. The sonnet is centred on the idea of a fusion of opposites as the requisite for harmony and spiritual regeneration.

The sonnet *Transmutations* [63] also deals with various transmutations, explicable in terms of alchemy. The significance of musical symbolism, previously mentioned in connection with the Tarot, is here extended to alchemical transmutations:

> Quelle est la harpe d'azur
> Vive aux abîmes du Harz
> A mettre un regard si pur
> Aux yeux biseautés du quartz

Music, by virtue of its orphic power, is shown to be capable of soothing and enchanting nature, and thus capable of effecting the liberation of imprisoned material. In this sonnet, as in other of Goll's poems, the rock is like a sibyl. The sphere of action of the transmutations is extended onto a cosmic level by the use of the words "azur" and "abîmes". The role played by music in the spiritualization of matter is stressed by the use of "azur", since blue is the colour associated with spirituality and infinity. The primeval darkness of the abyss ("abîmes") appears to represent the "prima materia" from which the spirit, imprisoned in matter, will rise in the form of music. The glance of the sibyl mingled with that of the quartz therefore represents an alchemical "coniunctio" which will engender this music. At the same time, the world of nature is participating in the transmutation, and appears shrouded in magic and mystery as a prelude to the Great Work:

> La montagne frissonna
> Aux pas des renards charmés
> Dans les prismes des grenats
> Saigne mon oeil enfermé

For Goll, the eye imprisoned in the garnets symbolizes spirit imprisoned in matter and awaiting liberation. By the use of the personal pronoun "mon" he seems to have projected himself into the material, thus signifying that, in addition, the transmutation is taking place on a microcosmic level. Regeneration is taking place both within nature and within man himself. The role played by fire in this process is indirectly alluded to in the image of the "étés de chrome": the melting heat of summer feeds the furnace in which the elements are undergoing transformation. The use of the word "chrome" is particularly apt in this context, since it expresses the idea of both brilliant luminosity and intense

[63] *Dicht.*, p. 418.

heat. Interestingly enough it is echoed in another poem entitled *Chrome*, again in connection with combustion:

> Descendu aux durs étés de chrome
> Étés inextinguibles Extases inassouvies
> J'ai soupesé le feu lourd
> Dans ma paume de soie ... [64]

In the sonnet, the cupped hand of the adept represents the hermetic vessel in which the egg (deduced from the use of "couvé") is being incubated. This will in turn give birth to the spirit, symbolized by the emergence of the alchemical phoenix:

> Un feu couvé dans ma paume
> Donne naissance à l'oiseau

Thus the liberation of spirit from matter is complete. Music occurs again in the final verse, and a feeling of calm ensues after the powerful vibrations and activity induced by the transmutations. This calming of the elements is symbolized in the decolorisation of sleep by the purifying sulphur of the passion-flowers. These flowers, like the rose, are a symbol of the alchemical Work itself. The flower is at one and the same time the Work and its completion:

> Au soufre des passiflores
> Mon sommeil se décolore
> Et mon chant calme les eaux

In this poem the alchemical processes do not seem to have been followed through by Goll in any logical order, despite the fact that they are more recognisable than those of the previous poem. The main difference lies in the colour sequence — so important in the Great Work, where the increasing perfection of the metals was supposed to be characterized by a change in colour from the initial blackening, to white, yellow and finally to red. Here the change is from dark ("abîmes") to yellow ("chrome"), to red ("feu") and finally to white (indicated by "décolore"). At times the final stage of the work was thought to be characterized by the colour white, and that generally in conjunction with red, as for example in the Sublimation symbolism indicated by the emergence of the Red King (i. e. dressed in red) and the White Queen (dressed in ermine). In Goll's case it is reasonable to assume that he was more concerned with the symbolic

---

[64] *Chrome* in YVAN GOLL, *Multiple Femme**, Paris 1956, p. 11. (*Multiple Femme**).

process of "spiritualization", than with the adherence to a strict alchemical sequence.

In the eighth sonnet *L'Oeuf Philosophique* [65], Goll makes use of well-known alchemical symbolism, this time utilizing the image of the philosophic egg, the "prima materia" which contains the imprisoned world soul. The process of extracting the "pneuma" present in the egg is to be understood both in alchemical and poetic terms. Again great emphasis is placed on the interrelationship between the macrocosm and the microcosm, which played such an important role in the general concept of alchemy. In alchemical terms the adept's skull ("crâne") represents the hermetic vessel and is a kind of matrix from which the "filius philosophorum", the miraculous Stone, will be born. On a poetic level the egg symbolizes the product of the poet's mind, the raw material ("pondaison jaune de ma déraison") from which the poem will be created. This poetic "liberation" is indicated by the use of alchemical symbols:

> Bientôt l'oiseau libéré du
> Poème oubliant sa prison
> Fait bondir les quatre horizons ...

The image of the bird indicates that spirit has been freed from matter: in other words, the poet has given definite shape and form to an amorphous mass of words and ideas, and has thus achieved what amounts to a liberation of language. During this process of "distillation" he loses his sense of identity and becomes merely a receptacle or agent by means of which this liberation is achieved. He is "depersonalized" to such an extent that his heart "n'est plus qu'un résidu". Goll's allusion to

> Plumage-prisme aux sept couleurs
> Ame allumée aux sept douleurs

might be an allusion to the stage in the Great Work in which the "cauda pavonis" (peacock's tail) appears, these many colours leading to the one white colour that contains all colours. On the other hand, Goll may again be making use of the occult science of numbers, according to which the number seven is chiefly concerned with the spiritual origins of things and with creative activity. Its essence is seen not in space but in time, in evolution and in transformations. Hence Goll's reference to "tout être se transfigurant" and to the seven colours of the rainbow, the

---

[65] *Dicht.*, p. 420.

rainbow itself being an example of the spiritual nature of the seven. In occult science man was regarded as having seven principles in his evolution: this could well explain Goll's allusion to "âme allumée aux sept douleurs". The final lines

> Tout être se transfigurant
> Échappe à sa mesure d'oeuf
> Vers l'univers surgi tout neuf
> Hors de la coque du néant

suggest that the poem should be understood not only in poetic and alchemical terms, but as a symbolic representation of man's spiritual development from the darkness of chaos ("coque du néant") to the splendour of regeneration ("l'univers surgi tout neuf").

It would seem from the following poem [66] that the poet no longer needs the word-systems of the cabbala, having exploited their potential to enlighten him, and now feels that he can illustrate by means of his poetic technique all that he has learned from them. He proceeds to do this in the sonnet La Rose des Roses which is an exercise on various aspects of that flower. In this poem can be seen Goll's growing predilection for compound-noun formations: "rose-roue", "rose-oeil", "rose-astre", "rose-eau". The increasing desire to use this construction as a poetic device may have been the cause of Goll's return to the German language in later years (as in Traumkraut), as this is a more natural construction in German than in French [67]. The images used in this sonnet are images which recur in Les Cercles Magiques *, and for this reason they will only be discussed briefly at this stage. The image "rose-roue au moyeu des âges" may well refer to the wheel of Fortune (cf. Key 10 of the Tarot pack), an emblem commonly used in Romanesque rose-windows. The Wheel combines both the idea of rotation: "Tournez tournez pour mon outrage", and that of destiny or fate. The image "Rose-astre enceinte de présages" seemingly alludes to the sibylline aspect of the flower, while "Rose à lots des mauvaises fêtes" re-emphasizes the idea of chance and destiny. "Rose-Saadi rose sadique . . ."[68] indicates the nature of the rose itself.

The reason for Goll's inclusion of La Rose des Roses in a cycle of sonnets supposedly "en quête de la Pierre Philosophale", must remain a

---

[66] Ibid., p. 422.

[67] Goll's return to the German language will be discussed in greater detail in Chapter IV.

[68] "Saadi" is an allusion to the Gulistan of the Persian SA'DI SCHIRAZI.

matter for speculation. However, the image of the rose did preoccupy Goll to a large extent during the composition of his later poetry. As noted above, it appears in *Les Cercles Magiques* *, but with more erotic implications than in *Le Char Triomphal*. In the poem *Die siebente Rose* [69] of 1928, the rose does not appear to have the significance as an "absolute" object that it had for Goll in later years. In *Les Cercles Magiques* * and *Fruit from Saturn* the rose and also the peach (another of Goll's "absolute" objects) are synthesized into eyes. These eyes in turn become portals through which the poet can pass into a realm of deeper perception, and through which he can return to the matrix. This will be considered in greater detail in Chapter II.

The sonnet *Le Dé* [70] turns to the role played by chance in the universe, as manifest in events defying scientific analysis. From this point of view the poem may be compared with one of the ideas behind Mallarmé's *Un coup de dés* [71], namely, that if one could predict the number that would appear when the dice is thrown, then one would have eliminated chance: but this is clearly impossible. In Goll's poem a god is said to be incarcerated within the cube (whose six sides, according to occult teaching, represent the physical world):

Dé! démence du dieu
En son cube incubé ...

The twenty-one "eyes" of the dice are described by Goll in a vivid manner as "hublots illuminés". Man must pit his wits against chance, embodied in the image of the rather malicious jinx within the dice:

Dardant les condamnés
Il chiffre leurs enjeux

The sestet then deals with the magical or occult associations of the numbers on the dice:

1 verbe solitaire
2 noce des contraires
3 règle et nombre d'or

4 dieu mis en cage
5 main d'ambre du mage
6 lasso de la mort

---

[69] *Dicht.*, p. 319.
[70] Ibid., p. 424.
[71] STÉPHANE MALLARMÉ, *Un coup de dés n'abolira jamais le hasard*, Paris 1914.

1, indicating the symbol of life and creation, "In the beginning was the Word"; 2 representing polarity and duality, the descent of spirit into matter; 3 representing the Golden Mean, the balance between two extremes; 4, the spirit imprisoned in the cage of matter; 5 signifying destiny (since Goll refers to "mage", he may also be thinking of the five-cards of the Tarot which signify the Star of the Wise Men); and finally, 6, which represents the number of death, the number in which creation perfects and exhausts itself. This sonnet, above all others, bears witness to Goll's interest in, and knowledge of numerology. In emphasizing the role of hazard, or the occult workings of chance in the universe, this particular poem provides an interesting contrast to the concept of causality explicit in the Tarot. Superficially, perhaps, the links with alchemy appear somewhat tenuous, although number symbolism does play a significant role in connection with alchemical concepts [72].

In the following three sonnets Goll utilizes images of various gigantic statues or oracles, images which also appear in *Les Cercles Magiques* * and *Le Mythe de la Roche Percée*. In *La Fille Chaste d'Héraclite* [73] Goll's interest in eyes is revealed in his description of the vast statue in which "Une comète en chaque orbite/S'érige en monument de braise". In this sonnet the gigantic statue of Diana of Ephesus appears to serve Goll as a point of departure for the symbol of fire. His interest in this symbol may have been stimulated by his reading of the Old Testament, particularly the Book of Kings; but on the other hand, since Goll mentions the philosopher Heraclitus, not only in the title of this poem, but in various other poems also [74], it might well be that he was thinking of Heraclitus' concept of fire as the primary principle from which all is made:

> Figuier de feu! Rosier d'Éphèse! ...
> S'érige en monument de braise ...
> Fourmis de feu ...
> Chiens de feu ...

Once again it is difficult to establish any direct links with alchemy; certainly a primary identification of the images in no way necessitates a

---

[72] For further reference see the entries under "Numbers" in JUNG, index, p. 541.
[73] *Dicht.*, p. 426.
[74] Cf. *Jean le Feu* in *Jean sans Terre*, p. 105: "Native de l'Asie élève d'Héraclite"; also the unpublished poem *Élégie sur le Feu*: "La danseuse de feu/La fille d'Héraclite"; and also the poem *Vultures* in the unpublished *Lackawanna Elegy**: "Du marbre moisissant de mon visage/Déjà s'effrite la nacre du rire et le doute héraclitien".

knowledge of alchemical imagery. The main idea behind the poem, however, could well be that of the importance of fire in the Great Work. Indeed, the Stone itself was frequently believed to have been created from fire. The poem is perhaps a symbolic illustration of the alchemical belief that fire represented the spirit concealed in matter: in this case, the statue (matter) would resemble a vast furnace, similar to that of the alchemists, and containing the fire of a divine presence (spirit). Why Goll should characterize it as "chaste" remains a matter for speculation, although the Stone was at times referred to as the Heavenly Virgin. The spirit appears to manifest itself in the form of music during a process of intense calcination:

> Harpe de cendre! Mandoline
> De feu! Musique à jamais tienne!
> En toi tout pense et te calcine!

For lack of any information on the part of Goll as to his intentions in this sonnet, *La Fille Chaste d'Héraclite* must inevitably rank as a prime example of "obscure" poetry.

Lilith, as will be seen in due course, has various functions in the poetry of Goll; but in the sonnet bearing her name in *Le Char Triomphal*[75], she is represented in her traditional guise as the Lilith of the Bible and of semitic legends. On a purely personal level Lilith represents the poet's temptress. Mme. Goll has described her role in Yvan's life thus: "Lilith, le problème de la femme qui joue un rôle capital dans la vie d'Yvan, était également pour lui: la Lilith du Vieux Testament, la femme fatale des Origines"[76]. In this particular poem she is portrayed as an eternal wanderer, a goddess of carnal desire and temptress of men. Possibly, too, like the legendary Lilith she is a murderess of children, and the burden of her guilt weighs heavily upon her:

> Lasse de sa lourde origine
> Vaine quêteuse de l'oubli

The extent of her evil influence on men is emphasized by Goll, as is the dark, demonic aspect of Lilith's character. By her passion and sensuality Lilith engenders sickness of mind:

---

[75] *Dicht.*, p. 428.
[76] Quoted in CARMODY, p. 142. That the idea of Lilith was suggested to Goll by his reading of TRACHTENBERG can be assumed from his note: "Trachtenberg, p. 9, Lilits, démones de la nuit".

> Son coeur délirant de gémir
> Enfante le mal de l'esprit

This lust of the flesh destroys both man's peace of mind and those spiritual qualities symbolized by the bird, the "chaste colibri". Goll's portrayal of Lilith as an equestrian appears to be a deviation from the traditional concept of Lilith,

> Quand sur son coursier qui s'échine ...

but it is one to which Goll adheres in several poems, among them *Lilith* in *Masques de Cendre*:

> J'attends que les sabots de ta monture ... [77]

and in *Fruit from Saturn:*

> Return o beautiful equestrian
> Astride the stallion of wind [78]

while in *Les Cercles Magiques* * she is referred to as:

> Écuyère de haute voltige sur la jument de feu [79]

In this sonnet of *Le Char Triomphal* Lilith is the androgynous figure so familiar in Goll's work:

> Lilith a fui de double lit
> Et s'est découverte androgyne ...
> Son sein unique se calcine

The androgyne appears again in *Les Cercles Magiques* *, *Masques de Cendre, Multiple Femme* * and *Neila,* and embodied by the Amazons, in *Le Mythe de la Roche Percée.* In *Masques de Cendre,* however, Lilith appears to symbolize Goll's wife Claire, and to exert a purifying influence upon the poet,

> Par les soleils semés dans tes rousseurs
> Par ton sang purificateur
> Annule le forfait des siècles [77]

and only in the last verse of the above poem is there an echo of the demonic aspect of Lilith:

> Oh toi qui couchais dans les tombes
> De tes amants plus nombreux que tes nuits
> Serai-je seul à coucher dans la tienne? [77]

---

[77] Yvan Goll, *Élégie d'Ihpétonga suivie de Masques de Cendre,* Paris 1949. The pages are not numbered in this edition. (*Masques de Cendre*).

[78] Yvan Goll, *Fruit from Saturn,* New York 1946, p. 31. (*Fruit from Saturn*).

[79] Yvan Goll, *Les Cercles Magiques*,* Paris 1951, p. 17. (*Les Cercles Magiques**).

Further aspects of Lilith will be discussed in connection with the poems in *Les Cercles Magiques* * (Chapter II).

Memnon, the subject of yet another "statue" sonnet in this cycle [80], is the singing stone, similarly portrayed in *Roche Chantante* of *Le Mythe de la Roche Percée* [81], and alluded to in the *Lilith* poem of *Les Cercles Magiques* * [82]. Goll was obviously acquainted with the legend of Memnon whose stones were reputed to utter strange musical sounds at the first rays of the rising sun — his mother Eos. Goll may have taken the idea from an interesting discussion of "Die Bedeutung des Memnonbildes" which he had read in J. J. Bachofen's *Der Mythus von Orient und Occident* [83]. In this sonnet Goll describes the rays of the rising sun striking the face of the rock:

> Captif une main de lumière
> Vient te frapper d'un double son
> Quand l'aurore surgit de son
> Abyssale et morne tanière

They are capable of effecting a transmutation of matter, and the poet therefore exhorts Memnon to respond to this and to free himself from his lapidary state:

> Pierre tu vengeras la pierre
> Scellée en un néfaste Non
> Perpétuel ô pur Memnon
> De ta souffrance lapidaire . . .
> Ébranle-toi grave statue

In *Le Mythe de la Roche Percée* Memnon is said to be "Rivé à sa pierreté" [81]. Thus imprisoned in his "souffrance lapidaire" Memnon has become silent and inert, but on account of this he is thought by Goll to be all the more powerful. The penetration of the rock (matter) by the rays of the sun (symbolizing spirit), in what constitutes an alchemical "coniunctio", releases the spirit from the rock in the form of music. The final state in this process of transmutation represents "Das Ende des Werkes: die lebendige Statue; der Stoff ganz Seele geworden, ganz Ton,

---

[80] *Dicht.*, p. 430.
[81] *Der Mythus*, p. 24.
[82] *Les Cercles Magiques**, p. 19.
[83] J. J. BACHOFEN, *Der Mythus von Orient und Occident*, Munich 1926, particularly pp. 102—104.

hörbares Gold" [84]. Memnon is thus no longer silent but has acquired the potential to become an oracle:

> Ton granit suant un sang rose
> Accepte sa métempsycose
> Guitare d'or à la voix humaine

The affinities between this transmutation and that of an alchemical experiment are obvious. Here, as in the Great Work, the final stage is characterized by the appearance of a reddish colour ("un sang rose").

In the following sonnet *Armoiries de la Parole* [85] Goll considers the active power of words, and this he expresses in a striking metaphor:

> Les mots sont les luisantes haches
> Pour creuser le puits d'une plaie

Words are capable of effecting great results:

> Un mot jeté dans la balance
> Fait déborder le lac qui stagne

A similar idea is expressed in *La Plaie* in similar images:

> Un seul mot jeté dans la balance du monde
> C'est insulter le volcan
> C'est faire déborder le lac
> Qui s'apprêtait à regarder en face le Dieu [86]

In *Armoiries* Goll states that it is only through the medium of words that the poet can hope to become aware of the life-force present in all things:

> Aveugle je ne m'approprie
> Que par le chant l'âme du seigle

Only thus is he able to apprehend the mysteries of nature which would otherwise remain unknown to him:

> Cents soleils dans ma panoplie
> Mais les barreaux de l'écriture
> M'ouvrent les bans de la nature

In the poem entitled *Pourquoi ne te perçois-je* Goll repeats this idea:

> Mais je ne m'approprie
> Que par le mot
> Ce qui m'échappe
> Par la passoire des cils et des mains [87]

---

[84] This is the explanatory note provided by the translator Kemp in *Dicht.*, p. 431.
[85] *Dicht.*, p. 432.
[86] *Multiple Femme**, p. 12.
[87] Ibid., p. 22.

The inclusion of *Armoiries de la Parole* in a cycle of sonnets designated by Goll as "hermétiques" is justifiable only in as far as the poet's task can be viewed as comparable to that of the alchemist. Working with their respective basic materials, both are attempting to transform them, to extract their essence. Poetry is the way of manipulating words to discover the "spirit" of things; alchemy is the procedure of manipulating matter in order to produce the Philosophers' Stone. It is, according to Goll's view, the process of "distillation" that provides a common link between the act of poetic creation and the Great Work of alchemy.

In the final sonnet of the cycle, *Chanson de Paracelse* [88], Goll applies the Word to various alchemical formulae used by the alchemist Paracelsus as remedies for different illnesses. In reality, however, these formulae merely represent the cant of medieval iatrochemistry:

> Avec le sang de l'éllébore
> J'ai guéri la démence
> Il faut cueillir la mandragore
> Au pied de la potence

Hellebore was apparently held in high esteem by the ancients, and its roots were often prepared as a drug which was indeed frequently used as an antidote to madness. The mandrake, too, has long been associated with the occult, and Goll's mention of it in connection with the gallows is by no means fortuitous [89]. The alchemical idea of the secret forces of minerals is illustrated in the verse:

> Du lac gelé de l'émeraude
> Jaillit un regard qui corrode
> Ma vanité de léopard

The glance emanating from the emerald exerts a cathartic and spiritualising influence upon the poet: its brightness and purity purge him of personal emotions. The jewel is equated with the human eye and resembles a frozen lake. The poet finally entreats Paracelsus to take him into his protection; the great alchemist is viewed by Goll as the embodiment of mystery and the posessor of so many occult secrets:

---

[88] *Dicht.*, p. 434.

[89] Cf. C. J. S. Thompson, *The Mystic Mandrake*, London 1934, particularly Chapter XV, "The Mandrake and the Gallows legend". "Another curious superstition that became associated with the mandrake, probably between the fifteenth and sixteenth centuries, was, that it sprang up and grew where the body of a criminal had polluted the ground, and generally beneath a gallows": p. 165.

Que nul tyran ne m'inféode
Étends sur moi ta main Vieillard
Impénétrable du Zohar

With his reference to "tyran" Goll may be thinking once again of the potential danger of the metals he is melting down. This idea was encountered in the second sonnet — "Tyran qu'innocemment je sers/Le métal est un grand dément". Goll therefore invokes the aid of the Grand Old Alchemist in order to assure the success of his undertaking.

A review of this cycle in its entirety establishes the fact that certain sonnets are directly linked by virtue of their imagery. Sonnets I, II, III, V, VI, VII, VIII and XV, all make use to some extent of identifiable alchemical or cabbalistic material. The fourth sonnet can be regarded as dealing indirectly with similar material, since the relationship between the Tarot and alchemy and cabbalism has already been noted. Sonnets XI, XII and XIII deal with mystic statues or oracles. Two of these statues, La Fille Chaste d'Héraclite and Memnon, appear to be undergoing some sort of transmutation similar to that of alchemy. The third, Lilith, seems to have little in common with alchemical concepts in this context, unless she is intended to represent the hermetic androgyne. If this is the case, however, it is far from obvious. Nevertheless, as the embodiment of sensuality and lust, Lilith might represent that aspect of man's nature which must be destroyed before purification and regeneration can take place. Sonnet XIV deals with the power of words to reveal the hidden laws of the universe. In this respect the subject-matter has affinities with cabbalistic concepts, according to which knowledge of God is possible only through the Word. The analogy between the processes of alchemy and those of poetry has already been noted. In sonnets IX and XV, the rhetoric which has been learned through experimentation is applied as an actual poetic technique, but the ninth sonnet can hardly be termed "hermetic". Sonnet X deals mainly with the magical attributes of numbers. From this point of view it can be linked with alchemical concepts, in which number symbolism plays an important role. What the dice undoubtedly does symbolize for Goll, is the inexplicable element of chance in life. He was continually fascinated by the element of chance present in such games as dice-throwing and roulette [90]. Sonnet VI can also be partially included in the category of numerology.

[90] This is mentioned lightheartedly in a letter written by Claire to Yvan from Boulogne sur Seine, dated September 1923. It is published in *Yvan Goll — Claire Goll:*

The principle of selection behind these poems is difficult to determine, despite the fact that many of them appear to be dealing, either directly or symbolically, with the liberation of spirit from matter. Goll's description of this cycle as "un recueil de sonnets hermétiques, en quête de la Pierre Philosophale" implies that he understood the term "hermetic" as specifically pertaining to alchemy, in which case it would be inadequate as a designation for the entire subject-matter of this cycle. On the other hand, general usage provides no such specific meaning for the term "hermetic", defining it as "belonging to magic or alchemy, magical" [91]. If Goll's statement is to be understood in the more general sense, it would be a more suitable description of the sonnets in Le Char Triomphal.

Briefe, Mainz and Berlin 1966, p. 44: "Wie oft konstatierte ich die magische Anziehungskraft, die sogar das Roulette einer Jahrmarktsbude auf Dich ausübt. Dann entdecke ich in deinem Gesicht jene französische Leidenschaft für den Zufall ..." (Briefe)
[91] Part of the definition given in Chambers's Twentieth Century Dictionary, ed. William Geddie, 4th ed., London 1960.

Chapter II

LES CERCLES MAGIQUES*

Unlike the poems of the previous cycle, those of *Les Cercles Magiques**
were apparently composed over a period of years. Although the majority
of them are of unknown date, there exists evidence to prove that one, at
least, was written as early as 1942. In contrast to this, however, the
imagery of certain poems suggests a much later date of composition,
possibly 1947 or 1948 [1].

That Goll was dealing with material similar in many respects to that
of *Le Char Triomphal* can be seen from a random glance at some of the
titles: *Métamorphose, Raziel, Lilith* and so on. Whether these poems
were conceived on the basis of a unity of subject-matter will be considered in due course. One critic sees in this cycle only the unity of circularity, but states that even this fails to correlate the poems to any
degree of satisfaction [2]. The title anticipates to a large extent the imagery of the cycle, for a dominant image is that of the circle (represented
by such spherical objects as rings, hoops, wheels, etc.); closely connected
with this is the concept of circular motion (rotation, torque, convolution,
and so on). Goll's own ideas on the subject of circularity appear in one
of his manuscripts, in English: "In the noose of cyclical generation we
garrot ourselves. All formulas fail, down and up are equal alternatives
to end strangulation. The tower stabs, once at the ring, and dwindles.
Pang recoils, in a last white place, in the fortress where beauty sonam-
bulates in an anaesthetized sleep. The fatal six is looped. The rattle is per-
sistent to the question: Who then? the fabulous imponderable, who then?
the carping piteous small, who? invincible and newly born as the new
moon, who? runner on the brink of tombs — Velocity turned our remem-

---

[1] According to Goll's notes the poem *Élégie sur une pêche* was written on August
12, 1942. The poem *Les Cercles Magiques* was published in Goll's magazine *Hémisphères* in 1945. When the imagery of certain poems appears to indicate a late date of
composition, this will be noted in the text.
[2] Cf. CARMODY, p. 147.

brance. Only tear and the tissue are history and testimonial that this devil has been exorcised before — A zenith is mounted above the horizon to hoop the eye the instant before it can pierce. Eternity feeding on its own tail binds up the sum of self-devouring. But the whirling instant of the fall's own halt: the egg has consumed the egg, has consumed the last, the umbilical cord that binds to circular law, and deletes itself.

Return is to inward, where circle is reconciled in non-Euclidean globe. The scorpion never was. There never was a circle" [3].

The text seems to relate the circle to a number of other ideas in Goll's poetry. Once again he refers to the magical properties of the number six, "the fatal six" as he calls it, a reminder of the "lasso de la mort" of Le Dé. "Runner on the brink of tombs" probably refers to Lilith and is reminiscent of the lines from Masques de Cendre, "Oh toi qui couchais dans les tombes ...". The allusion to "eternity feeding on its own tail" appears to link the circles to alchemical symbolism, according to which the serpent or dragon eating its own tail represents the alchemical process itself, the rebirth of things by means of their apparent destruction. The connection between the "magic circles" of Goll and the Great Work of alchemy is further indicated by the wood-cut which, together with Goll's poem Les Cercles Magiques, appeared in his magazine Hémisphères in 1945. Ideas such as the eye that can pierce, velocity, involution, "the noose of cyclical generation", the scorpion etc., appear frequently in this cycle.

Images connected with circularity appear from the outset of the cycle. The circle is, of course, the figure that best represents totality or the absolute. As the perfect geometrical form it illustrates Goll's concept of the "absolute object" or the "Ding an sich". In its eternal rotation it embodies the fundamental laws of energy; it represents time, and the cessation of its motion would signify death.

In the first poem, Les Cercles Magiques, [4] the poet is depicted as caught in the circle which determines his position in time and space. He is at the mercy of forces beyond his control, for he desires to escape from this cyclic motion, but cannot. The speed of the rotation can increase to such an extent that it crushes and destroys man as if he were corn in a mill-wheel:

---

[3] Quoted in CARMODY, pp. 147—148.
[4] Cf. Les Cercles Magiques*, pp. 11—14.

Pris dans le cercle de mon astre
Tournant avec la roue qui tourne dans mon cœur
Et la meule de l'univers qui moud les grains du temps

Once again the interplay between macrocosm and microcosm is illustrated in these lines. References to astrology [5], itself an occult science based on an analogy between the macrocosm and the microcosm, are indicated by the "cercle du bélier", the Ram as the possessor of occult secrets (just as all the twelve constellations of the Zodiac were regarded as an external expression of spiritual forces). "Rien ne va plus: croupier du zodiac" links the theme to that of games of chance, as do the lines:

Hélas le démon de mon dé
Me perce de ses vingt et un yeux noirs

The poet desires to escape both from the circles and from the darkness surrounding him, the latter indicated by the images "quartz des nuits" and "ombre". Such an escape is apparently offered him by Lilith, whose eyes are the gateway to knowledge or oblivion. Thus in his search for ultimate knowledge, and in his desire to escape from the cyclic process of cosmic time, the poet attempts to plunge through the eyes of the vast statue:

Dans ton oeil bleu Lilith comme un cerceau d'azur
Je tente le saut de la mort
Et je descends vers le gond de tes sangs
Je descends l'escalier sans fin des siècles

The image "cerceau d'azur" contains the idea of an open spherical form, a circus hoop, and eyes of an intense shade of blue. This colour is particularly significant in this context since, according to Kandinsky, "Depth is found in blue, first in its physical movements (1) of retreat from the spectator, (2) of turning in upon its own centre. It affects us likewise mentally in any geometrical form. The deeper its tone, the more intense and characteristic the effect. We feel a call to the infinite, a desire for purity and transcendence" [6]. Such is the feeling experienced by the poet. "Le saut de la mort" evokes the world of the circus again and the constant fear and danger experienced by the acrobatic performers.

[5] Cf. E. Tylor, *Primitive Culture*, London 1920, vol. 1, pp. 128—129: "Astrology, in the immensity of its delusive influence on mankind, and by the comparatively modern period to which it remained an honoured branch of philosophy, may claim the highest rank among the occult sciences".

[6] Wassily Kandinsky, *Concerning the Spiritual in Art*, Vol. 5 of the series 'Documents of Modern Art', Geo. Wittenborn, New York 1966, p. 58.

In the last two lines quoted above, Goll emphasizes the idea of descent (both spatial and temporal); but since "up and down are equal alternatives to end strangulation", the poet is given the alternative of ascending:

> Ou monterai-je l'échelle de jeu
> Qu'entourent les ailes des anges?

The concepts of descent and ascent which appear from time to time in Goll's poetry are usually expressed in images of steps and ladders; the latter sometimes represent a kind of Jacob's ladder, surrounded by spiritual beings and linking the world below with the world above. The use of the word "gond" (hinge) in connection with Lilith reinforces the idea of the eye as a door, an entrance or exit. The poet then proceeds to enumerate various occultisms he thought he had mastered. In reality such occultisms symbolize the poet's attempts to escape from the perpetual rotation of the circles, since all of them involve the construction or inhabitation of static, non-circular structures: "tour, le 1 vertical, pyramide, hexagone, pentacle, le dé carré, la forteresse où capter l'ange/Dans un sommeil d'ivoire un sommeil sans paupières". In the final example Goll implies that the angel would be capable of protecting him from the circles; the subsequent cessation of motion implied by "sommeil d'ivoire" would then resemble the "anaesthetized sleep" mentioned previously. However, all his ventures into the occult have been to no avail for the marks on the dice suddenly take on the aspect of eyes. A similar idea of the inescapable gaze of the dice appears in one of Goll's unpublished poems:

> Hélas tous ces dés ont des yeux d'épouvante
> Qui ne se ferment pas comme ceux des morts
> Des yeux qui te fixent à travers tous les granits
> A travers toutes les tombes [7]

In *Les Cercles Magiques* the poet becomes increasingly enmeshed in new circles, which in turn become associated in his mind with the wheeling movements of hovering vultures and thus with the idea of death itself:

> Des yeux d'oiseaux des yeux de serpents des yeux de femmes
> M'enroulent dans de nouveaux cercles
> Des cercles de vautours virent au-dessus de ma vie
> Des spirales de spirilles tracent le 6 de ma mort
> Des yeux de tout feu s'ouvrent se ferment

[7] Unpublished poem in the possession of Mme. Goll.

Once again the number six appears in connection with the idea of death, while the eyes "de tout feu" resemble the vast fiery orbits of Diana of Ephesus (*La Fille Chaste d'Héraclite*). Suddenly, however, Goll's attention turns again to alchemical matters, with images of the "dragon d'or", a variant of mercury symbolizing the vision and experience of alchemy; and "cet aigle qui pond ses oeufs . . .", the eagle being synonymous in alchemical symbolism with the phoenix rising from the egg. The image of "ce personnage qui court sur le bord de la roue" recalls the Tarot emblem of the Wheel of Fortune, but also recalls to a certain extent the mythological figure of Sisyphus. Nevertheless, despite all his attempts to penetrate the mysteries of the universe, the poet does not expect to receive an answer, for he says "Le vent de la voûte astrale nous coupe la mémoire". Goll voiced the same idea in his manuscript when he stated that "velocity turned our remembrance". Again he attempts to halt the circular movement by various means:

> J'essaie toutes les clefs usées pour briser le cercle
> Je lance les lettres de l'alphabet comme des ancres dans l'oubli
> Je plante les racines des mots dans les sillons de mon front
> Je jardine la roseraie magique
> La rose des vents la rose de sable

These lines, apart from their allusion to the word-manipulations of cabbalism ("Je lance les lettres de l'alphabet . . ."), also appear to refer to the Tarot, in which features a secret rose-garden to which one only has access by means of the Key. It must be borne in mind, however, that the rose is also a well-known alchemical symbol. The final line quoted above anticipates the imagery used by Goll, particularly in *Traumkraut*, where similar images express both desolation and transience, and also physical disintegration, as in the poem *Rosentum* [8].

If the poet were able to penetrate the veil of reality and enter the realm beyond, he feels that he still would not be free from the circles:

> Et si je tente le plongeon en ange dans le miroir
> Mille nouveaux cercles couvent vers le bord du monde

Like the eyes themselves the "mirror" represents a passageway to knowledge, but just as the poet is in the process of contemplating whether or not to plunge through it, he perceives Lilith, now a figure of cosmic proportions:

---

[8] *Dicht.*, p. 450.

> Mais quelle est cette déesse parée des bracelets de Saturne?
> Quelle est cette énergie qui fouette les ellipses?

The energy behind the perpetual movement of circular objects emanates from Lilith. She is the activating principle of the universe, maintaining both the movement of the planetary system and that of the microcosm. Similarly in *Lilith* of *Multiple Femme** she is referred to as:

> Écuyère du manège du monde
> Enfourchant le cheval du vent
> Et dirigeant d'un seul élan des cuisses
> Le cours des ellipses fatales
>
> Les soleils obéissent et bondissent autour de toi . . . [9]

Thus it can be seen that Lilith has acquired a new significance for Goll. She is no longer merely the demon and temptress of men but has become a vast figuration of the universe, holding sway over the macrocosm itself. This concept is extended into the poem — *Lilith* [10] — in which Goll enlarges upon Lilith as a symbol of cosmic forces; but it is only at night, when everything has slackened speed, that the poet is able to call upon Lilith within his own consciousness. This is yet a further illustration of the macrocosm-microcosm situation, for the external events of the cosmos are projected into the mind of the poet:

> Les nuits où les cercles magiques perdent leur centre
> Où les planètes semblent ralentir . . .
> Je t'appelle Lilith tournant dans le cirque de ma tête

Lilith has assumed enormous proportions in the poet's mind, and is now portrayed as:

> Écuyère de haute voltige sur la jument de feu
> Toi qui jongle avec les œufs du monde
> Balançant le soleil sur ta tête hiératique
> Qui fait virer Mercure sur l'index gauche
> Et tourner à ton bras droit les six anneaux de Saturne

As an equestrian Lilith is the embodiment of the elemental forces of the universe. She supplies the energy to keep it in perpetual motion. Once again Goll makes use of circus images: "le cirque de ma tête, écuyère, jument de feu, jongle, balançant, virer, tourner", for Lilith's despotic control of the cosmos, her direction of the planets, is reminiscent of a

[9] *Multiple Femme**, p. 24.
[10] *Lilith* in *Les Cercles Magiques**, pp. 17—24.

circus act. In this poem she retains her evil powers; indeed, she appears more menacing than ever. Goll heightens this impression of evil by his depiction of her eyes as rotating:

> Tes yeux tournent comme des miroirs d'alouettes
> Méduse qui transforme le coeur en granit

These eyes, which are in spontaneous movement, resemble a "larking-glass", for they entice men to danger and death. Lilith also possesses the power to destroy men by turning their hearts to stone. In contrast to this she has the ability to maintain life by perpetual motion. She is the "frisson centrifuge "and her influence is apparent both within the microcosm, "au-dedans du diamant", and within the macrocosm, "au dehors du zodiaque". Thus her function is both negative and positive.

The reference to sellers of dreams, "celles qui vendaient le rêve" and to "celles qui cueillaient les médicines odorées sur les tombes", appears to have been taken from Trachtenberg, who mentions the medicinal value of herbs, their associations with the spirits and their consequent occult potency [11]. Lilith's associations with occult rites connected with nature are indicated in the lines:

> Amante des métaux reine des herbes
> Avec le hibou au poing
> Tu exorcises les démons

The allusion to the anti-demonic rite performed by Lilith is somewhat ironic since, according to various legends, such rites were often performed against Lilith herself. Lilith appears elsewhere in Goll's poetry in a similar role:

> Tu nourris tes amants d'herbes précieuses ... [12]

and likewise:

> J'ai soupesé la pierre occulte où tu habites [13]

and in *Baala II:*

> C'est toi qu'attendaient les herbes savantes
> Et les onyx mystiques [14]

---

[11] TRACHTENBERG, pp. 206 f. Also in connection with this point, see *Jean sans Terre,* p. 177, where the editor Carmody quotes from Goll's notebook.

[12] *Lilith* in *Les Cercles Magiques* *, p. 23.

[13] *Lilith* in *Masques de Cendre.*

[14] *Multiple Femme*, p. 27.

Despite the enormous power she now wields, Lilith is unable to escape from tradition and from the authority of the past:

> Cependant tu souffres quand te regardent les Mères
> Assises en rond dans l'amphithéâtre des siècles
> Devineresses sûres de leur réussite
> En attendant que tournent tournent
> Les tournesols jusqu'à la fin du jour

The idea of infinite, monotonous circular motion is expressed in the image of the sunflowers: it is an idea which is aptly conveyed by the French word "tournesols" but lost to a great extent by the German rendering "Sonnenblumen", since this conjures up no associations with rotation.

In Part II of this poem great emphasis is placed on Lilith's function as a seer. Her eyes, still in constant rotation, are compared with a mirror in which man is able to recognise himself. In desiring to penetrate beyond these eyes, he is seeking not only truth and knowledge, but freedom from human limitations, freedom from self:

> J'ai voulu éteindre ces yeux ces cercles qui m'enferment
> Un oeil comme un cerceau tendu de papier de soie
> Au travers duquel le clown fait le saut de la mort
> Oeil rond, oeil monstre de Lilith

Echoing Part I of the poem, the circus images reappear: "cerceau tendu de papier de soie, le clown, le saut de la mort". Lilith, as a world figuration, symbolizes the earth, and thus the poet's "death-leap" through her eyes constitutes a descent to the centre of the earth, comparable to the alchemist's return to the matrix or primeval chaos. The return from "death" alluded to in the lines

> Je rentre, Lilith, et tu peux m'aimer à nouveau
> Je reviens de ma tombe . . .

is in reality a return to life and the perpetual motion of the circles, which in no way constitutes a regeneration analogous to that of alchemy. It is a return to his former life rather than a spiritual regeneration. Once again the poet's ventures into the realms of the occult have caused him to draw a blank. He has now returned from that mysterious region beyond the realm of human experience. This idea is emphasized by Goll's reference to birds and crocodiles, which were believed, particularly in Egyptian mythology, to be vested with some mysterious inscrutable force related to the extra-human world:

Je viens de là-bas . . .
Où l'oiseau était du complot et le crocodile était dieu

The poet even compares himself to Memnon, yet an additional reference
to indicate the extent of his explorations. He now believes that he has
subjugated Lilith by means of all the knowledge he has gained through
his experiments in various branches of the occult. Lilith is now like the
god imprisoned in the dice and her imprisonment appears to have brought
about a temporary cessation of movement:

A présent tu m'aimes, Lilith, fille des vents,
Le démon de mon dé t'a subjuguée
Tu vis enfermée dans le donjon carré du dé . . .
Tu dors d'un sommeil d'ivoire d'un sommeil sans paupières

But despite his apparent victory he cannot escape from her eyes and
their perpetual movement:

Mais tes yeux me regardent
Tes yeux innombrables emplis d'eau noire
Hublots à jamais fermés du chaland de Charon
Yeux à jamais ouverts des serpents
Tes yeux, Lilith, qui me perforent à mort tous les jours

Lilith's associations with death are heavily stressed in these lines,
while the description of her eyes as "Hublots à jamais fermés . . ."
recalls the similar image of the "hublots illuminés" in Le Dé. Man's
inability to evade the scrutiny of such eyes and thus escape from life
itself is the subject of one of Goll's unpublished poems entitled L'Heure
du Passeur, in which he says:

Et je suis vu de tous ces yeux
J'en suis vu j'en suis perforé et mis à nu
Il n'y a pas d'échappatoire du monde [15]

In terms similar to those used in the first poem of this cycle, the circles reappear. Goll speaks of "vautours fermant ma spirale", "cercles du
soleil", "la roue du Zodiaque", and of "Cercles qui lentement font de
moi le scorpion" (this latter alluding to the fallacious belief that scorpions
commit suicide by stinging themselves to death if tortured by fire). The
conclusion to be drawn from all this is obvious; namely, that images
of circularity evoke associations with death for the poet. More specifically, Goll's "magic circles" are connected with the lethiferous eyes of

---

[15] This unpublished poem belongs to Lackawanna Elegy*.

Lilith. She is accorded insight into the mysteries of the universe, the secrets of life and death. For Goll the way to attainment of a higher reality (equated with "death") proceeds from the world of the senses; thus as the embodiment of physical forces, Lilith is indispensable to the poet in his search for the absolute. However, all man's gropings towards self-knowledge are shown to be futile, since so many questions remain to which man can find no answers. According to Goll, Abulafia alone possessed the secret key with which to open the "door of doors", since he lived in the "cercle intérieur".

With the mention of the alchemist Abulafia, Goll returns once again to familiar subject-matter and imagery. He stresses the idea of descent involved in the alchemist's search:

> Il descendit en soi-même l'escalier sans degrés

Goll himself despairs of ever finding the names of God. The futility of his search and his subsequent despondency are apparent in the final lines of the poem:

> Mais combien de vies fallut-il pour trouver le chiffre
> Du nom de Dieu
> Combien de clefs se brisèrent dans les mains friables de l'homme
> Pense pense pense jusqu'au bout de la folie
> Que la fleur gonflée de sens s'élève comme une danseuse rose ...

Despite man's attempts to attain self-knowledge and spiritualisation, the perpetual rotation of the circles, i. e. time or "life", and the proliferation of the organic world (the evil aspect of which is symbolized by the "sphex (qui) pond ses oeufs, dans le cadavre d'un ange") prove too much for him.

After so many speculations Goll returns again (*Lilith* III) to a consideration of Lilith. Now he visualizes her as a monarch exhorting her brothers, the winds (for whom Goll invented the names Orr, Kabawak, Kiffi and Mirabad), to transport her back into the past to the land of her origin, which Goll associates with various aspects of the Near-East (Semiramis, Birs-Nimrod, the Hanging Gardens of Babylon), and also with such monsters as Medea and the Eumenides. The theme of ancestry and of a return to one's ancestors is common to several of Goll's poems of this period, and was possibly inspired by the alchemical concept of a return to primal matter. The poet's desire to portray everything in its totality is illustrated by his use of contrast, as for example in "la porte de Jade" and "le Pont de Cendre". He finally addresses Lilith (IV) in erotic tones, using images similar to those of *La Rose des Roses*. He lays particular stress on her associations with the occult:

Ton sein est la rose des roses des roses
Tu nourris tes amants d'herbes précieuses . . .

Lilith is once again the goddess of carnal desire in whose arms the poet attempts to lose himself and experience "death". But the unreality of this experience is indicated by the images "bras de poussière" and "chair de rose". His return to life from his "death" is referred to in the lines:

J'ai vécu de mourir
Et je suis mort de vivre

Life itself is like death for him since he is unable to escape from the perpetual motion of the circles. The allusions to death are numerous: for example, "tête morte", "masque", the "bataille féroce" between opposing forces in the universe, and the reference to man's fight for survival. The element of evil is hinted at in the images of wasps and of spiders' eggs. It finally appears that the experiences described have brought the poet to the borders of insanity for he speaks of "le cirque démoli de ma tête".

Images connected with circularity appear in the poem *Élégie sur une Pêche* [16]. Goll's interest in circles as purely geometric symbols dates back to the Cubist influence of Cendrars and Apollinaire, and only in later years do they become vested with some sort of esoteric significance for him. This particular poem is in fact a good illustration of Goll's concept of "réisme", although his ideas on the subject were not formulated concisely until many years later in the manifesto, *Le Réisme*, of 1950 [17]. Nevertheless, it is obvious that the peach, as a perfect autonomous sphere, is a pertinent example of what Goll later termed the "absolute object" or the "Ding an sich". Moreover, in its capacity as a spontaneously rotating object, it illustrates his theory of the "objet végétatif en action". Objects such as the peach of this poem, or the rose, are set in motion and are thus drawn into a vast rotatory system linking the microcosm and the macrocosm; it is precisely by means of this rotatory system as a source of energy, that the "absolute object" is maintained in constant motion.

[16] *Les Cercles Magiques**, pp. 27—29.
[17] GOLL's manifesto, *Le Réisme*, appears in *Quatre Études*, pp. 206—207.

In the opening lines of the poem the peach is addressed in tones even more erotic than those of *La Rose des Roses*. The peach is more suggestive of eroticism on account of its fullness and texture — "pêche de volupté" and pêche d'amour" are indications of this quality and its accompanying associations with woman and love. As the embodiment of sensuality, the peach turns and spins like a dancer, "ballerine qui tourne comme un miroir aux anges". By its ability to reflect external reality, the mirror thus provides a link between the microcosm and macrocosm, an identification of subject and object. The angels, hovering between the upper and lower spheres, perform a similar function. Thus the peach itself is set in relation to the macrocosm. It ripens to a perfect autonomous sphere, and as the spontaneously rotating "fleur à l'hélice rose", it is Goll's "objet végétatif en action". The peach is described as being:

Solidement vissé à la loi sidérale
Par les écrous et les noeuds de la branche
Respirant sous la tente laquée du feuillage
Travaillant nuit et jour
Dans l'atelier astral dont les courroies invisibles
Fournissent le courant cosmique

Thus Goll reinforces the idea that the finite is subject to the same laws of motion as the infinite. The peaches (later referred to as "planètes-fruits") reach up into the planetary system like branches of the universal tree. They are directed by the movement of the planets into the "ballet impérial du monde", which in this case symbolizes the regulated order of the cosmos. The significant factor in the second verse of Goll's poem is his use of technical words, words connected with machinery: "vissé, écrous, travaillant, atelier, courroies". By comparing the peach (which as part of the organic world is subject to the eternal process of growth and decay) with the solid, unchangeable form of machines, Goll is attempting to lessen the "organic" aspect of the fruit and to render it more "absolute". Likewise, the accordance of microcosm and macrocosm summarized in the image "ton noyau cœur de l'univers" (cf. "Die Nuss in deren Schale der Ursinn wohnt") [18] centralises the action and thus makes it more absolute.

The peach has at one and the same time the qualities of eroticism and innocence, "innocence des vierges et gobelet de sang". This dual aspect

---

[18] From *Die Sonnen-Kantate* in *Dicht.*, p. 456.

is emphasized by the poet in such phrases as "fruit d'amour et du crime", "plus solide que roc et plus mortel que mousse". The poet rejoices in his possession of the "untouchable fruit". Finally, however, he abandons specific references; he extends the action spatially ("vergers, Orient, Olympe" etc.) in order to present a more general concept of the peach, culminating in the image of "pêche de toutes les chairs!" In the closing lines of the poem Goll alludes to the peach's ability to propagate:

Mythologie du coeur du monde
Je te mange
Et crache ton noyau aux lendemains

This seems to belie the poet's previous statement that the peaches "N'avaient qu'une raison d'être", namely, "Tomber à la terre vétuste/ Et pourrir". Possibly Goll finds consolation in the final indication of permanence assured by the generative process. Furthermore, this ability for self-propagation is an important attribute of the Philosophers' Stone. This, together with the emphasis placed on the interrelationship between the macrocosm and the microcosm, appears to indicate that the subject-matter is based to a certain extent on alchemical premises, which have of course been both modified and poetized. Thus the peach has various functions in this poem: (1) in its capacity as a spherical, "absolute" object; (2) as an illustration of that object in motion; (3) as a symbol of woman and love; (4) as an object capable of self-propagation, and thus analogous to the hermaphroditic Stone which fertilizes, creates and brings itself forth; (5) as a rotating spherical object the peach provides a link between the macrocosm and the microcosm, and as such, is an adaptation of the alchemical belief "as above, so below".

In the following poem, *Élégie de la Liberté* [19], the word "liberté" might almost be equated with "nothingness" or "infinity" and can therefore be related to the concepts symbolized by the statues of Lilith and Vénus des Ténèbres; both statues offer the poet escape from self into the "abyss". Since the poem was almost certainly composed during Goll's exile in the United States of America, he may have been tempted to incorporate into it various aspects of the Statue of Liberty, which, incidentally, he could see from his apartment. Goll introduces a slightly exotic note into the poem, however, by referring to his "liberty" as:

---

[19] *Les Cercles Magiques**, pp. 30—31.

> ... l'enfant de la mousson
> Et d'un vieux sage du désert
> Sur les pentes du Liban
> Elle garda la chèvre sacrée
> Dont les yeux enfumés recelaient
> La folie des déesses invengées

As in previous poems the image of the eye appears. The eye, absorbing as it does the totality of the external world, provides a link between the world above and the world below. In the second verse the poet states his willingness to go to any lengths in order to achieve his aim of liberty (in this instance an amalgam of sensuality and fate):

> O mon amante Liberté
> Conduis-moi au bord du cratère
> Où je brûlerai ma dernière rose ...

He is prepared to sever his last contact with reality (symbolized here by the "dernière rose") and to follow wherever he is led. However, the sea appears to him as the only unbiased region, and it is there that he proposes to erect a "mirror-palace" which will then serve as a refuge from hostile reality and even from death itself:

> Nous construirons au sein de l'océan impassible
> Avec un peu de chaux et de salive
> Le palais de miroir aux cent portes
> Aux cent escaliers vrillant vers le vieux ciel
> Qui sert à rescaper les anges en danger

The image of the palace or castle is one which recurs in *Traumkraut*. Such buildings represent a permanent stabilising factor for Goll in the face of transience and the threat of encroaching non-entity. The brightness of the interior of the palace is indicated by "miroir", and its many exits by the "cent portes" and "cent escaliers".

In the final verse the poet's "liberty" is made more concrete:

> O ma belle petite Liberté rouge
> D'un rouge entre le minium et le géranium

He addresses it in terms which suggest that he envisages its tangible representation in the form of such objects as the rose or the peach of the previous elegy. In the final lines there is a tender, melancholy note in contrast to the almost jubilant tone of the previous poem. In the final instance the poet is still prepared to take the irrevocable step towards self-extinction:

Je suis prêt à fendre la foule des vagues
Qui me piétineront

However, neither the goal itself nor the measures he proposes to take in order to achieve it are clearly defined here. Thus the poem closes with the question of the poet's fate left unanswered.

At this stage in the cycle the subject-matter of the poems becomes increasingly autobiographical, since in them Goll expresses his emotions concerning his fatal illness, leukemia. Both *Le Moulin de la Mort*[20] and the *Élégie du Pauvre Égo*[21] deal expressly with the idea of approaching death. They are purely personal records of Goll's thoughts and reactions and therefore cannot be fully understood and interpreted without a knowledge of Goll's personal circumstances. For example, the significance in *Le Moulin de la Mort* of such images as

O jardins blancs du soleil albinos
Sangs blêmes du circuit matinal . . .

must necessarily be lost on the reader who is unaware of the fact that they symbolize an excess of white corpuscles in the poet's blood.

By their insistence on the ideas of transience and death, these two poems anticipate to a large extent the themes of *Traumkraut*. *Le Moulin de la Mort* emphasizes the idea of death in images connected with circularity. In this respect it is reminiscent of the first poem, *Les Cercles Magiques,* in which Goll mentions the "meule de l'univers qui moud les grains du temps". Here Death itself is envisaged as a "Belle meunière" who is grinding both the poet's bones and his remaining hours. Just as he was unable to escape from the rotation of the circles, so here he is unable to evade death — it has begun to appropriate his body, "O ma mort allongée en moi", and has become his "mariée irrémédiable". The entire poem is a horrible testimony to the ebbing-away of the poet's power of consciousness: the advent of insanity (which occasionally accompanies leukemia) is indicated by the image "rosiers de ma frénésie". The emphasis on dryness, disintegration and the white, chalky quality of everything is all too familiar in Goll's last poems and has its origin in the poet's vision of the destructive lymphocytes consuming his blood: "plâtre, jardins blancs, soleil albinos, sangs blêmes, copeaux blancs, blé blanc, farine, l'oiseau de cendre" etc. The poet's strength is gra-

[20] Ibid., pp. 32—35.
[21] Ibid., pp. 36—38.

dually being sapped away and he begins to resemble a lifeless, sightless statue; his eyes have become "incrusted"; the "doors" of his heart no longer open. In his awareness of approaching death he no longer dares to look upon a rose (again the symbol of life and consciousness), for fear that it should wither. Even the external world of nature is projected into the body of the poet and participates in his suffering:

L'eucalyptus éclot en mes yeux éclatés
L'agave s'arrache le coeur

The image of the angels reappears. The poet speaks of them as being "Les anges à la face double qui sont coupables d'innocence", thus emphasizing their dual function, which was originally to bring life and awareness to the poet ("L'idée de ma première rose"), and is now to announce his death (symbolized by "le vieillissement soudain des anémones"). Thus the angels resemble Janus and their influence extends back into the past and forward into the future.

The poem finally closes with the poet's entreaty to the mill to quicken the advent of oblivion and thus end his suffering:

Moulin, mouds l'eau du néant!

In *Élégie du Pauvre Égo* [21] the poet is again dealing with the theme of bodily disintegration and decay, but in this instance he lays greater stress on the solitary state of man, imprisoned in the "tower" of his flesh which daily becomes more odious to him. The human body is viewed as a crumbling structure built of "cinquante douleurs/Entre des murailles moisissantes". (Goll later refers to the "ruines de mes clavicules"). The "fire-proof angel" he should have kept with him for spiritual assistance has departed, and the "fire-angel" (symbolizing his illness, and possibly reflecting Goll's reading of Heraclitus) has appeared in its place. Goll's increasing horror and disgust is reflected in his attitude towards his body, progressing from "Je ne t'aime plus, mon pauvre Égo" to "Je ne t'aime plus étranger ... Je ne t'aime plus, toi qui oublias/Toutes les félicités de l'ange"; his body has forgotten all the joys of life. It now resembles a rusty, broken-down machine, covered in dust: "Tout occupé de ta poussière ...". In the delirium of his illness, (symbolized again by fire images, "un goût calciné ... depuis que l'aile de pourpre prit feu") Goll feels completely isolated and abandoned, as if the hand of friendship were no longer stretched out to him, but had withered like an elm in October, "laissant voir les veines sans amour". The intensity of this feeling of solitude, symbolized by the departure of the angel, is mirrored in his cry of despair:

Je suis seul, je suis seul dans ma tour de chair . . .
Je suis seul, je suis seul
Car l'ange m'a quitté

The truth of the statement from *Lucifer Vieillissant* that "La solitude est le seul état qui se transmette de la vie à la mort" [22] was never more relevant than at this moment when the poet, completely alone, hovers on the brink of life and death. Only occasionally is he driven from his "prison" by physical needs such as hunger. The transience of man's existence is indicated by images such as "babylones de fourmis", while the desire for permanence and retribution is reflected in the final lines of the poem:

Un jour, quand la roche ne se changera plus en sable
Quand la mer se retirera de mon coeur
L'ange à la chevelure de feu
Reviendra-t-il pour rendre justice?

The following poem *Métamorphose* [23] is one of the most obscure poems in this cycle. Superficially, at least, it appears to offer little illumination apart from the title, which relates the subject-matter to the theme of change, and the indication that the "Voix de l'Éternel" is the culminating point in the process. However, an unpublished, modified version of the poem (beginning "Et le chant de Raziel . . .") indicates that the subject-matter is connected with Raziel and thus indirectly with alchemy or cabbalism. The references in this poem to the Archangel, (possibly Michael or Gabriel) to Absalom and Isaac, point to a biblical or semitic source. Since there is throughout the poem an emphasis on movement, sounds and vibrations ("Et le chant, le mol reproche, la voix des violoncelles, la voix sexuelle du jonc, parole de la peur de sable, la Voix de l'Éternel") [24], it is possible that the poem relates to the occult theory that everything in the universe vibrates or undulates. This theory of vibration as the basis of manifestation is connected with numerology and linked to Key 14 of the Tarot pack, which in turn signifies adaptation and coordination. This interpretation does not purport to be anything other than conjecture, and if not conclusive, is certainly plausible. The

---

[22] YVAN GOLL, *Lucifer Vieillissant*, Paris 1934, p. 69. (*Lucifer Vieillissant*).
[23] *Les Cercles Magiques**, pp. 39—40.
[24] Cf. *Bahir*, p. 33, note 6, in which the editor Scholem writes: "Die Mystik der 'Stimme' ist ein alter Gegenstand der Spekulation, und spielt auch in der deutschen Richtung der Kabbala eine sehr große Rolle . . .".

emphasis on various changes taking place in nature is reinforced by what appears to be an indirect allusion to the change-theory of Heraclitus; "La veulerie du fleuve qui nous quitte/Qui nous quittera toujours". It is by means of the metamorphoses of the external world that God is finally made manifest and dwells in the "oreilles de la rose". (Christ was believed by the Gnostics to dwell in the rose; Buddha and Shiva were thought to dwell in the lotus).

This poem is difficult to interpret because of the apparently syncretic nature of the imagery. It is almost impossible to relate it to any one branch of the occult sciences, and for this reason, only general indications of possible interpretations can be given.

The poem *Loterie* [25] proves more intelligible. As the title indicates, its main theme is that of hazard or a game of chance. In some respects the imagery anticipates that of *Traumkraut*, for in the opening verse Goll has created a hallucinatory effect by means of images which engender a disturbing sense of unreality, or perhaps more appropriately, of surreality:

> Des os de mon père déterré de la ville de sel
> Je forme un temple où la ruine sera légué aux futurs barbares
> Dans la levure de ma chair naissent les forêts du songe
> De saines moisissures où couve le printemps quadruple
> Dans une orgie de molènes et d'argynnes

Images such as "ville de sel", "temple", "ruine", "forêts du songe" seem to indicate a fairly late date of composition for this poem, possibly 1948 or 1949. Reference in the second verse to the Tarot links it to a certain extent with concepts in *Le Char Triomphal de l'Antimoine*:

> J'ai bu au cinq de coupes et tué d'une quarte d'épée

"Coupes" (cups) represent the passive principle of air, and the union of air and the active principle earth produces fire, which is symbolized by "épées" (swords). However, Goll does not elaborate upon the symbolism of the Tarot, but proceeds to create a chain of associations from the familiar image of the eye (cf. *Les Cercles Magiques, Lilith, Oeil*). Again, too, the various images are held together by the concept of circular motion:

> Mon frère au mauvais oeil qui tourne comme la roue
> Du monde, la roue de mon vieux vélodor, de mon soleil crevé
> Où je tourne, je tourne empalé par une flamme rousse
> Cueillie dans tes boucles, ô femme

[25] *Les Cercles Magiques**, pp. 41—42.

Now the eye is visualized as turning like the wheel of the universe or like that of an old bicycle; the wheel has become an instrument of torture to which the poet is strapped, licked by flames which have been plucked from a woman's hair (doubtless an allusion to Claire Goll's red hair). The poet himself seems to be spinning like a top, "Je tourne, toupie d'un dieu fou . . .", almost suspended in the void, and the game of chance has taken on universal proportions. The chain of associations connected with the eye is created by reference to purely spherical objects: "oeil, roue du monde, vélodor, soleil" and in the final verse: "toupie, sansara, molécules étoilées, cymbales, cercles, roues, meules, zéro central". There is a constant alternation between images pertaining to the microcosm and those pertaining to the macrocosm. Finally the poet is crushed by the perpetual circular movement:

> Les yeux des cercles les roues me broient comme des meules
> Activées par le zéro central

The eye reappears as a dominant image in the poem bearing the title *Oeil* [26]. Here the poet appears to be contemplating his own eyes, perhaps in a mirror, and they seem to him to be mysterious and unfathomable, full of knowledge and timeless secrets [27],

> Je te regarde me regarder: mon oeil
> Monté je ne sais d'où
> A la surface de mon visage . . .

A similar idea is expressed in another poem bearing the same title:

> Te regardant me regarder
> Oeil de ma nuit Oeil de mon dé
>
> Oeil de ma face Oeil de terreur
> Surgi de quel profondeur [28]

The eye is like a lake or a mirror, both of which absorb and reflect the external world. The eye and the circle are once again synthesized, and thus the idea of magic associated with the circle is correspondingly transferred to the eye:

[26] Ibid., pp. 45—47.
[27] Cf. GÉRARD DE NERVAL's concept of the eye as shown in his poem *Le Christ aux Oliviers*, *Oeuvres* I, Bibliothèque de la Pléiade, Paris 1956, p. 37:
"En cherchant l'oeil de Dieu, je n'ai vu qu'une orbite
Vaste, noire et sans fond, d'où la nuit qui l'habite
Rayonne sur le monde et s'épaissit toujours".
(NERVAL: I)
[28] Cf. *Oeil* in *Masques de Cendre*.

> O cercle magique: oeil de tout être!
> Oeil de volcan tout injecté des sangs malsains
> Oeil de ce lotus noir
> Surgi des calmes du songe
> Oeil diamant taillé sur trente-six faces

The dual aspect of the eye, its purity and impurity, is indicated by "diamant" and "sangs malsains". Faceted like a diamond it glitters and shines, yet like a volcano, it constantly threatens to erupt. The dark, mysterious centre of the eye is surrounded by light; the eye is therefore referred to as a "lotus noir". (Goll may be thinking of the Indian lotus whose calyx was regarded as the seat and birth-place of the gods — a dark centre giving birth to light and consciousness). Omniscient, the eye is now situated at the centre of the universe and has become its focal point — a position previously occupied by the statues:

> L'univers tourne autour de toi
> Oeil à facettes qui chasses les yeux des étoiles
> Et les impliques dans ton système giratoire

Like the vast statue of Lilith, the eye draws the stars into its rotatory system. It represents both a place of union and of termination:

> Oeil magnétique où les hivers hypnotisés convolent
> Où les engoulevants terminent leur voyage
> Où des régimes de lunes s'éteignent

It is acclaimed by the poet as "tout-puissant". The eye has become a kind of repository for Goll's experiences, for past souvenirs and future hopes:

> J'ai jeté dans cet oeil
> Toutes mes reliques
> La montre en or de mon grand-père
> Et les soleils fertiles de mes petits-enfants

The eye represents the gateway to knowledge. In its function as a mirror, it enables man to see and recognise himself. The paradoxical idea of the eye as dark and deep is indicated by the use of "abîme". According to Goll the eye resembles a crystal, and its purity and brightness are emphasized by "reflets chatoyants, noisette de cristal, source de ce matin, pureté". In the same way as the translucent crystal is the product of black carbon, however, the pure, shining crystal-eye is the product of the blackness of "houille" and "nuit". The alchemical implications of this imagery are obvious. Despite the brightness of its periphery, the centre of the eye remains dark and contains the rotating "scarabée des origines". The scarab is, of course, the sacred beetle of the ancient Egyptians, but it also plays a significant, if little-known role in alchemy as a variant of mercury. Goll's adaptation of alchemical concepts is particularly apparent in the final verse of the poem. The poet descends into the depths of the earth and returns to his origins:

> Je descends, je descends l'escalier des sommeils synthétiques
> Vers les mondes d'onyx où repose la matrice

This is tantamount to the alchemists' concept of descent and return to the "matrix". This return to primeval chaos necessitates destruction, "J'écrase/Des crânes des dieux et des oeufs de l'avenir". By descending into the darkness of the "abyss", the poet hopes to find a new day in the mirror of the eye:

> Cherchant le jour
> Tout au fond des miroirs

This day would represent a rebirth to light and awareness from the darkness of the earth, a process analogous to alchemical sublimation.

Goll's interest in the eye as the gateway to knowledge is apparent in several other poems, many of which will be discussed in the course of this thesis. It is also apparent in *Jean sans Terre devant le miroir:*

> Ferme les paupières
> Et tu trouveras
> Entre les frontières
> Le clair au-delà
>
> . . .
> Mais dans les orbites
> De tes yeux déserts
> Une peur habite
> Montée des enfers [29]

and in *L'Oeil (Métro de la Mort):*

> Je plonge dans un œil . . .
> Oeil de joie et d'effroi
> Source de toute vie
> Puits de toute mort
> Astre aussi proche aussi lointain
> Que l'Uranus [30]

---

[29] Cf. *Jean sans Terre*, p. 18.
[30] Yvan Goll, *Métro de la Mort*, Brussels 1936, p. 31. (*Métro*)

In addition, Goll's collection of souvenirs which included eyes (*Jean sans Terre l'homme à tiroirs*) comes to mind: "la collection d'yeux rares" [31]. Similarly, the image of the eye occurs in some of Goll's novels. In *Die Eurokokke* he states: "ich sammelte die Augen, die aus Honig waren, aus Silber, aus Saphir, aus Petroleum, aus Mahogonie, aus Zink, aus Vergissmeinnicht" [32]. In this case, however, it is the technique of enumeration that is all-important, since eyes had no "esoteric" associations for Goll at that time (1927). However, in his novel *Gala* of 1930, Goll appears to be moving towards a more esoteric application of the image: "Mes yeux sont deux hémisphères d'une géographie toute spéciale, avec des volcans de colère, des mers de peur, des rivages d'amour; deux rondes étoiles, visibles seulement avec les instruments astronomiques de la sympathie, deux roues de bicyclette qui tournent si vite que jamais on ne comptera les raies et les sentiments qui les composent" [33], and elsewhere, "et mes yeux sont comme ceux du sphinx, vides et clos, et cependant la source inépuisable d'une sagesse divine" [34].

The next poem *Alose* [35] remains somewhat enigmatic. From a thematic point of view it is difficult to see why it has been included in this cycle of poems. The reference in it to "le sommeil vert de ma métempsycose" could be merely an allusion to metempsychosis, but could also indicate some sort of atavistic identification on the part of Goll. His interest in ancestry has already been mentioned briefly. It is possible that he found source-material for this poem in some primitive myth or other, for atavistic identification plays an important role in certain primitive rites of renewal. A statement that might substantiate the claim of atavism appears in a letter written by Goll to his wife in 1937: "Je ne pus retenir un de ces cris rauques coutumiers à mes ancêtres les hiboux" [36]. Similar ideas occur in *Jean sans Terre atterrit*: "des buffles ancestraux" [37], and in *Jean sans Terre découvre l'ange*: "mes arbres-ancêtres" [38]. However, such statements in the poem as

---

[31] *Jean sans Terre*, p. 81.
[32] *Dicht.*, p. 206.
[33] Yvan Goll, *Gala*, Paris 1930, p. 220.
[34] Ibid., p. 222.
[35] *Les Cercles Magiques**, p. 48.
[36] *Briefe*, p. 203: letter from Yvan to Claire, Nice, Mardi Gras 1937.
[37] *Jean sans Terre*, p. 91.
[38] Ibid., p. 69.

Je suis alose
Car j'ai mangé de sa mélancolie
Le chant horizontal qui nous relie
Et je poissonne déjà toute chose ...
Mangeur mangé et saturé d'hypnose

might be intended by Goll to be an illustration of a process of empathy, and may be compared with his statement in the manifesto *Le Réisme:* "Le Réiste dit: 'Entrez dedans! Intégrez-vous à l'Objet, devenez cet objet jusqu'à ce qu'il vous ait dévoré' " [39]. This integration of subject and object is none other than "cet élément panique qui transforme le poète en ces objets mêmes qu'il contemple, qu'il touche" [40]. The poet has identified himself with the shad, and the use of the verbalized noun "poissonner" serves to underline this identification. A similar process is illustrated in the poem *Oseille (Multiple Femme*):*

Je m'enoseille
Je convertis le carburant soleil
En liqueur à mouches en émeraude à vent
J'ai fermé mes paupières d'oiseau
Pour mieux voir pour mieux sentir
Le secret de la terre [41]

The verbalized noun "*enoseiller*" illustrates more clearly than the verb "poissonner" the active direction of this process of empathy. The desire to reach the essence of nature through a process of empathy is shared by other artists, notably Franz Marc: "Ich suche mein Empfinden für den organischen Rhythmus aller Dinge zu steigern, suche mich pantheistisch einzufühlen in das Zittern und Rinnen des Blutes in der Natur, in den Bäumen, in den Tieren, in der Luft ... Ich sehe kein glücklicheres Mittel zur 'Animalisierung' der Kunst als das Tierbild ... Wir werden nicht mehr den Wald oder das Pferd malen, wie sie uns gefallen oder erscheinen, sondern wie sie wirklich sind, wie sich der Wald oder das Pferd selbst fühlen, ihr absolutes Wesen, das hinter dem Schein lebt, den wir sehen" [42].

Numéro Treize [43] returns to various familiar themes, and the opening lines are reminiscent of some of the *Jean sans Terre* quatrains:

---

[39] *Quatre Études*, p. 206.
[40] Quoted from an article by MARCEL BRION in *Quatre Études*, p. 14.
[41] *Multiple Femme**, p. 15.
[42] Quoted in W. HESS, *Dokumente zum Verständnis der modernen Malerei*, Reinbek bei Hamburg, 1956, pp. 78 & 79.
[43] *Les Cercles Magiques**, pp. 49—50.

J'ai distribué mes sourires aux pauvres
J'ai vendu le château des Tantalides ...

One critic has suggested that the title echoes lines from a sonnet by Gérard de Nerval,

Le treizième revient, c'est encore la première
Et c'est toujours la Seule — ou c'est le seul moment [44]

and is a possible reference to the thirteenth hour or to Key 13 (Death) of the Tarot pack. Certainly there is a strong emphasis on death throughout the poem, conveyed in images of a sea-passage, a passage from the plane of a dismal and solitary existence,

Nous avons eu notre mesure de malheurs
A la lueur morbide des chandeliers

to a dismal and solitary death (again recalling Goll's statement that "La solitude est le seul état qui se transmette de la vie à mort") [45]:

J'ai le numéro 13 et j'attends toujours
Là-bas au terminus de la solitude
Mon nom blanchit sur les régistres lourds
Et mes empreintes digitales corrodent

The idea of solitude and death is reinforced in the poem Ports Perdus [46], in which the "terminus" is more explicitly recognisable as the place of death:

Et me voici au terminus de la solitude
Où s'arrêtent toutes les courses des hommes

The poet's sense of isolation and despair increases, since even the little he possessed has been taken from him:

Il s'agit de partir les mains vides ...
Ils ont ouvert tous mes silences
Et la pierre merveilleuse a été confisquée
Les derniers songes aussi de mes paupières
Et dans mes mains les cercles brouillés

Images connected with the customs (douane, douaniers etc.) occur frequently in Goll's poems of the New York period, for example in Ports Perdus,

---

[44] This is suggested in CARMODY, p. 157. The poem Artémis appears in NERVAL: I, pp. 35—36.
[45] See note 22.
[46] This poem belongs to the Lackawanna Elegy*.

> A la maison de la douane j'ai ouvert tous mes silences
> Et la pierre merveilleuse a été confisquée . . .

perhaps reflecting Goll's personal experiences on his journey from Europe to the United States of America. Since his most treasured possessions have been taken from him, the poet finally appears to resign himself to the loss, and to put his faith in future generations:

> Mon cœur lâche enfin le rêve chimique;
> Que le sel bleu de mes larmes séchées
> Mêlé à celui des ancêtres d'Érèbe
> Améliore l'alchimie d'une terre rêvée!

The final verse suggests an alchemical procedure (as does the "pierre merveilleuse"), with its imagery of the intermingling of past and present, by means of which a better future may be assured.

The poem *Les Portes* [47] employs the image of the door as the gateway to knowledge or to the unknown (cf. "Je suis la porte sur l'abîme" in *Vénus des Ténèbres* [48]). In this short poem the poet summarizes the extent of his wanderings and explorations into the occult (cf. *Les Cercles Magiques, Lilith, Élégie de la Liberté, Oeil, Vénus des Ténèbres* etc., in which these explorations are described):

> J'ai passé devant tant de portes
> Dans le couloir des peurs perdues et des rêves séquestrés . . .
> J'ai passé devant la porte dorée de la connaissance
> Devant des portes qui brûlaient et qui ne s'ouvraient pas
> Devant des portes lasses de s'être trop fermées
> D'autres comme des miroirs où ne passaient que les anges

The significant factor here is the inference that the poet has always passed in front of the doors ("J'ai passé devant . . . j'ai passé devant . . .") but has never succeeded in opening them ("Devant des portes . . . qui ne s'ouvraient pas/Devant des portes lasses de s'être trop fermées"). Only angels, in their capacity as spiritual beings, have been able to open those doors which resembled mirrors. Finally, however, the poet is offered a hitherto unthought-of possibility of escape. In his quest for knowledge, having explored the remotest possibilities, he has overlooked the simplest of them all:

---

[47] *Les Cercles Magiques**, p. 53.
[48] Ibid., p. 54.

> Mais il est une porte simple, sans verrou ni loquet
> Tout au fond du couloir, à l'opposé du cadran
> La porte qui conduit hors de toi
> Personne ne la pousse jamais

This undoubtedly indicates a return to his wife Claire, and reveals the fact that Goll is turning away from all his esoteric studies and explorations of occultisms, since he appears to have profited so little from them, to the simpler and more obvious escape that love offers him.

In *Vénus des Ténèbres* [49] Goll is offered liberation from himself. This poem is a modified version of *Vénus Cubaine* [50], a poem composed by Goll round about 1940 and modelled on his experiences in Cuba, which he visited in April of that year. *Vénus Cubaine* is probably the first of Goll's vast statue poems, some of which are included in this cycle. It is, however, less abstract and more erotic in tone than *Vénus des Ténèbres*. Like the vast statue of Lilith, Vénus des Ténèbres entices the poet into the abyss:

> Passager du Néant: je suis la porte sur l'abîme
> Le pont sur la nuit que tu cherches partout
> A l'appel des sources démentes

By renouncing his identity, the poet is given the opportunity of leaping into the darkness of the gulf, and of returning to the origin of things ("abîme, nuit, sources démentes, gouffre"). Like Lilith, Vénus is full of energy and movement, and this ceaseless motion is reflected in the rotation of her eyes. By penetrating beyond them, the poet can hope to hear the "soupir suprême". In terms similar to those used in *Vénus Cubaine* and *Parménia* [51], Vénus invites man to enter the tower of her body:

> Je suis ta tour mystérieuse
> Ta Tour Penchée habillée de frissons
> D'où sans danger tu sautes dans le gouffre

Like Parménia, Vénus is "la Femme Universelle", and her ubiquity is indicated by the extension of her body in the direction of the points of the compass (cf. the lines later in the poem, "Je suis ta mer étale et ton ressac", which give the same idea of spatial extension):

> Monte à ma tour pour te croire plus grand
> Écoute: elle parle la langue des ouragons en déroute
> Monte à mon Épaule Nord où gîte l'archange déchu

[49] Ibid., pp. 54—55.
[50] This appears in *Quatre Études*, pp. 153—157.
[51] Ibid., pp. 152—153.

Similarly in *Vénus Cubaine:*

Monte à mon Épaule Nord où gîtent les anges en disgrace
Ma Hanche Ouest est la vallée de tes sommeils
Mon Genou Sud se souvient de tes prières
Ma Main Est est l'étoile sous laquelle on meurt [52]

Thus Vénus is portrayed as reaching out in all directions like the central tree, "L'Arbre Central" *(Parménia)* [53].

The idea of the statue as an oracle recurs in *Vénus des Ténèbres.* Vénus possesses extra-sensory powers, by means of which she can help man to escape from the laws of time and space and find forgetfulness:

Je suis la Clairvoyante
L'écriture dans mes paumes t'enseigne la magie
Veux-tu gagner enfin le chiffre de l'oubli?

In *Vénus Cubaine,* as in some of the Lilith poems, the idea of the oracle is more closely linked to images of the eye and the concept of circular motion:

Je suis ta Voyante
Tourne tourne les roues de mes yeux verts
Pour déchiffrer l'énigme hélas démonétisée [52]

The poet must be prepared, as he was in the *Élégie de La Liberté,* to renounce all personal claims and desires if he is ever to find refuge and security in Vénus. Realising that the poet's previous attempts to escape, both from himself and from the perpetual motion of the circles, have been unsuccessful, Vénus invites him to return to the world, i.e. to "life" on a higher plane, through her:

O fils qui a perdu sa mort
Reviens au monde en moi

The significance of the poet's "life" and "death" has already been discussed in connection with the poem *Lilith.* Paradoxically, the perpetual movement and energy of Vénus offer the poet a means of escape from himself, i.e. liberty, in the cage of her body:

Je suis le départ de toi-même
Ton mouvement perpétuel
Ta cage où toujours rugira ta liberté

Many of the ideas expressed in this poem, and likewise many of the images, are similar to those in *Lilith,* but in this case the ultimate signi-

[52] Ibid., p. 154.
[53] Ibid., p. 152.

ficance of the poet's descent into the abyss is to be understood in sexual rather than alchemical terms.

At this stage Goll turns once again to cabbalistic material in the poem *Raziel* [54]. The basic situation — the cabbalist's search for the names of God — is the same as that described in *Raziel* of *Le Char Triomphal de l'Antimoine*. There is, however, an important additional concept, namely, the construction of a castle. In many versions the castle is replaced by a tower, but their significance is identical. The function of the castle/tower is two-fold: (i) it represents the place of action — isolated from external reality — to which Raziel retires to seek the names of God; (ii) it can be equated with the Word itself (cf. "le château du Verbe"), i. e. it is the means by which the cabbalist hopes to discover God. A statement of Goll's serves to illustrate the validity of the second point: "Car n'est-ce pas que la Kabbale est un échafaudage gigantesque pour l'érection d'une tour qui atteindrait les nues. Et de quel matériau cette Tour est-elle construite? De mots et de verbes. C'est uniquement par le Verbe et par la Connaissance que les Kabbalistes espèrent parvenir à leur but suprême: celui de découvrir Dieu, à travers le nom de Dieu. Celui qui nommera Dieu, le connaîtra" [55].

The poem opens with a description of Raziel beginning his task:

> Raziel! Drape-toi du manteau occulte doublé d'éclairs!
> Déplace les monts de l'orgueil! Découvre
> Le fleuve Sambation qui n'existe pas
> Et mélange à minuit les signes de l'alphabet!

Significantly, Raziel is dressed in an occult cloak lined with lightning, indicating that he is isolated from external influences, but in contact with the upper world. By mixing and combining the letters of the alphabet, Raziel seeks to reveal the hidden connections between them which will yield the numerical value of seventy-two (each letter of the Hebrew alphabet possessed a numerical value), and thus disclose the name(s) of God. There is only a faint trace of specific links between this task and that of alchemy (links heavily stressed in *Raziel of Le Char Triomphal*), namely, the combining of opposites: "Des lettres jaunes et rouges de soufre et de sang ...". The materials used by Raziel in the construction of the castle reflect its mysterious, ethereal quality, while their brillance and purity further emphasize its spiritual attributes:

[54] *Les Cercles Magiques**, pp. 56—57.
[55] Quoted by CARMODY, p. 127.

De nuit en nuit avec les cristaux des nébuleuses
La poussière des météores le lait de l'aurore australe
Raziel édifia en vingt ans le château du Verbe
Où Dieu était captif dans ses soixante-douze noms

Since the names of God are captive in the castle, the castle itself is fitted accordingly with

Les soixante-douze chambres de l'extase
La chambre du saphir et la salle des tempêtes . . .

as a reflection of His spiritual illumination and power. The similarity between Raziel and the Hermit of the Tarot is reinforced by the reference to the magic lanterns: "Il alluma les lampes du Yod magique", for the Hermit is portrayed as carrying such a lantern in which a six-pointed star is shining. This lantern represents the light of knowledge, and it is with the help of similar lanterns that Raziel is able to open, and finally discover the secret behind the "door of doors". Chaboseau's discussion of the Hermit could well apply to Raziel: "Ici nous sommes en présence de l'Adepte, isolé dans l'étude de soi-même, replié dans son manteau qui l'isole des influences extérieures, et l'étude qu'il propose est précisément indiquée par la lumière voilée qu'il porte . . ." [56]. Goll, in using the image of the mirrors, has extended the sphere of action into infinity and symbolically indicated the revelation of God Himself:

Et des miroirs pour fontaines et pour lacs perdus
Et des miroirs verticaux pour les générations d'oiseaux
Et des miroirs perplexes pour la mise en grâce des enfants
Dieu sortit vêtu de soixante-douze noms

The cabbalist's construction of the castle and his search for God is intended by Goll to be interpreted in terms of the poet's search for a method. Thus the poetic process signifies the construction of a Word-castle ("château du Verbe") by means of the twenty-two letter-pillars of the Hebrew alphabet. The poet's long and arduous search for the Word is viewed as comparable to the cabbalist's twenty year-long search for the seventy-two names of God. Thus Goll states in his notes: "Raziel . . . se fixa à Barcelone pour se consacrer aux recherches kabbalistiques, qui devaient lui révéler Dieu dans les noms émanés de l'alphabet héb-reu. Il découvrit 72 noms de Dieu. *Triomphe du poète*" [57].

---

[56] CHABOSEAU, p. 58.
[57] Unpublished note in the possession of Mme. Goll.

In the case of this poem, Goll's adaptation of general alchemical concepts is obvious; the affinities between the cabbalist's search for God, the poet's search for the Word, and the alchemist's search for the Philosophers' Stone, are unmistakable.

In the final poem of this cycle, *Les Cercles* [58], Goll returns to his point of departure — those circles which have plagued him since his youth:

> Depuis mon enfance tu me tentes de tes cercles
> Pour quel saut, belluaire, o Dieu dément
> Du cerceau naïf à la bague de Saturne
> De la torque gauloise aux hublots du chaland de Charon
> Moi, cycliste de quel cirque sur mon vélo d'or
> Veux rattraper l'avance de l'O parfait

Many of the images are similar to those of *Les Cercles Magiques* and *Lilith*. The circus images reappear ("saut, belluaire, cerceau, cycliste, cirque"), together with images of circularity related to the concept of macrocosm and microcosm, and also indications of danger and death. Having questioned himself as to the point of it all, the poet finally comes to the conclusion that he is

> . . . le Fou qui songe songe
> Attaché à la roue des roses

The "roue des roses" (cf. "rose-roue au moyeu des âges") [59] brings to mind the Wheel of Fortune which is a symbol of the world. Man himself (in this case "le Fou") is attached to the circumference and is therefore in constant rotation. The poet compares himself to a cyclist competing in a futile race against time — symbolized by the circles:

> O vaine course contre le soleil
> Galop effréné du zéro autour du rien
> Autour d'un rêve nécrosé d'avance
> Autour des bornes occultes placées sur les routes

A similar image of the cyclist appears in *Le Cycliste* (*Métro de la Mort*):

> Il roule il roule
> Sur son vélocipède en or
> Il boit le vent
> Il mange l'espace

---

[58] *Les Cercles Magiques**, pp. 58—61.
[59] *Dicht.*, p. 422.

Il bat des records
En vain: il ne rattrapera jamais
Le vieux soleil
Déjà au but des aubépines [60]

The poet now realizes that his search for occultisms has been to no avail, and that time is rushing by bringing death in its wake:

Hélas le Temps est le chariot qui me devance
Tournant si vite qu'on le croirait arrêté pour toujours
Telle est la mort qui fait tourner tes globes nacrés

The same idea recurs in the poem *Course de Fond (Multiple Femme*):*

Tandis que la main de ma montre pointe vers la mort
L'hélice du navire a fait l'amour avec combien de vagues
Et la roue du cycliste s'est accrochée à la roue du soleil . . .
Je n'en peux plus Je lâche prise
La Terre a une trop grande avance sur moi [61]

Thus the transience of human existence and the futility of human aspirations become apparent: death comes to all men. In death the eye would be quiescent and passively reflect external reality:

Où tout soleil et sirius
Reposent calmement sur ton oeil retourné

All things, from the most powerful to the most insignificant, are subject to the eternal process of growth and decay; all must return to their origins:

Couronnes d'empereurs, couronnes de myosotis
Roulent au même gouffre des genèses
Airelles, mimosas aux mêmes vins d'enfer
Que les disques bruns, les yeux des biches
Et les paillettes de mica des serpents

The poet finally addresses the circles thus:

Cercle invisible des nouvelles lunes
Cercle d'ellipse aux festons purulents
Qui rythmez mon destin
Et la pesanteur de mes mots

The processes of growth and decay are emphasized in the contrasting images of the new moons ("nouvelles lunes") and the decomposing garlands ("festons purulents"). From this it is evident that the circles are no

---

[60] *Métro*, p. 22.
[61] *Multiple Femme**, p. 16.

longer mere geometric symbols for Goll, but are the determining factors of his existence. In symbolizing life, they symbolize time itself. Furthermore, they represent that which is beyond human comprehension. In the face of such overwhelming odds, the poet has but one last stand — the power of human thought:

> Rouleriez-vous sans ma pensée centrale?

In a way this resembles the question asked by Rilke:

> Was wirst du tun, Gott, wenn ich sterbe [62]

Both Rilke's God and Goll's circles are given meaning only by the poets' awareness of, and need for them. Goll concludes his poem with the observation:

> Oui tout s'arrêtera au repos de mon oeil

As a variant of the circle, the rotating eye is a vital principle, and the cessation of its motion would bring the universe itself to an end.

In retrospect, it does not seem likely that the poems discussed in this chapter were conceived by Goll as an integrated cycle. The uncertainty of the chronological order of the poems, together with the fact that they were apparently selected from a larger group, of which the *Multiple Femme** poems are the residue, only adds to the confusion. From the point of view of subject-matter it is clear that Goll was concerned to a great extent with themes and images which occupied him in *Le Char Triomphal*, but a difference in attitude towards the material of the two cycles emerges. The poems of *Les Cercles Magiques** are basically much more personal than those of *Le Char Triomphal*: they are correspondingly more pessimistic, for the further Goll advances in his personal search for illumination, the more evident it becomes that he will never succeed in finding it.

It is difficult to determine the extent to which Goll's "magic circles" were influenced by alchemical concepts. General links between the two have already been mentioned briefly. Superficially at least, alchemy appears to play a lesser role in this cycle than in *Le Char Triomphal*, for direct references to alchemical processes are brief and sporadic. However, various examples of Goll's adaptation of alchemical concepts have been pointed out in the course of this chapter.

---

[62] RAINER MARIA RILKE, *Das Stunden-Buch*, Frankfurt am Main, 1962, p. 29.

A discussion of the poems in *Les Cercles Magiques** according to the order in which they were selected for publication, has undoubtedly served to illustrate the complex nature of the material. It is tempting to classify the poems under various "headings", but a mere consideration of the first two poems in the cycle (in which allusions to circularity, death, alchemy, cabbalism, astrology, dice, eyes, Lilith, ancestry, etc. appear), clearly shows the impossibility of such a task. Goll is evidently trying to create a chain of associations out of the numerous images and ideas with which he is preoccupied, but the results are all too often merely confusing. In certain poems he has attempted to link far too many disparate elements together, and it becomes increasingly difficult to extricate the themes, since they can no longer be clearly defined.

Only two themes emerge as being common to the majority of poems in the cycle — firstly, that of time (symbolized by images of circularity and circular motion), and secondly, that of death. Allusions to death are certainly numerous enough to permit its classification as a major theme. It can, however, be subdivided into two categories: the theme of the impending death of the poet, evident in such poems as *Élégie du Pauvre Égo*, *Le Moulin de La Mort*, *Numéro Treize*; and the experience of death or infinity implicit in his search for illumination, as illustrated in such poems as *Les Cercles Magiques*, *Lilith*, *Élégie de la Liberté*, *Vénus des Ténèbres*. This second aspect of death is frequently represented in images connected with circularity.

Goll's treatment of the symbol of circularity shows a marked development. Whereas in earlier years the circle had represented a purely scientific or geometric concept for him, it now becomes "esoteric" by virtue of its links with various occult or magic ideas. This theory is substantiated by the fact that the cycle itself is entitled *Les Cercles Magiques**. Goll proceeds to synthesize the circle with eyes (*Les Cercles Magiques*, *Lilith*, *Loterie*, *Oeil*, *Les Cercles* etc.), and particularly with the eyes of female statues through which he desires to plunge into infinity (*Les Cerles Magiques*, *Lilith*). Finally the eyes become symbols of the microcosm and Goll sets them in motion (*Oeil*, *Lilith*, *Loterie*, *Vénus des Ténèbres*). The eye, the peach, and to a lesser extent the rose, (*Lilith*, *Les Cercles*) are examples of what Goll termed "absolute" objects, and when set in motion (as for example in *Élégie sur une pêche*), they illustrate what he later formulated as "l'objet végétatif en action".

A comparison between the poems of *Le Char Triomphal* and those of *Les Cercles Magiques** reveals that Goll was making use, to a greater or lesser degree, of the same kind of subject-matter in both. This repetitive use of material could indicate a limitation of his imaginative powers, but it is far more likely that Goll's excessive preoccupation with esoteric material was due to the fact that it provided him with infinite scope for speculation on the mysteries of the universe, on man himself and his beliefs.

The majority of poems appear to be the product of the poet's general interest in cosmogony. Alchemy, cabbalism, the Tarot, and so forth, and even Goll's own cosmic statues and magic circles are all attempts to describe the great moving forces underlying reality. As such, they could all be classified under the general generic term of magic, which is itself concerned with the secret forces of nature. In a similar way, all branches of occultisms — and correspondingly those of Goll's poems which deal with them — can be related to magic since "The secret of the occult sciences is that of Nature herself" [63], or again, "Every branch of the occult or secret sciences may be included under the word MAGIC ... the doctrines concerning the nature and power of angels, ghosts and spirits; the methods of evoking and controlling the shades of the dead, elementary spirits and demons; the compositon of talismans; the manufacture of gold by alchemy; all forms of divination, including clairvoyance in the crystal and all the mysterious calculations which make up kabbalistic science, are all parts of magic" [64].

[63] ÉLIPHAS LÉVI, *The History of Magic*, trans. Waite, London 1963 ed., p. 358.
[64] WAITE: *O. S.*, p. 9.

Chapter III

FRUIT FROM SATURN

The reader who proceeds from *Le Char Triomphal de l'Antimoine*
and *Les Cercles Magiques** to Goll's English cycle *Fruit from Saturn* [1]
cannot fail to be struck by the close resemblance between the three cycles.
Indeed, some of the English poems are virtually verbatim translations of
Goll's French poems in *Les Cercles Magiques** [2]. From a poetic point of
view, however, they are neither as interesting nor as striking as many of
Goll's French poems. Although the salient impression of this particular
cycle upon the reader must inevitably be one of repetition and perhaps of
monotony, it is nevertheless worthy of consideration because it introduces
a new concept in the form of atomism, which then assumes great importance in the final chant of *Le Mythe de la Roche Percée.* [3]
Once again the actual date of composition of *Fruit from Saturn* proves
somewhat difficult to determine. In one list of sources [4] the poems are
recorded as having been composed in 1942, and while there is justifiable,
but not necessarily conclusive evidence that this might apply to the last
five poems, it is clearly impossible in the case of the opening poem *Atom
Elegy*, in which Goll refers specifically to Alamogordo, the site in New
Mexico where the first atomic bomb test was held in July 1945! It is
highly unlikely that Goll would have had any interest in Alamogordo
prior to 1945, and that he could have foreseen the first atomic explosion

[1] The New York 1946 edition of *Fruit from Saturn* is used for purposes of quotation, but the poem *Atom Elegy* can be found in *Dicht.*, pp. 796—800. In the later edition, however, the poem published as section VI of the *Atom Elegy*, p. 801, does in
fact belong to the *Élégie d'Ihpétonga* cycle.
[2] This idea is supported by RICHARD EXNER in *Dicht.*, p. 830, note 7: "Ausgenom-
men vielleicht die Lukas Foss gewidmete 'Atom Elegy', handelt es sich in diesem Band
um Adaptionen von im Französischen zuvor und nachher besser ausgedrückten Gedanken. Eine dichterisch viel gültigere Aussage dieser Atom-Elegie findet sich in
Le Mythe de la Roche Percée im Gedicht 'Roche Atome'".
[3] *Der Mythus*, p. 42.
[4] Cf. *Dicht.*, p. 833. The source for the German translation of this poem is listed
as "Englische Originalfassung 'Atom Elegy' 1942".

as early as 1942, would be to credit him with uncanny powers of pre-cognition. It is probable that the atomic bomb test acted as a catalyst (albeit purely temporary) on Goll's poetry, inspiring him to compose the *Atom Elegy* and also the final chant of *Le Mythe de la Roche Percée* (1946). In no other poems, however, does Goll take atomic fission as his theme — surely an indication that he was only briefly preoccupied with that topic. Obviously this theme cannot be regarded as "esoteric" in the same way as alchemy or cabbalism, but Goll has intermingled purely scientific concepts with familiar occult themes and images in such a way that the end product undoubtedly justifies the claim to esotericism.

The title of the cycle is open to various interpretations. In an unpublished note [5] Goll himself provides one interpretation of the significance of Saturn: "Saturne des Alchimistes. Avec la libération de l'atome on rejoint le rêve des anciens à transformer le plomb en or, mais à la place de l'or, on a trouvé l'énergie".

These poems describe yet again the poet's attempts to escape from his incongruous situation, determined in time and space, as he feels himself to be, by the "magic circles".

In the first part of the opening poem, *Atom Elegy* [6], Goll deals solely with the subject implied by the title — namely, the atom:

> In pitchblende orchards grew the holy fruit
> Sweet atom fissioned in its foetal center
> To fate's twin death-birth

It seems clear from this that Goll is fairly well acquainted with the processes of atomic fission. He refers to the process during which the atomic nucleus disintegrates into two parts, a procedure signifying at one and the same time the "death" of the atom and the "birth" of energy. The "pitchblende orchards" represent the ore from which uranium is extracted, and when the latter is bombarded with neutrons, fission takes place and a vast amount of energy is released:

> High frequency of wrath
> Hath made rock run like oil
> Steel boil to vapour

The poet's own desire for spiritual regeneration is apparent in his metaphorical application of the neutron-bombardment process:

---

[5] This unpublished note is in the possession of Mme. Goll.
[6] *Fruit from Saturn*, pp. 11—19.

Atomic deity
Bombard my heart at will
With neutrons of your truth

Already Goll is moving towards a personal application of the atomic disintegration-reintegration process, for he says:

I secretly accept with wisdom of the dove
My death and resurrection

In other words, he is fully prepared to accept "death" (renunciation of human passions etc.) as a necessary prelude to "resurrection" (spiritual regeneration). The similarity between this idea and the alchemical concept of Putrefaction and Sublimation is obvious. It is clear from the first section of the poem that Goll is evaluating positively the recent advances of science, not for their intrinsic potentiality, but rather for their application to his own particular situation. This is illustrated by the fact that the scientific aspects of atomic fission are minimized in favour of a more esoteric description of the process, which approximates it to Goll's descriptions of alchemical and cabbalistic processes.

The second part of the poem must again be interpreted both on a scientific and a personal level:

The ray of rays shatters my insane soul
And feeds me with inhuman energy

O new nativity in the protean cradle
O death festival for the old sore thighs of earth
Unlocking the concentric love

On the one hand, these verses present a description of the process of nuclear fission; on the other hand, they reveal Goll's welcoming of the latest scientific discoveries, since these discoveries provide him with a new concept of the universe and thus with a new method of acquiring knowledge. His previous beliefs, which in this context may be termed "irrational", are superseded by this latest concept of the structure of the universe, and previous explanations of the nature of the universe, such as the alchemical or cabbalistic, are replaced by the scientific. The "death festival" signifies the termination of the old cosmic order, and the "new nativity", the birth of the atomic era. This process of dissolution and regeneration is dependent on the destruction of his former beliefs (cf. "Atomic deity ... Transform my eyes to yellow nitric stars/I secretly accept with wisdom of the dove/ My death and resurrection").

The imagery again reveals Goll's knowledge of the actual process of atomic fission. The "cradle" is in fact the bomb itself, in which new elements are being formed. The fact that uranium can be transformed into a number of different elements during atomic fission undoubtedly prompted Goll to use the adjective "protean". However, the "cradle" could also represent a hermetic vessel in which the alchemical substances are dissolved, prior to their re-formation. In this case, Goll's reference to the "concentric love" could be considered as an allusion to the concentric circles as a symbol of the universe and of the Great Work of alchemy. [7]

The developments in science from its early beginnings are seen by Goll to be achieved at the expense of former beliefs. Goll's personal concept of the cyclic progression of scientific knowledge, based on the principle of rebirth from destruction, is presented in images from the organic world — "Tree of Science saturn-blossoming". Science offers the poet the opportunity of acquiring ultimate knowledge of the motivating forces of the universe ("real trinity") which, as in previous poems, are symbolized by spherical objects such as wheels, circles, roses, etc. All these objects may be considered as examples of Goll's concept of the "absolute object":

Spiritual rose from aged centuries
The master wheel among the world of wheels
This rose was light
This rose was round
As is the rose of universe
As is my eye in which all eyes are hidden

The imagery develops from a universal to a personal level, from macrocosm to microcosm, with the introduction of the image of the poet's eye which absorbs and contains all external reality. In a similar manner, the atoms of the universe are contained in the mind of the poet himself:

Round as the dew
Round as my head
In which the stars of million atoms ripen

The final line quoted above indicates that Goll was familiar with the frequently-drawn comparison between the nucleus of an atom and a star. The reference later in the poem to "withering stars" (i.e. decaying atoms) appears to substantiate this, as does the allusion to "yellow nitric stars"

[7] BERTHELOT, p. 61, states that "Le serpent, aussi bien que le système des cercles concentriques, est au fond l'emblème des mêmes idées que de l'oeuf philosophique, symbole de l'univers et symbole de l'alchimie".

in the first section of the poem. Similarly, the use of the adjective "yellow" in this context is hardly fortuitous and indicates that Goll had probably seen a compound of uranium, remarkable because of its brilliant yellow crystals.

Occult sciences such as alchemy and cabbalism are reintroduced in Section III of *Atom Elegy,* and represent the poet's earlier attempts to acquire knowledge of the nature of the universe:

> In the beginning was the word
> In the beginning was the number
>
> The word: prime essence out of which
> Through seven thousand nights of labor
> The Kabbalist compounded seventy names of God

Goll himself explained the significance of the Kabbalist's task thus: "The Kabbalist ... sought to achieve the highest degree of perception by the close study of the names of God, through the symbolical employment of letters and numerals". [8] This theme is already familiar to the reader (cf. *Raziel* in *Le Char Triomphal,* and *Raziel* in *Les Cercles Magiques**.) In this poem the Word can be interpreted on various levels: the most obvious of these interpretations is the cabbalistic. Here, the Word is the basic material which the cabbalist manipulates in his search for the essence, the inexpressible name of God. A second interpretation is the alchemical. Here, the Word is the "element of elements/Poured in the mental furnace", an image which conveys the idea of the melting of the elements in the hermetic vessel. The Word thus represents a transforming substance, by means of which the hermetic spirit will be liberated from the darkness of primeval chaos, "the coal of memory". It is therefore a "Guide to the Perplexed", that is to say, it offers the means of illumination to those who aspire to know the essential nature of the universe. The "Guide to the Perplexed" is also an allusion to the principal work of Maimonides, in which he seeks to reconcile the teachings of Aristotle and the Greek scientists with Old Testament truths. [9] Interpreted in a poetic sense, the Word is the poet's basic material, which as in cabbalism, is manipulated in the search for essentials, and which, as in alchemy, must undergo the process of distillation in the "furnace" of the poet's mind.

[8] From an unpublished note in the possession of Mme. Goll.
[9] See Chapter I, note 6.

In the final stanza, the various occultisms hitherto embraced by the poet in his search for knowledge are rejected in favour of the new prospects offered by atomic science:

O to the music of the withering stars
To the delirium of pregnant gongs
Out of my algebraic dreams
And old old fears
Dance: my beloved atom
Transfigured carnotite

The stanza represents an analogy, not only with the alchemical process of Putrefaction and Sublimation, but also with Goll's own view of the development of science. The destruction of previous concepts and explanations of the universe is the necessary condition for the emergence of atomic science. The "pregnant gongs, algebraic dreams, and old fears" represent the previous occultisms from whose destruction in the athanor emerges the poet's new belief in the power of the atom.

The significance of atomic science is assessed in cabbalistic terms in section IV. Goll begins with the cabbalistic theory of the divine plan of the world. The Word or spirit of God, the "Divine Garment", [10] is made manifest by the ten Sephiroth. These are the medium through which intelligence perceives the world's existence and the divine action. According to the cabbala (as noted previously), these ten Sephiroth are contained in the heavenly Adam, Adam Kadmon:

And the 10 numbers sprang from Adam's forehead
The spheric fruit of the Sephiroth
Became the emblem of his crown

The cipher:

The Sephiroth, signified throughout the poem by the number 10, are the divine emanations, the aspects of the Infinite. They are changeless and timeless. Goll takes the reader through the various stages in the history of man's search for knowledge of the plan of the universe, stages in which he perceives the presence of the 10, the cipher:

---

[10] This idea is illustrated by a quotation from the Zohar given in ABELSON, p. 121: "The narratives (or words) of the Law are the garment of the Law. Woe unto him who takes this garment for the Law itself! ... There are fools who, seeing a man covered with a beautiful garment, look no further than that; and yet that which gives a worth to the garments is his body, and what is even more precious than that, his soul".

Past Delphi's tripod and cathedral domes
Pythagoras' revolving harmonies
Past Bruno's pyre and Einstein's time [11]

Finally, Goll finds the 10 manifest once more in atomic science:

Riding the wheel
The 10 again in sweet uranium 235

Thus the cyclic appearance of the 10 is conveyed in the image of the wheel. This wheel can also be interpreted as the tenth key of the Tarot, the Wheel of Fortune. The idea that atomic science is the latest example of the recurring search for knowledge of the Infinite is emphasized by Goll's own statement: "The mystic numbers of 'sweet uranium 235' are foreshadowed by the 10 of the tarot pack and by the 70 names of God sought by Raziel". [12] Although Goll has managed to justify atomic science as the latest phase in a cyclic development, the negative and destructive aspects of the new advance now begin to attract his attention:

The seven-colored ray
Bursting from dying self
The Infinite raped in Alamogordo

This idea is developed further in the final section of the poem. Goll begins by stressing the unity of all things, a belief which is to be found at the basis of many religious and philosophical systems:

Substance and Emanation One: Ibn Arabi
God in Us We in Him: Santa Teresa
One in All All in One: Zosimus [13]

[11] *Pythagoras*: lived in the sixth century B.C. Greek philosopher whose Pythagorean brotherhood had much in common with the Orphic communities who sought to purify the believer's soul and thus to enable it to escape from the "wheel of birth". Certain doctrines may be traced to Pythagoras, first and foremost among these being the theory of immortality and the transmigration of the soul. The Pythagorean school also holds an important place in the history of mathematical and astronomical science. *Giordano Bruno*: c. 1548—1600. Italian philosopher of the Renaissance. He was a student of ancient mathematics, Pythagorean philosopher, astronomer and scientist. His views approached those of pantheism. He was burned at the stake. *Einstein*: 1897—1955. Physician and mathematician, whose main achievements lay in the theory of relativity, statistical mechanics and the photon theory of light. He left to the world of physics a new viewpoint — the aim of the geometrization of physics.

[12] Unpublished note in the possession of Mme. Goll.

[13] *Ibn Arabi*: 1165—1240. Moslem theologian and mystic born in Murcia. In law he was a Zahirite, in theology a mystic of the extreme order, although professing orthodox Ash'arite theology. He was against many aspects of the Indo-Persian mysticism (Pantheism), and was regarded by many as a heretic.

Atomic science is seen as the charge whose detonation will destroy the "ancient rock of contemplation", that is to say, the ancient foundation of the belief in the unity of the physical and spiritual world. At the same time it will destroy the poet's belief in such a unity, leaving him disillusioned and abandoned:

> Beloved molecule
> Shot from the past into the future
> Straight through my heart

> The blue gas globe above my fontanelled skull
> Abruptly void
> Void as a rusty rivet atom-laden
> Bearing God's corpse

> And man alone alone

The reference to "God's corpse" indicates Goll's former beliefs, similar to those expressed in the first stanza, beliefs which have been shattered by the implications of atomic fission. In this poem Goll has passed through various stages of emotion ranging from joy to utter despair. Even the advent of the atomic age which he had first greeted with optimism, finally proves unable to evoke any reaction other than dejection in the poet. [14]

The second poem, entitled *The Magic Circles,* [15] is almost a verbatim translation of the French poem *Les Cercles Magiques.* [16] In some cases the order of the verses and the construction of sentences have been altered, while elsewhere, verses have been appropriated from other poems of *Les Cercles Magiques**. The main ideas, however, are basically the same in both poems. It is therefore conceivable that Goll composed this poem at the same time as the French version — that is to say, during the year 1945.

As in the French version, the poet is enmeshed in the same magic circles which determine his position in time and space. Likewise, he desires to escape from them by plunging through the eyes of Lilith to the world beyond:

St. Theresa: Spanish nun born at Avila in Old Castile. Her "conversion" took place in 1554 and effected a total transformation and sanctification of character. Her works contain various treatises of mystical religion, in which she describes the progress of the soul towards perfect union with God.

Zosimus: Writer who lived at Constantinople during the fifth century. Besides being a historian, he was an apologist of alchemy.

[14] On the subject of the atom, A. G. van Melsen's book *From Atomos to Atom,* trans. H. J. Koren, New York 1952, was consulted.

[15] *Fruit from Saturn,* pp. 23—26.

> Through your blue eye Lilith as through a hoop of azure
> I try the death leap
> I descend I descend your blood
> Descend the floorless staircase of the centuries
> Unless I climb the ladder of fire
> At whose end burn the feathers of angels

The familiar idea of descent, both spatial and temporal, is expressed in "Descend the floorless staircase of the centuries". The poet also has the alternative of ascent, he has the possibility of climbing "the ladder of fire ...". This recalls Goll's statement that "down and up are equal alternatives to end strangulation". Whichever alternative he chooses, however, the poet's main desire is "O to break one circle!" Once again Goll utilizes familiar material in the form of the Memnon legend, here comparing himself with Memnon who was freed from the prison of matter. This time Goll has drawn upon verses from *Lilith (Les Cercles Magiques*)*:

> Was I not Memnon the speaking pillar
> Who sang at dawn on the mountain of skulls?

This is almost an identical rendering of the French version:

> Tel jour ne fus-je pas Memnon, la pierre parlante
> Qui chantait à l'aube sur la montagne des crânes [17]

Again the poet attempts to escape from the perpetual motion of the circles by building or inhabiting non-circular structures:

> I built the tower
> The vertical 1 ...
> Pyramid builder
> I lived in the hexagon of snow in the pentacle of anemone

This idea is continued in the lines:

> And I measured the square dice
> The fortress where to keep the angel
> In an ivory sleep a sleep without eyelids

However, the state of immobility implicit in the reference to the "ivory sleep a sleep without eyelids" is not to be, for the poet cannot escape from the eyes of the dice:

> Alas the demon of my dice
> Pierces me with his 21 black eyes
> Eyes of lakes of serpents of birds ...
> Draw the 6 of my death

[16] *Les Cercles Magiques**, pp. 11—14.
[17] Ibid., p. 19.

Alchemical symbolism occurs again in Goll's reference to "this fulgent dragon ..." and "this eagle laying eggs ..."; the former probably refers to the spirit of Saturn, the latter to the spirit of Jupiter. Goll's allusion to "this runner of the edge of the wheel" evokes the emblem of the Wheel of Fortune:

> Who is this fulgent dragon flying
> Without disturbing the bouquet of comets?
> But a beetle between his teeth
> Stops the clock of universe?
> Who is this eagle laying eggs on the tree felled by thunder
> And its brood drinks at the new moon?
> Who is this runner on the edge of the wheel
> Who climbing the mountain falls to the gap of his tomb?

The implications of these references are clear. The poet desires to "stop the clock of universe", to destroy the concept of time, as the alchemical "dragon" and "eagle" are able to do, but he is attached to the edge of a constantly rotating wheel and can do nothing to halt its perpetual motion. Like Sisyphus, no sooner has the poet reached the summit of the mountain than he finds himself at the bottom once more. As before, the poet does not expect an answer, for "the wind of the volute blew up our memory". He tries every means at his disposal to unlock the circles, and finally jumps into the mirror:

> And while I dive into the mirror
> A thousand circles scatter to the border of the world

But the mirror resembles a lake, and the poet's plunge into it merely produces a thousand new circles in the form of ripples. After this descent, a "coniunctio" takes place, as in the alchemical process. Here the poet actually marries Lilith, whereas the idea of marriage is by no means explicit in the French version of Les Cercles Magiques: [18]

> I marry the goddess who wears the sapphire bracelets of Saturn
> With energy that whips the ellipses

However, this marriage bodes no good for the poet, since Lilith is still represented as the source of energy keeping both macrocosm and microcosm in constant motion. This being so, the poet's hopes of escaping from the circles are shattered. In desperation he attempts to halt the perpetual

---

[18] Ibid., p. 14: "Mais quelle est cette déesse parée des bracelets de Saturne?/ Quelle est cette énergie qui fouette les ellipses?"

motion by appealing personally to the circles; he invokes two new concepts:

Azimuth! Samsara! Stop!
Viper: release your tail

Azimuth, as explained in the notes accompanying these poems, is "one of the circles of the sphere intersecting each other in the zenith and nadir and cutting the horizon at right angles". Samsara signifies "the perpetual mental awakening, i. e. enlightenment" in occult Hindu philosophy. [19] Mme. Goll, discussing it in its context in *Fruit from Saturn*, defines Samsara as "the rising and falling of existence, the never-ending and continual series of births and deaths in the phenomenal world from which there is no escape. It is the absolute opposite of Nirvana, although in some Buddhist teachings there is a profound doctrine that Samsara *is* Nirvana". [20] In his book *Le Tarot*, Jean Chaboseau has pointed out the affinities between the Tarot key, the Wheel of Fortune, and the Wheel of Samsara: "La Roue (i.e. the wheel of Fortune) est un symbole du Monde, la circonférence représentant la manifestation produite par les rayons émanés du centre ... L'image de la Roue du Samsara s'impose: du sein de ce tournoiement surgit l'espoir de l'être purifié qui s'élève en Brahma et y demeure". [21] Significantly, this passage is marked in Goll's copy of *Le Tarot*. The similarities between the ideas expressed at the end of this passage and those of alchemy are striking. Chaboseau himself states further that "ce cycle des lois de la nature présente l'analogie alchimique de l'ordre incessant des évolutions et des involutions atomiques et de leur désintégration consécutive à leur régrégation". [22] Goll is attempting to break the eternal cycle, which is symbolized in alchemy by the serpent/dragon devouring its own tail, and he therefore appeals to the serpent to release its tail from its mouth. He finally attempts to rid himself of the circles by closing his eyes, but even this fails:

With my lids I shut you down
Eye of the sun or egg of the batrachian
And still the scorpion kills himself in the circle of chalk

He is still caught in the circles like "a scorpion in the circle of chalk".

[19] *Fruit from Saturn*, p. 52, notes.
[20] In a letter to the authoress dated November 13, 1967.
[21] CHABOSEAU, p. 61.
[22] Ibid., p. 62.

In section I of the poem *Lilith*, [23] Goll stresses the double aspect of Lilith's character; on the one hand Lilith embodies beauty and desire, on the other, she embodies danger and death. This double aspect is accentuated by Goll's reference to her as a "Bird-Woman". As a "bird" she resembles a bird of prey, while as a "woman" she is beautiful and desirable. However, Goll's characterisation of Lilith as a winged creature, ("eagle-bred daughter of an occult womb"), and his emphasis on the dual aspect of her character, follow the tradition of Jewish demonology, according to which Lilith gave her name to a class of winged demons. Furthermore, "Lilith herself is conceived of as a beautiful woman, with long flowing hair; it is at nights that she seeks her prey. She is dangerous to men because of her beauty; but she does not appear to molest women". [24] In Jewish demonology Lilith is sometimes represented as male, sometimes as female, and Goll has combined the two ideas in his depiction of her as "Lilith Androgyne", an image which assumes alchemical connotations later in the poem.

The dangerous aspect of Lilith's character is indicated in several images. In common with the Lilith of *Les Cercles Magiques**, Lilith here retains her Medusa-like ability to turn men to stone, [25] an idea implicit in the phrase "The Algol of your eyes" (Algol being a twin star in the head of Medusa). It is interesting to note that Goll mentions Algol and Saturn as early as 1917 in a poem entitled *Astral*: [26]

> Durchs Geäst blinkte Algol das brünstige Paar aus der Schlucht der Nacht
> Saturn schleuderte seinen Diskus durch die Ebene [27]

Similarly in *Dix Mille Aubes**:

> Tes yeux d'étoiles
> Qui forment le couple d'Algoll [28]

Goll's interest in classical mythology was clearly one of long standing. The demonic aspect of Lilith's character is emphasized by the image of her rapidly rotating eyes, in conjunction with the Algol image:

---

[23] *Fruit from Saturn*, pp. 29—32.
[24] See OESTERLEY, p. 71.
[25] Cf. the lines from the poem *Lilith* in *Les Cercles Magiques**: "Tes yeux tournent comme des miroirs d'alouettes/Méduse qui transforme le coeur en granit", p. 17.
[26] *Dicht.*, pp. 141—146.
[27] Ibid., p. 141.
[28] These lines from YVAN and CLAIRE GOLL's *Dix Milles Aubes** are quoted in *Quatre Études*, p. 103.

> The Algol of your eyes
> Rotating at high dementia

Her association with death and decay is conveyed in images which imply her relationship with birds of prey and scavengers,

> Eagle-bred daughter of an occult womb
> Royal with lice-ridden wings

while the negative aspects of her womanhood are indicated by her inability to reciprocate love:

> Damnation of all love

As an androgyne Lilith is insufficient both as a man and as a woman. She signifies for Goll "A new sex calling from the edge of nothing". In a similar manner, Lilith's sensuality is unproductive:

> Double-mouthed orchid
> Tomb of the colibri
> Berth of the thought

Despite her exotic beauty ("orchid"), her attraction is that of a poisonous flower. She kills spirituality, embodied in the bird, the "colibri", and dulls man's intellect ("Berth of the thought"). Her negative aspects belie her apparent eroticism:

> Pearl unrobed skin by skin
> For the dance of the idea
> In pristine nakedness

She is only capable of creating the "idea" of love, as opposed to its actuality. Thus the poet's desire remains unfulfilled and he is left in solitude:

> O universal solitude
> Infinite desire
> Pregnant with the bird of death

> At last a golden feather
> Plummeting to the empty sands

In the second section of the poem Goll appears to desire the return of Lilith as a positive motivating force of the universe:

> Return: o beautiful equestrian
> Astride the stallion of wind
> Let the hoof of your charger
> Kindle stars from my heart's ecstasy

> Turn the wheel of our circus again

As in *Lilith* (I) of *Les Cercles Magiques**, [29] Lilith is once again portrayed as a proud and magnificent equestrian. The poet implies that she is the traditional wind-spirit of Jewish folklore, for she is "astride the stallion of wind". Goll goes on to speak of the many secrets he has learned during the absence of Lilith:

> In your long absence Lilith
> Women taught me the secrets of earth
>
> They fed me the spirit of grain
> They whirled the white chicken above my head
> To redeem my crime

The "spirit of grain" and the "white chicken" obviously refer to specific occult rites. An explanation of the latter can be found in Trachtenberg's *Jewish Magic and Superstition*: "Fowl are closely associated with the spirits in Jewish and non-Jewish lore, and are the commonest oblation to them". [30] The lines

> I learned to defile the rain with my flute
> I drove the youngest of volcanos
> Graze on violet lava

indicate an assumed mastery over the secrets of nature. Through occult powers the poet has been able to accomplish many things, but his one desire is to free himself from the concept of time (here the idea of tradition and "Time-past" is embodied in the "Mothers"), and he entreats Lilith to help him accomplish this:

> But now return to free the son from his mothers
> Who gravely sit in the amphitheatre of the past
> Sad mountains
> Keeping Time tied to their withered udders

The idea that the "mothers" have outlived their usefulness is expressed in the image of their "withered udders". Goll then stresses the polarity of existence, the opposing principles of life and death:

> ... the young bull in the arena of day
> Exposed to both laws mortal
> Sol y sombra
> To the dagger of light
> And the veil of shadow
> In the death circle

[29] Cf. *Les Cercles Magiques**, p. 17: "Écuyère de haute voltige sur la jument de feu".

[30] TRACHTENBERG, p. 164.

The doctrine of opposites plays an important role in alchemical concepts, and it is therefore not surprising that Goll should refer to Lilith in terms applicable to the alchemical androgyne:

Return o Matriarch
From your breasts: sun and moon
Churn the two principles
The milk the wine
The strength the weakness

The androgyne symbolizes the Philosophers' Stone, born from the union of the active male element (Sun) and the passive female element (Moon). An interpretation of the above-quoted lines in terms of alchemy is justified by the fact that the same ideas are expressed in a French poem, significantly entitled *Sollune* (symbolizing the alchemical union of Sol and Luna):

De tes deux seins
Verse les deux principes:
Lait rouge de la force
Vin blanc de la faiblesse [31]

In this poem, however, Goll goes a step further than in *Lilith*, and associates the opposing principles of milk and wine, strength and weakness, with the colours red and white. In alchemical literature the colour red was frequently associated with the Philosophers' Stone, the colour white slightly less so. "Red was however not the only symbol of perfection employed in alchemical literature. White was almost equally prominent, and the Stone was often said to be both red and white at once ... In using these two symbols together, the alchemists intended to emphasize the hermaphrodite nature of the Stone". [32] Moreover, red denoted the male principle, while white denoted the female principle.

In using such alchemical symbolism in connection with Lilith in *Fruit from Saturn*, it becomes obvious that Goll identifies her with the alchemical hermaphrodite, and thus indirectly with the Philosophers' Stone. This idea is reinforced by Goll's use of the adjective "fiery",

---

[31] *Multiple Femme**, p. 23.
[32] Quoted from GRAY, pp. 123—124, from the chapter "The theory of colours" in which the author discusses the role of alchemy in Goethe's *Zur Farbenlehre*.
A discussion of "Wein" and "Milch" also appears in *Bahir*, p. 100; the significance of their respective colours is discussed by the editor Scholem p. 101, note 5: "Rot und weiß nämlich sind die alten symbolischen Farben der Strenge und der Gnade, der linken und rechten Seite".

In your fiery embrace let me find
Ever new freedom from flesh
Ever older growing God

since the Stone itself was believed to come from fire and to be fire — a
concept illustrated in the following quotation from the *Rosarium*: "This
our stone is fire, created of fire, and turns into fire; its soul dwells in
fire". [33] Goll expresses the desire for liberation from his human limitations,
for an escape from his body, and a revelation of the absolute through
union with Lilith.

The final stanza could also be interpreted in alchemical terms. The
poet's embracing of Lilith in an attempt to reach the absolute requires the
division of his spiritual self from his physical self, a process resembling
the alchemical "separatio":

At last remains the insect's hull
Closing the compass of its legs
In a prayer to the Absolute

This separation is symbolized by the self-dismemberment of the beetle/
dragon prior to regeneration. [34]

In the fourth poem of the cycle, *Raziel*, [35] Goll makes use of familiar
cabbalistic material. Raziel's significance has already been discussed in
the previous chapters. In this instance Raziel is undoubtedly the alchemist
Abulafia, a conclusion drawn from Goll's reference to one of Abulafia's
works, the *Book of Signs*. [36] It is now evident just how far Goll has
digressed from his initial theme of the atom, turning once again to former
preoccupations. This poem is not a translation of the French versions of
Raziel, although many of the ideas expressed in it appear in *Le Char Triomphal*, in *Les Cercles Magiques** and in the unpublished French versions of
Raziel. [37]

In section I of the poem the emphasis falls once again on Raziel's search
for the Word as the essence of the Infinite. The purity and absoluteness of
the Word are stressed by Goll's description of it as "immaculate" and
"primal as snow/And conclusive as a raindrop". Goll further stresses the
need for solitude and personal sacrifice, if Raziel's task is to be accomplished:

[33] Quoted from the *Rosarium* by JUNG, p. 116, note 31.
[34] This process is discussed by JUNG, p. 431.
[35] *Fruit from Saturn*, pp. 35—38.
[36] See Chapter I, note 7.
[37] The German translations of these poems are given in *Dicht.*, pp. 544—551.

By implacable sacrifice

Though the tithe is inhuman
And redeems no safe laughter ...
Raziel with his albatross heart
Rose to the realm of solitude

Similar ideas are expressed in various unpublished French versions of *Raziel*: [38]

Raziel maigrit comme un spectre
Et se fixa dans la tour d'un saphir
Taillé comme un bastion contre toute réalité
Lui si jeune était sorti du monde

and in a further version:

Ha! Raziel qui était sorti du monde ...
Maigrit soudain comme un amoureux

and similarly:

Et Raziel s'enferma de nouveau dans la salle de solitude

The references to the Eastern Mountain and the river Sambation [39] appear in various versions, as does the mention of midnight as the hour at which Raziel commences his work:

Having displaced the Eastern Mountain
And late discovered the river Sambation
He leaned back toward midnight ...
Through seven thousand midnights ...

Midnight is stressed, for example, in *Lilith* (*Les Cercles Magiques**), "Lorsqu'il se leva à minuit"; [40] in *Raziel* (*Les Cercles Magiques**), "Et mélange à minuit les signes de l'alphabet"; [41] in an unpublished version of *Raziel*, "Raziel en montant chaque minuit dans son crâne"; Goll probably adopted the idea from the *Zohar* in which great emphasis is placed on midnight as the holy hour, and as the hour of judgement and mercy. [42] The initial source is the Bible: "At midnight I will give thanks unto thee

[38] These versions are all in the possession of Mme. Goll.

[39] *Sambation*: In rabbinical literature the river across which the ten tribes were transported by Shalmaneser, King of Assyria. In later legends this river was confused with the Sabbatic River described by Josephus and Pliny, which was said to flow for six days and stop on the seventh.

[40] *Les Cercles Magiques**, p. 21.

[41] Ibid., p. 56.

[42] See *Zohar: Basic Readings*, pp. 45—48 for a discussion of the significance of midnight.

because of thy righteous judgements"; [43] "And it came to pass at midnight ..."; [44] "And Moses said, Thus saith the Lord, About midnight I will go out into the land of Egypt", [45] and so forth.

In section II of the poem Raziel becomes the "Insane king of the abstract"; this idea recurs in yet another version: the cabbalist is called "Roi fou de l'abstraction". [46] In a process similar to that of the Great Work, Raziel is "recreating creation" by means of the "alchemy of sounds". He is extracting the essence of words and of nature:

> With roots of words with roots of trees
> Wringing wisdom from the earth

Thus he hopes to span the vast distance between "silence" and "prophecy". Finally, the idea of the Word as the Divine Garment reappears:

> Word: cloth of the infinite
> Mantle of azure around the thought
> Beyond rapture beyond death

The Word is both the substance and the means by which man can attain knowledge of the Infinite.

Section III is a recapitulation of Raziel's search for the seventy names of God, but with specific references to the Hebrew alphabet:

> Under colonnades of Shins
> Under golden roofs of Daletus

The characters of the Hebrew letters Shin and Daleth are שׁ and ד respectively, [47] thus evoking the idea of "colonnades" and "roofs". The sacrificial aspect of Raziel's task is again emphasized in the final stanza of the section:

> Implacable sacrifice
> For he bled more than those children
> Iphigenia Quetzalcoatl

The idea of the sacrifice of the individual to the common good is reinforced by the references to Iphigenia [48] and Quetzalcoatl. [49]

[43] Psalm 119, v. 62.
[44] Exodus 12, v. 29.
[45] Exodus 11, v. 4.
[46] Unpublished version of *Raziel*.
[47] See WAITE: *D. L. K.*, p. 61.
[48] *Iphigenia*: In Greek legend, daughter of Agamemnon and Clytemnestra. Agamemnon had offended Artemis, who prevented the Greek fleet from sailing for Troy, and could only be appeased by the sacrifice of Agamemnon's daughter.
[49] *Quetzalcoatl*: Mexican deity whose name signifies "feathered snake"; was said to have left Mexico and departed for heaven, being superseded by Jesus.

In section IV Raziel finally achieves his goal, a goal normally beyond the reach of any human, "At last he heard the name". In the *Zohar*, the reasons for man's inability to achieve such a goal are stated thus: " . . . it is the higher firmament above which none can see because all that is there passes understanding. Why? Because all is enveloped in the Thought, and the Thought of the Holy One, blessed be his name, is hidden, secret and too exalted for man's understanding to reach and comprehend . . . vain are all questionings and all ponderings which seek to grasp the essence of the supreme Thought, centre of all, secret of all secrets, without beginning and without end, infinite". [50] The similarity between Goll's concept of the infinite (as illustrated in the quotation "Word: cloth of the infinite . . ."), and that expressed in the *Zohar* is striking. In the poem Raziel has penetrated the secrets of the "higher firmament", but death is the price he must pay for his illumination:

> From earth arose the flaming Name
> From floral whorls from spectral horns
> On the high hour of death

The implication of the final section of this poem is that Raziel perceives the essence of God in all the manifestations of the physical world, in the "depths of sapphires/In the blood-count of weary rubies/In the fear of waterfalls/In the geometry of butterflies . . .", since the physical world is but a replica of the spiritual world.

The next poem in this cycle, *Peach Elegy*, [51] is reminiscent of the poem *Élégie sur une pêche*, [52] but is more erotic in tone and by no means as interesting as the latter. Whereas the idea of circularity and rotatory motion was predominant in the French poem, this is not the case in the English version, in which Goll appears to be more preoccupied with the peach as a symbol of woman and fertility. This idea was present to a lesser extent in the *Élégie sur une pêche*. Goll's preoccupation with circularity and associated concepts (such as the peach as an example of the "objet végétatif en action") is only apparent in such references as

> Globe of the peach-planetary system
> Sovereign of the noon empire
>
> Producing its own energy
> Scheduled for the rotation of love

---

[50] Quoted by SAURAT, p. 78.
[51] *Fruit from Saturn*, pp. 41—46.
[52] *Élégie sur une pêche* from *Les Cercles Magiques**, pp. 27—29.

where the peach is a motivating force of the universe, producing life-giving energy. In the first part of the poem there is a certain innocent quality about the fruit:

> Fruit stemmed to the tree
> Yet independent as a girl's green breast
>
> Purity long untouchable
> Even to dryad's eye

Its gradual loss of innocence is marked by the increasingly erotic tone of the poem. The peach ripens to maturity, passing through the stage "Till slow knowledge grows" to the point where it is addressed by the poet as "Flesh luminary flesh/Ripened by the full moon". Goll describes the texture of the peach, "Clad in woollen mist animal silk", and it has a voluptuous, over-ripe quality about it:

> O free to flare free to deteriorate
> As sore a flesh as that of wandering whores
> Aflame with beautiful wounds

Its sensuality is described with increasing eroticism by the poet, and no doubt is left as to the peach's identification with woman:

> Like a garden of burning carnations
> And beneath it the hidden law
> The inner mountain

The life-producing centre of the fruit/woman is described in "technical" terms. In its generative capacity, it is the "workshop of eternity":

> Beneath it the workshop of eternity
> The furnace fusing the rocky medallion
> Cemented fortress
> Keeping the almond virgin
> Far from finality

but it is kept intact, and therefore "virgin". The poet has tasted many fruits — the geographical references in section III ("Olympus, Dalmatian, Rumanian, Jewish, Korean") indicate the extent of his experience. However, the final lines of the poem suggest that he has never completely possessed those fruits:

> I bought I ate the purple flesh of dawns
> And threw their adamant heart
> Back to the old earth
> The pure refuse

The peach cannot really be considered as "refuse" (i.e. as something that has been rejected because it is no longer of any use), for through its stone, still intact and therefore still "pure", it has the means of self-propagation.

Goll's reason for including this poem in *Fruit from Saturn* remains a matter for speculation. A plausible explanation of his choice of subject-matter, however, is that he regarded the peach as a microcosmic example of the eternal generative principle of the macrocosm. In its capacity for infinite self-propagation, the peach might be said to resemble the andro-gynous Stone of the alchemists.

In the final poem of this cycle, *The Eye of Eyes,* [53] Goll again makes use of familiar imagery. His increasing preoccupation with time, and with man's race against death, is expressed in images associated with circularity and rotatory motion:

> Runner on monocycle around my Self
> To overtake the lead of veteran ancestors
>
> First in the dash to death
> Riding the wheel of wheels
>
> To win the race of zero around nothingness
> The race of thought against the Matter God

He is once again the cyclist, riding the wheel of destiny, in an attempt to outrun death. This race is taking place in the macrocosm, "Within the vortex of the cosmic storm", recalling the poet's "montée dans l'orage cosmique" [54] in *Les Cercles*. As in that poem, the contrasting ideas of death and rebirth are expressed in contrasting images, this time of "old suns" and "new moons". The poet desires to outrun time and thus conquer death itself, but he doubts his ability to achieve this aim:

> While time's four-wheeled chariot tumbles
> Along the tamed horizon
>
> Will the lilac rim shrink
> To the luminary eye of man?

Will he be able to contain within himself, within his own sphere of consciousness (symbolized by the eye), the totality of the external world? Were he able to do so, he would himself become the vital moving force of the universe, and thus free himself from the threat of death. The poet develops the associations connected with the eye; the eye now appears to him, not as a part of his body, but almost as an external object:

[53] *Fruit from Saturn*, pp. 47—50.
[54] *Les Cercles Magiques**, p. 61.

> Eye riveted under the forehead
> My own eye so afraid of me

Whereas in *Oeil (Les Cercles Magiques*)*, he had known nothing of its origins — "mon oeil/Monté je ne sais d'où . . ." [55] — he now addresses it as:

> Regal nymphea emerged from deep remembrance
> To the lucid surface of my face
> With the bold look of lakes

The association of the eye with a lake is reinforced by Goll's description of it as "nymphea": he visualizes the eye emerging to the surface of his face like a water-lily appearing on the surface of the water. It is surging from the dark recesses of his mind, "from deep remembrance", with the "bold look of lakes". But, as in previous poems, Goll also regards the eye as a mirror through which he can enter into a realm of deeper perception; the eye emerges

> With the command of mirrors staring
> From behind the infinite

The eye is also dangerous, in that it is capable of luring both man and beast to death:

> Beware the magnet of the owl
> The powers of the Southern Cross
>
> Dementia and premonition
> In the bull's eye brewing with torero's blood

A further association of the eyes with lakes is indicated in the lines:

> I throw into this eye the stone of guilt
> And a million rings enclose me in my fate

Thus, with the idea of the "stone of guilt" causing ever-widening ripples in the lake which is his eye, Goll reintroduces, by implication, the idea of the magic circles enclosing him and preventing his escape:

> Encircled by my circles
> I clutch in vain the beads of prayer
> And toss in vain the ball of the roulette

Perhaps Goll hopes that he may read his fate in the eyes of other creatures:

> Yet let me ride the brightest wheel of fortune
> In creature's peerless eye
> Blue discs of Diana black discs of pheasants and serpents

[55] Ibid., p. 45.

Or golden arcs of toads
Yea from an insect's eye
May the phosphorean verdict flash

Goll desires to destroy the concept of time, either by making things return to their original state, or by sending them to the "dump-heap of oblivion":

Whip all the mad clocks against time
Whip the hoops of childhood
Crowns of kings and rings of lovers
To the dump-heap of oblivion

He desires to set all the spherical objects — clocks, hoops, crowns, rings, roses — in motion until their revolutions become so rapid that

... the central atom splits
Making my eye the sun of all the worlds

When this happens, the poet himself will become the focal point of the universe: he will be omniscient. Time will cease to have any meaning for him — indeed, it will seem to have stopped altogether. But this state of apparent immobility will be like that induced by the rapid revolutions of Time's chariot, whose wheels turn so quickly "qu'on le croirait arrêté pour toujours". [56] Such, says Goll, is the state of death itself, "Telle est la mort qui fait tourner tes globes nacrés". [56] Goll's idea of death as being an escape from time recurs in one of his unpublished poems — "C'est cela mourir: s'exclure du temps". [57]

It is clear from the preceding discussion of the poems that Goll was pursuing his customary practice of revising, and in this case, translating his own poems. *Fruit from Saturn* does not contribute anything very new as regards esoteric subject-matter. Atomism emerges as the only notable new theme. Basically, however, atomism is a "scientific" rather than "esoteric" concept, and it is only by virtue of Goll's essentially personal application of it, that it can justifiably be associated with the latter term. Apart from atomism, the majority of themes and images in this cycle have already been encountered in *Le Char Triomphal* and *Les Cercles Magiques**. A slight variation occurs in Goll's more overt identification of Lilith with the alchemical hermaphrodite, while his invocation to "Samsara" adds a new dimension to the subject-matter and bears witness to his interest in Oriental religion and philosophy. [58]

---

[56] Ibid., p. 58.
[57] From the poem *East River* in the *Lackawanna Elegy**.
[58] This interest is affirmed by Mme. Goll, and also by Goll's reading lists.

The congruence of macrocosm and microcosm (noted in connection with *Les Cercles Magiques**) is particularly evident in *Atom Elegy, The Magic Circles, Peach Elegy, The Eye of Eyes*, and to a lesser extent in *Raziel*. This aspect is corroborated by Louis-Marcel Raymond's statement that, in *Fruit from Saturn*, "C'est le poète rêvant sur l'infiniment petit avec le même tremblement que le savant. Que chaque grain de matière, le plus petit soit-il, soit le centre d'un système planétaire aussi perfectionné que cette mécanique qui gravite autour du soleil, quel sujet d'inspiration pour un poète!" [59]

In Chapter II it was concluded that the subject-matter of Goll's poems indicated a general interest in magic on the part of the poet. The same is undoubtedly true of *Fruit from Saturn*. In this case the conclusion is substantiated in two ways: firstly, by the fact that the English poems are based to a large extent on the same subject-matter as *Le Char Triomphal* and *Les Cercles Magiques**; and secondly, by the fact that all forms of magic presuppose a belief in the uniformity of the microcosm and the macrocosm. As Ronald Gray observes: "The microcosm and the macrocosm are replicas of one another, or better, both are animated by the same Spirit. This sympathy between subject and object, man and Nature, the part and the whole, belief in which lies at the basis of all magic ..." [60]. Such a belief is an integral part of Yvan Goll's poetry.

LE MYTHE DE LA ROCHE PERCÉE

Le Mythe de la Roche Percée, [61] composed in 1946, represents a two-fold departure from material already discussed in Chapters I and II: (a) in a formal sense, and (b) from a thematic point of view. Formally it represents Goll's most highly integrated cycle and constitutes a kind of literary exercise. Thematically it differs from the previous cycles in that the entire subject-matter is based on an actual physical and geographical phenomenon — the Roche Percée, which is situated off the coast of Gaspé in Canada. [62] This rock provides a central theme or focal point around

---

[59] Louis-Marcel Raymond, *Yvan Goll — Choix de poèmes précédé par la vie et l'oeuvre*, Quebec 1948.

[60] Gray, pp. 8—9.

[61] For information on the edition used, see Chapter I, note 42.

[62] In a short foreword to these poems Goll describes the geographical position of the Rock, gives a brief geological description of it, and tells how it received its name. See *Der Mythus*, p. 9.

which Goll has grouped fifteen chants, and throughout the cycle he proceeds to attribute mysterious qualities and occult powers to the rock. This poetic technique is discussed by Richard Exner in an article entitled "Surrealist Elements in Yvan Goll's Franco-German Poetry", [63] in which he writes: "One must, however, not lose sight of the main process of Goll's poetic expression. He does not draw on outside events for his serious production. In 1930 he subscribed to Apollinaire's programme 'Jusqu'à nous l'art était un parasite de la réalité: le poème doit être lui-même son sujet', and has adhered to this idea ever since. In 1951 Benn described this manner of creation at length in his *Probleme der Lyrik*. The poem, Benn states, starts with a psychic nucleus which then almost magnetically attracts associations from the conscious or unconscious experience of the poet. This might well take place in the realm designated as absurd. The best illustration for this process is Goll's cycle *Le Mythe de la Roche Percée*." And indeed, the "psychic nucleus", or what Exner terms the "Urbild" (in this case the Roche Percée) has attracted geological, geographical, paleontological, spagyric and magical associations. Moreover, Goll's apparent inability to free himself from ideas and images which had preoccupied him in previous cycles may be explained, in the light of the above statement, by the fact that he is drawing involuntarily upon his "conscious or unconscious experience". Still on the subject of the Roche Percée, the same critic writes elsewhere that *"Le Mythe de la Roche Percée ist ein ausgezeichnetes Beispiel für das Hineinnehmen anorganischer Phänomene in den lebendigen dichterischen Raum und für das Besessen-sein vom Sujet ... Hier ist der Fels: Göttin, Geliebte, Symbol des Lebens — die Objektgrenzen gehen ineinander über, und der Dichter, der diesen Fels besingt, leistet wieder die Titanen-Arbeit: die Welt zu kompromieren, stilisieren und in ein paar Zeilen auszusagen. Sein Wort meisselt in das Geheimnis des Steines".* [64]

In the *Triptyque de la Pierre* [65] Goll describes this cycle as "un chant de la pierre première, apparemment morte et immobile pour toujours: le

[63] RICHARD EXNER, article in *Symposium*, Vol. XI, no. 1, Syracuse Univ., New York 1957, pp. 92—99.

[64] From an article by RICHARD EXNER entitled "Yvan Goll: Zu seiner deutschen Lyrik", in *German Life and Letters*, VIII, London 1955, pp. 257—258.

[65] GOLL's *Triptyque de la Pierre* is a group of unpublished notes in which the poet discusses the significance of three of his cycles, *Le Mythe de la Roche Percée*, *Le Char Triomphal de l'Antimoine* and the *Élégie d'Ihpétonga*.

poète en découvre la vie occulte et profonde. Il en décèle la vie intérieure, elle devient Roche Chantante, roche danseuse, sibylline, dans la chair de laquelle grouillent fossiles et arbres d'ères préhistoriques, roche magicienne, roche occulte, et finalement roche atome dont la fission et l'explosion inaugurent une nouvelle ère du monde". In his *Kleiner Führer zur Ersteigung des durchbrochenen Felsens*, he describes it further as "die Suche nach dem Stein der Weisen", and states that "Der Dichter hat in seine Retorte zwei Teile Geologie und einen Teil Magie geworfen, um daraus die poetische Essenz zu gewinnen". [66] In this instance, the use of alchemical symbolism has been appropriated by Goll to illustrate the poet's personal view of his method of poetic creation.

Goll attributes an inner life and spirit to the Roche Percée, thus heralding a new theme in the form of animism. Animism, defined as "the doctrine that a great part of the inanimate kingdom is endowed with reason, intelligence and volition, identical with that of man", [67] is a primitive explanation of phenomena, and played an important role in primitive semitic religions, for example. The relevance of such a definition to the subject-matter of these poems will become apparent in due course. Moreover, the animistic interpretation of matter is further strengthened by Goll's opening quotation from the lapidary of Marbode, [68] "Lapidibus in-esse vires".

Animism plays an important role in the *Élégie d'Ihpétonga* cycle, in which Goll attributes animistic qualities to stone and perceives the presence of evil within it:

> Mais la pierre enceinte de mort
> Est plus perfide qu'un mont de termites
> La pierre couve les oeufs d'un soleil
> Au jaune vénéneux [69]

The theme of the rock is developed in *Jean sans Terre achète Manhattan*, [70] and sporadic references to rock appear elsewhere. Goll speaks of the "Schweigen der Steine", [71] and at times seems to feel an affinity

[66] *Der Mythus*, p. 45.
[67] Part of the definition given in the *Encyclopedia Britannica*, New ed., 1964.
[68] The edition used by Goll was MARBODEUS GALLUS, *De Lapidibus Preciosis*, Paris 1531.
[69] YVAN GOLL, *Élégie d'Ihpétonga suivie de Masques de Cendre*, Paris 1949; there are no page references in this edition. (*Masques de Cendre*)
[70] *Jean sans Terre*, pp. 102—103.
[71] From the poem *Astral* in *Dicht.*, p. 143.

with stone: "Und spüre die gute Verwandtschaft/Des greisen Granits". [72] In *Montagne* he alludes to its great age, "Rocher qui m'attend depuis cent mille ans", [73] and similarly in *Pics*: "Siècles fiers de la primitive pierre". [74] In *Les Cercles Magiques** Goll refers to the wisdom of stones: "les rochers savants", [75] and this idea recurs in the poem *Der Obelisk*: "Es ist ein Stein unter Steinen .../Er trägt noch in seinem Blut das Wissen des Ur-bergs .../Wir ahnen nicht dass er Gott ist". [76]

In contrast to the "primitive" view of animism, Goll finally offers the twentieth-century atomic theory as a "modern" explanation of matter. The thematic progression in *Le Mythe de la Roche Percée* from animism to atomism is explained by Goll himself in the *Kleiner Führer*: "Das Thema der Dichtung ist das Leben und der Tod eines Felsens, sein dunkles, schein-bar steriles Exil mitten im Meer, das im ewigen Zirkus der Hochzeiten Leben ausbrütet, sein Tanz inmitten kostbarer Steine, sehnsüchtiges Lied von verlockenden Morgenröten und schliesslich seine Befreiung und Auf-lösung im atomischen Zeitalter". [77] The words "scheinbar steriles" in the above passage are highly significant for they hint at the dichotomy be-tween the stark, apparently immutable exterior of the rock, and its inner depths seething with life — so aptly illustrated by Tanguy in the sketches accompanying these poems. The Rock had a dual significance for Goll, on the one hand as a phenomenon of permanence, since it had been a witness to thousands of years of events dating back to prehistoric times; on the other hand as a symbol of change, a "Symbol der Wandlung ... in dem er (Goll) sein Innerstes als ein Gleichnis für die erst in diesem Welt-augenblick entdeckte Wahrheit der Untrennbarkeit von Werden und Sein im Atom enthüllt". [78]

The first poem of the cycle [79] opens with the theme of prehistory and tells of the original formation of physical phenomena such as rocks, mountains, plains, etc., caused by the breaking of the earth's crust. The birth of the Rock itself is described:

---

[72] From the poem *Der Ölbaum, Dicht.*, p. 193.
[73] This poem appears in YVAN GOLL, *Le Nouvel Orphée**, Paris 1923, p. 198.
[74] Ibid., p. 195.
[75] *Les Cercles Magiques**, p. 38.
[76] *Dicht.*, p. 564.
[77] *Der Mythus*, p. 46.
[78] HELMUT UHLIG, essay entitled "Yvan Goll" in *Expressionismus — Gestalten einer literarischen Bewegung*, eds. H. Friedmann and Otto Mann, Heidelberg 1956, p. 202.
[79] *Der Mythus*, p. 10.

Roche
Née de l'Oeuf de la Tempête
Au temps des migrations de la pierre

In as far as this cycle is to be understood in alchemical terms as "die Suche nach dem Stein der Weisen", so the birth of the Rock corresponds to the alchemical idea of the birth of the universe from the Philosophic Egg (chaos). The emphasis on the element Water — "Tempête . . . la première aile d'après-déluge . . . toboggan de l'océan . . . Et l'océan descendit . . .", seems to indicate a belief that the primeval world was entirely covered by the ocean, and that rocks had been formed by precipitation of some sort during a storm. Significantly, too, the belief in the emergence of the world from the waters is a feature of Judaism (cf. Genesis I, vv. 7—9). The biblical overtones appear again in the lines

Alors que l'Aghri-Tagh lui-même
Ouvrait à peine la première aile d'après-déluge
Pamir un citronnier entre les dents glissa sur le toboggan de l'océan

which are reminiscent of the story of Noah and the Flood, and the release of the dove from the Arc (Genesis 8, vv. 9—11).

Already in the opening poem, the poet attributes animistic qualities to rocks and mountains, for example: "L'Oural ne dressait pas ses poings de neige/Mais Élbrouz souffrait dans sa chair/Des mêmes pyrites que sa soeur Ande/L'Appalache avait ses crampes d'anthracite . . .". Here Goll indicates the great age of the Roche Percée, since the Rock already stands formed, while other rock formations (the Urals, Elbruz, the Andes, etc.) are still inchoate masses. Finally, the poet raises the question of the origin of the Roche Percée:

Roche Percée
Quelle terreur te fit geler dans le bras du Labrador
Appelant en vain au secours avec tes milliers de fossiles
Entre Malbaie et la Baie des Chaleurs

The poet seems to infer that the geographical position of the Roche Percée was brought about by some sort of shock which caused it to freeze or solidify ("geler"). An extremely interesting point concerning the formation of rocks is discussed by Ronald Gray in connection with the geological theories of Goethe. [80] In his discussion of Die Entstehung der Erde, [81]

---

[80] GRAY, pp. 142 f. Gray finally draws a parallel between this concept of "solidification" and the final stages of the Great Work of alchemy, pp. 144 f.

Goethe advanced the theory that rocks were formed by a process of "solidification", by means of which they were changed from an inchoate mass into a definite shape. The interesting factor in connection with this process is illustrated by Goethe's statement that "Solidescenz ist mit Erschütterung verbunden"; [82] in other words, the process of solidification is brought to a rapid conclusion by a sudden tremor or shock. By indicating that the Roche Percée received its formation in this manner, Goll is clearly thinking along the same lines as Goethe in this respect. [83]

In the second poem, [84] the poet's opening address to the Rock as "Roche Vivante" indicates that the birth of the Rock is accomplished. It is now a well-known geographical phenomenon, described by Goll in its three dimensions. It is a "totem with the three faces of eagle, lion and snake": [85]

De face Aigle
De flanc Lionne
Des airs Serpent

The Rock presents a constantly changing appearance, determined by the time of day or night, or by the play of light upon its stones:

Chimère du Nord
Qui change selon l'angle selon l'oeil selon l'heure

Its strangeness is emphasized by its personification as "Chimère du Nord", since chimaera is the name of a fish of extraordinary appearance inhabiting the northern seas. The Rock now possesses definite vital attributes and is no longer merely inert matter. "La Roche Percée ... n'est point minéral mort, mais substance bouillonnante de vie, présence presque animale, presque humaine". [86]

Pierre plus agitée que les vivants
Plus rancunière que la mer
Plus démente que tes oiseaux

The last line quoted above bears out Goll's own statement that the summit of the Rock "ist von Tausenden von Vögeln bewohnt, die dem Gestein

[81] J. W. von GOETHE, *Die Entstehung der Erde* in J. W. von GOETHE, Gedenkausgabe der Werke, Briefe und Gespräche, ed. E. Beutler, Zürich 1952, Bd. 17, pp. 464—484.
[82] Ibid., p. 472.
[83] There is no indication that Goll had read Goethe's *Naturwissenschaftliche Schriften*, but the similarity between their ideas in this respect provides an interesting subject for discussion.
[84] *Der Mythus*, p. 12.
[85] CARMODY, p. 119.
[86] This is taken from MARCEL BRION's article "Yvan Goll" in *Quatre Études*, p. 17.

einen Anschein von aussergewöhnlichem Leben verleihen". [87] By his reference to the actual structure of the Rock, with its lava ("L'Aigle au plumage de lave . . ."), metamorphic rocks ("gneiss"), its dark mysterious depths and seething subterrenes ("la nuit chthonienne"), Goll gives the idea of life trapped within the Rock and awaiting liberation ("L'attente de la créature/La patience du futur").

Geological material forms the basis of the next chant, "Roche Précieuse", [88] in which the Rock is addressed with great tenderness by the poet, almost as if it were his beloved. The poet is aware of the constant motion within the delicate network of convoluted rock. The Rock is

> Plus fine que la fleur de l'arbre de foudre
> Plus inquiète que la branchie du squale

Goll enumerates the countless precious stones within the Rock — mica, amber, quartz, jasper, agate, turquoise etc., thus creating an impression of the richness of colour and the intricate inner structure of the Rock. The almost human characteristics of the Rock are illustrated by such references as "Torse anfractueux, seins de mica, coeur, mains, paupières, yeux, sang", [89] while the inner life of the Rock is indicated by the lines

> Ton sang s'est mis à circuler
> Riche de l'hémoglobine des aubes cambriennes

It is a living creature with a blood-stream, rich and red from the light of Cambrian dawns. The above lines also reinforce Goll's statement about the colours in the Rock: "Die ganze Masse besteht aus einem Konglomerat von leuchtendem gelbem und rötlichem Eisen . . .". [90] In one instance, the animal-like attributes of the Rock are emphasized:

> J'ai touché ta chair de jaspe plus juteuse que la chair d'orignal

In another, its "scientific" nature is stressed, thus anticipating the revelation of chant XV:

> Et pris ta main d'agate radioactive dans la mienne

---

[87] *Der Mythus*, p. 9.
[88] Ibid., p. 14.
[89] *Cf.* Mircea Eliade, *Forgerons et Alchimistes*, Paris 1956, p. 8, "Les substances minérales participaient à la sacralité de la Terre-Mère. Nous rencontrons très tôt l'idée que les minerais "croissent" dans le ventre de la terre, ni plus ni moins que les embryons". (Eliade: *Forgerons*)
[90] *Der Mythus*, p. 9.

This particular chant is in fact a kind of lapidary. In a very general way it was probably inspired by that of Marbode. However, the claim of gemmology to a rank among the occult sciences is a doubtful one. In his book *Jewish Magic and Superstition*, Joshua Trachtenberg states that "Precious and semi-precious stones, in particular, have been credited with superior occult powers by many peoples. In medieval Europe this was an unquestioned dogma of the religion of superstition, as well as a subject of theological speculation; a heated debate centered about the question whether their peculiar virtues were divinely implanted, or simply part of the nature of gems". [91] In Greek and Oriental science, gems were linked with astrology. [92] Interestingly enough, there is a passage in the *Zohar* in which this same idea is expressed: "The book of the higher wisdom of the East tells of stars with trailing tails, comets, which from the skies hold sway over and direct the growth of certain herbs on earth, of the sort known as 'elixirs of life', and influence also the growth of precious stones and gold to be found under shallow water, within the bosom of high mountains; and the growth of these is brought about by the flash of that luminous tail trailing after these stars across the firmament ... That this is true (i.e. that stones will not grow without the light of the stars) is likewise shown in the book of King Solomon, which, dealing with the science of precious stones, asserts that certain such stones are stunted in their development, never attaining their most perfect completion, if the light and dazzle of certain stars are withheld from them". [93]

Goll himself makes no reference to such a link in this poem, although an interesting illustration of this idea is to be found in the poem *Hiob*, "Tief aus den Sternfossilien der Erde". [94] In "Roche Précieuse", however, there is no evidence that Goll believes the "peculiar virtues" of stones to have been implanted by some external force, but rather that such virtues are part of the nature of the stones themselves, for in the final line of the poem he talks of "la tendresse des pierres" which had been revealed by the turquoise. [95]

[91] TRACHTENBERG, p. 136.
[92] Quoted from CROLLIUS, *Royale Chimie*, Lyons 1624, by G. BACHELARD, *La Terre et les rêveries de la volonté*, Paris 1948, p. 291.
[93] See *Zohar: Basic Readings*, pp. 101—102.
[94] See *Dicht.*, p. 375.
[95] The turquoise was apparently attributed with the occult virtue of sympathy; see G. F. KUNZ, *The Magic of Jewels and Charms*, Philadelphia 1915, p. 337. (KUNZ)

In the fourth poem, [96] Goll laments the inertia of the Rock, now addressed as "Roche Vierge". It is depicted by the poet as essentially lonely, a pariah forced to bear witness to the union of others, while itself being a non-participant in the "cirque des noces":

> Roche Vierge
> O combien seule dans le cirque des noces
> Seule et non exempte du délire des migrations

Everything bears witness to the cyclic process of union and fertility: "les tentations de la marée les cycles de la sainte ponte/L'hémorragie des nébuleuses ... les cris fêlés des goélands le convol des cormorans les gestations des homards des harengs ... les saumons amoureux ...", while the virgin Rock stands alone, "solitaire", and unproductive, excluded from the nuptial activities. There is in the final lines a suggestion of bitterness and the idea of usefulness outlived. The Rock is now "an idol in frustrating inertia, a silent oracle outlived its day": [97]

> Tandis que ton sein déserté
> Pourrit du cancer du grès

This theme of the silent oracle has already been encountered in connection with Memnon, and will be encountered again in the course of this cycle.

In the fifth chant [98] the Rock is depicted not merely as an outcast, but also as a potential danger to man. By its very nature the Rock is alien to man, "Étrangère", and for this reason the poet addresses it as "Roche Malhumaine":

> Roche Malhumaine
> Étrangère au village qui porte ton nom
> Obsédante aux pêcheurs qui te contournent à grandes ramées

The Rock resembles the Lorelei and must be avoided at all costs. Goll himself explains the reference to the "village" and emphasizes the strangeness and isolation of the Rock's situation: "Der 'Durchbrochene Fels' ist eine isolierte Masse von devonischem Kalk, in Canada, an der Gaspesischen Küste, gegenüber dem Dorf Percé gelegen. Der indianische Name 'Gaspé' bedeutet: 'Ende der Welt'. Die Klippen des Felsens sind glatt und so vertikal, dass ihre Ersteigung durch ein Gemeindegesetz verboten ist". [99]

---

[96] *Der Mythus*, p. 16.
[97] CARMODY, p. 119.
[98] *Der Mythus*, p. 18.
[99] Ibid., p. 9.

The mysterious inscrutability of the Rock, an inscrutability heightened by its ever-changing aspects, causes it to be scorned by man:

Qui es tu? Égyptienne au regard d'amphibole
Chaldéenne à la peau d'aurore?
Changeant à tout vent à toute paupière
Changeant d'oiseau et de tristesse à chaque clivage
Oui l'Étrangère à qui l'on jette
Ses têtes de morues et ses échines de chats

Goll emphasizes its non-human appearance (cf. the use of "mamelles" rather than "seins"), and heightens the mystery surrounding the Rock by weird descriptions:

Et quand la lune de sang sort de ton crâne cornu
Quand de tes mamelles rongées s'évadent les lézards de la connaissance
Les hommes te chassent à coups de cloches noires

The strangeness of the Rock occasions both man's scorn and his fear, and the above lines convey the idea of a ritual exorcism.

Despite its ability to produce beautiful stones, the Rock is of no use to man, of no use to the "pauvres-de-faim" and the "pauvres-de-rêve". Thus rejected by man, its treasures are never possessed nor its true worth ever realized:

Les enfants jouent à rejeter tes bijoux à la vague
Les maçons enferment dans les murs le polypier magique
Les fossoyeurs entassent dans les tombes
Le trésor jamais possédé

In the sixth chant of the cycle [100] Goll makes use of paleontological material ("Man sagt, der Fels schliesse 44 Arten von Fossilien ein"). [99] He visualizes the Rock amidst the lush undergrowth of a tropical jungle. A drowsy, voluptuous atmosphere is captured in the opening lines:

Roche Tropique
Dormeuse passionnée
Repue d'arbres-fougères aux filigranes d'orages

The Rock is now portrayed as a sleeper after a heavy meal, the meal in this case being the innumerable fossils it contains:

D'innombrables sommeils
Meublent tes chambres de nitrate

[100] Ibid., p. 20.

The idea of drowsiness and timelessness is then conveyed by Goll in an enumeration of various fossils trapped within the stones, and thus freed from the external world and the concept of time:

Dans une larme de béryl
Le pur insecte
Seul connaît l'immortalité
L'échine du bambou-dieu frissonne encore
Et ce colibri tertiaire
Boira toujours au gobelet d'une campanule

The mineral deposits within the Rock are described in organic terms, "herbiers de houille ... le dahlia bitumineux le phlox de naphte", and provide a setting in which the fossilized insects and birds appear, "colibri tertiaire" etc. In the final lines Goll returns to the idea of the Rock as a passive sibyl whose eyes bear witness to the dreadful "still-births" of the fossils:

Derrière ton éventail de patelles
Tes yeux de saphir rouge
Transpercent la montagne et sont témoins d'enfantements terribles

In the seventh chant, [101] the Rock is considered as an earlier Memnon, whose spirit was released from its lapidary state in the form of music:

Roche Chantante
Bien avant Memnon dont la double pierre
Se faisait harpe au toucher de l'aurore
Oh voix de la longue mémoire
Lamentation de l'être en partance
Et rivé à sa pierreté

Its great age is indicated by the fact that it existed long before other oracles, long before Acrocorinth and Mount Hor. [102] The Rock is able to reveal its secrets only to those who can hear:

Roche tu joues pour ceux qui savent entendre ...

Its spirituality is released from imprisonment and transformed into music, not by the rays of the rising sun, as was the case with Memnon, but by the light of the moon ("mains lunaires"). This music is produced on the various types of rock, thus creating varying sounds:

[101] Ibid., p. 24.

[102] *Acrocorinth*: citadel of the ancient city of Corinth. The most imposing of the remains are the seven thick-set columns of the temple of Apollo, possibly the oldest remains of Greece, dating from about 585 B. C.

Mount Hor: twin-peaked mountain in the Edomite Mts. on the eastern side of the Jordan-Arabah valley. The scene of Aaron's death according to the Bible. On the summit a shrine is said to cover the grave of Aaron.

Roche tu joues . . .
De mille violons cachés dans les draperies de porphyre
De clavecin de nacre sous des mains lunaires
De la grande orgue aux pédales de mer

The differences in sound are indicated, for example, by the tender tones of the "clavecin de nacre" and the sonorous notes of the "grande orgue aux pédales de mer".

The evocation of music in the above poem conjures up associations with dancing for the poet. A note of gaiety is struck in the eighth chant [103] in which the Rock is depicted as a beautiful dancer bedecking herself in swirls of different colours, trapping the light on her stones and making them glitter:

Roche Danseuse
Voleuse de soleil
Pillant le prisme pour vêtir ta chair calcaire
Des sept voiles de l'aurore . . .
Te maquillant du mauve au lilas à l'orange

The dance resembles Salome's Dance of the Seven Veils, but in this case the veils have been stolen from the sun and are in fact the seven colours of the rainbow, or of the prism. All the birds nesting on the Rock become the skirts of the dancer:

Danse danse
Dans tes mousselines de gannets tes dentelles de mouettes tes volants de
cormorans dans tes soieries de cobalt.

The glittering spectacle is conveyed in images of precious stones, "onyx, diamant, opales", which trap the light and reflect all the other colours. It is hardly surprising that the poet should then associate such brilliance with the frigid beauty of snow; thus he exhorts the Rock to yield the secrets frozen in its depths:

Ah Belle aux Rêves . . .
Ouvre tes neigeries de silice
Où l'arc-en-ciel est congelé pour les hivers de mort

The emphasis on glittering whiteness and coldness provides an interesting contrast with the rank and sultry atmosphere of the "Roche Tropique", although both incorporate the idea of lifelessness. [104]

---

[103] *Der Mythus*, p. 26.
[104] This idea of lifelessness is reinforced in an unpublished alternative version of "Roche Tropique", in which Goll wrote "Roche au masque de tête de mort".

Developing the legend of the Rock, Goll alludes in the following poem [105] to various characters from classical mythology — Perseus, Andromeda, Prometheus — all of whom, according to legend, were connected in some way with rocks or stones:

Roche! Persée
S'approche de toi
Armé de la méduse pétrifiante
Pour punir le dragon stellaire

These lines recall the legend in which Perseus was said to have captured the head of Medusa, the head which had the power to turn men to stone. On his homeward journey Perseus was reputed to have rescued Andromeda, who was chained to a rock awaiting her death from a sea-serpent. The German translation of the original French poem is revealing in that the translator (Mme. Goll) has rendered the original "Roche" as "Felsen-jungfrau", thus alluding, it would seem, to the Andromeda legend. In addition, the final lines of the poem allude to the enchainment of Andromeda and Prometheus to rocks, and to their subsequent delivery from their fate:

Hélas Andromède délivrée
Gardera toujours dans ses chairs la douce terreur éthiopienne
Hélas de quoi se nourriront les vautours chauves
Privés du foie de Prométhée?

However, the Rock does not need Perseus' aid in repulsing the waves, ("le dragon stellaire") since their pounding is not devouring it, but rather feeding it:

L'océan qui s'acharne qui s'acharne ...
Mais il ajoute de la pierre à de la pierre
Au lieu d'abolir le poids des montagnes

In the tenth chant, [106] the Rock is equated with the Philosophers' Stone, and thus the poet's statement that Le Mythe de la Roche Percée is "die Suche nach dem Stein der Weisen" is substantiated:

Roche Philosophale
Roche acide qui détiens le cristal de la liberté

The Rock has the power of illumination, and is characterized by one critic as "révélatrice même du divin". [107] As in alchemy, where the "seed" of

---

[105] Der Mythus, p. 28.
[106] Ibid., p. 30.
[107] MARCEL BRION, loc. cit., p. 17.

gold contained in the Stone transforms all other substances into gold, so the light within the Rock finally consumes and transforms the Rock itself,

> Mais le coeur dévoré
> Par ta propre lumière . . .

and the power generated within it is constantly seeking liberation:

> Migatrice en toi-même
> Chasseresse de l'ion
> Écuyère de ta finalité

The link with alchemy is particularly apparent in the poet's entreaty

> Verse à nos alembics tes magnésies
> A nos coeurs tes connaissances
> Aide-nous à vendanger le vin de grenats . . .

The "vin de grenats", being red, symbolizes the final stage of the Work. Moreover, the cyclical process of the Great Work is called to mind in the final part of the poem:

> Transfigurée transfigurante
> Recommence à rebours la spirale inspirée

Marcel Brion explains the transmutation in these terms: "Transfigurée par l'esprit, la Roche Percée devient le symbole de la connaissance par la communion cosmique". [107] Goll finally invokes the aid of the Rock/Stone in his search for the essence of God:

> Déchiffre-nous le sanskrit des desmides
> Lis-nous à haute voix le quartz hébraïque
> Pour que nous percevions enfin
> Le souffle pétrifié de Dieu

In this he is helped by the "Hebraic quartz" which is basically a technical term, but which also, in Goll's words, "wird zur Magie und zur Definition des Steins der Weisen." [108]

In chant XI, "Roche Sybille", [109] Goll once again utilizes the theme of the oracle in terms reminiscent of some of the poems discussed in the preceding chapters:

> Roche Sybille
> Assise à Delphes au Harz ou à Gaspé
> Enceinte du cri
> Qui gonfle ta gorge démente

[108] *Der Mythus*, p. 45.
[109] Ibid., p. 32.

The poet recalls a more famous oracle — the Pythian oracle at Delphi, and also the haunted Brocken;[110] but his description of this particular oracle appears to suggest that although it is pregnant with utterances, it is nevertheless incapable of giving birth to them. "Wie eine Sybille schliesst sie (die Felswand) sich ein in ihren seherischen Mythus, wie ihre Schwestern von Delphi oder vom Harz oder soviele andere verwunschene Felsen". [111]

Goll entreats the Rock to break the long and sorrowful silence, ("tes années de sanglots") and to emerge from the mythic primeval level into the present. He exhorts it to speak and thus console its "sisters", those oracles condemned to complete silence:

> Remonte de ton âge occulte
> Et console tes soeurs damnées
> Qui te guettent dans leurs abîmes

The "Roche Sybille" must defend them against the "tribunal des Mères":

> Car tu les défendras devant le tribunal des Mères
> Assises dans l'amphithéâtre des montagnes
> Frappant leurs seins et leurs volcans éteints

Just who these "mothers" are is somewhat obscure. They appear in several of Goll's poems and probably represent the authority of the past. [112] They are reminiscent in some ways of the Squaw in the *Élégie d'Ihpétonga*, who symbolizes a past culture, and is described by Goll as having "Les seins rongés par les taupes et les comètes". [113] Goll's concept of circularity appears in the final image of their rotating eyes:

[110] *Brocken*: the highest point of the Harz Mts. It remained a place of worship long after Christianity had penetrated to the region. The curious rites enacted there annually on Walpurgis night — 1st May — led to the belief that the devil and witches held their orgies there.

[111] *Der Mythus*, p. 46.

[112] The "Mothers" appear, for example, in the poem *Multiple Femme I*: "Tes mères inconnues, avec des gestes rouges/Discutent notre amour dans la forêt publique", *Multiple Femme**, p. 9; and in *Multiple Femme II*: "Dans les ruelles de ton être/Tes mères se rassemblent/Discutant notre amour selon leur loi obscure", in *Multiple Femme**, p. 38. They appear in the poem *Liliane*: "In nächtlicher Arena hocken die Richterinnen/Deiner Mütter drei, nein, dreissig Mütter/Oder dreitausend, die das Dunkel füllen", *Dicht.*, p. 571.

Cf. also *Fruit from Saturn*, p. 32 and *Les Cercles Magiques**, p. 18.

For a possible interpretation of the significance of the "Mothers" see SALOMON REINACH, *Cultes, Mythes et Religions*, Paris 1908, vol. 3, p. 382, where the author discusses certain heaps of stone known as "Mères".

[113] *Élégie d'Ihpétonga I*.

Et qui tournent sans pitié
Leurs yeux leurs rouets leurs moulins de torture

Moreover, the fact that the Rock has to defend the "sisters" before this tribunal indicates that the "mothers" are in some way an ultimate authority. The images indicate that the merciless judgements of this tribunal take place on a cosmic plane ("dans l'amphithéâtre des montagnes").

The idea of cosmic forces, coupled with that of circularity, conjures up associations with Lilith for the poet, and the following chant is correspondingly entitled "Roche Lilith". [114] Originally Goll had planned a cycle similar to *Le Mythe de la Roche Percée*, based entirely on an identification of the Rock with Lilith. In the unpublished *Roche-Lilith* cycle, [115] Lilith possesses the various attributes (geological, hermaphroditic, paleontological, alchemical etc.), which are dealt with separately in the various chants of *Le Mythe de la Roche Percée*. In addition, there are some unpublished versions of the chant "Roche Lilith". Indeed, chant XII may be regarded as a condensation of the various aspects of Lilith dealt with in the unpublished material. As in the unpublished cycle Lilith here retains her evil characteristics:

Roche Lilith
Atteinte du haut mal
Et du délire de l'abîme

The alternative cycle, written in a narrative style, deals with the sickness and evil Lilith is capable of producing:

Lilith devient la statue du Mal
Ses menstrues de lave polluent les eaux jusqu'à la Malbaie [115]

Lilith is characterized as a temptress, preying on men and sowing the seeds of decay and pollution:

Et Lilith la chasseuse d'hommes
Descend à minuit dans les châteaux à dormir ...
Son sein roule de main en main comme une orange de feu ...
Et les hommes hagards la suivent
Hors des vallées fumantes de sang [115]

In chant XII, however, Lilith herself is infected by the evil she has sown. Like the traditional Lilith she descends into the abyss in search of her prey:

[114] *Der Mythus,* p. 34.
[115] This unpublished cycle is in the possession of Mme. Goll.

> Descends descends
> Dans les vallées du désir labouré
> Et fumantes de la rosée impure

The erotic aspect of Lilith and its attendant dangers appear in the various unpublished poems and are retained in the published poem:

> Réveille les hommes hagards de leur moiteur
> Qui sentent brûler dans leurs paumes
> Ton sein plus chaud qu'une orange de lave

The idea of Lilith as a Medusa — absent in the unpublished versions — appears in the final lines of chant XII:

> Et montre-leur ta tête de gorgocéphale
> Sur un beau mannequin de sel

The final line, by its allusion to the story of Lot's wife (cf. Genesis 19, vv. 22—26), reinforces the dangerous aspect of Lilith's sensuality. It is interesting to note in this context that Goll begins one of his alternative versions in the following manner:

> Roche Lilith
> Fille de Lot . . . [115]

In the same way as the circles conjured up associations with Lilith in the poet's mind, so Lilith in turn evokes associations with the androgyne, as is evident from the following chant "Roche Androgyne". [116] The poet entreats the Rock

> Appelle tes soeurs sévères
> Appelle à toi toutes les solitudes

and he invokes Atalanta and Penthesilea, both of whom were reputed to possess the unnatural strength of Amazons, and thus to have resembled men rather than women:

> Atalante! Penthésilée!
> Plus fortes que leurs coursiers! Plus mâles que leurs amantes!

In this poem the familiar idea of descent back through the ages recurs. The Amazons are pictured as rushing down the steps of the centuries, unable to escape from themselves and their state:

> Descendant quatre à quatre l'escalier des millénaires
> Sans trouver l'exit de leurs corps

Such Amazons are doomed by their strength and beauty to loneliness and flight — elsewhere Goll speaks of "l'outrageante royauté/De ce sein solitaire", [117] and of the "atroce solitude du sein seul de l'amazone". [118] The Amazons are nagged by the fear that they might have to submit to men, and tormented by the idea of losing their youth:

Volant de promontoire en promontoire . . .
Un soleil d'antimoine à la place du sein
Les Amazones torturées par une beauté vaine . . .
Par crainte d'obéir et de vieillir
N'adorent qu'elles-mêmes . . .

Their unnatural appearance is emphasized by Goll's rather unexpected use of an alchemical image, "un soleil d'antimoine à la place du sein". This could be an indication that Goll's concept of the androgyne is still closely associated with that of the alchemical hermaphrodite. The link between them, and between the Amazons and the oracles, is constituted by their insufficiency and resultant solitude. These "sisters in solitude" are brought together by Goll in the unpublished cycle *Roche-Lilith*:

Elle (Lilith) cherche refuge dans la nuit chthonienne
Où l'attendent les soeurs damnées
Princesses de Crète, sorcières du Harz . . .
Mais elles sont des cendres froides des urnes vides
Dans une atroce solitude
Car l'Amazone est seule avec son sein unique
Elle n'a que sa lance pour la caresser
Et son orgie est une mort [119]

In the final lines of chant XIII, Goll depicts the Amazons seeking refuge in the incestuous embrace of the waters ("l'étreinte incestueuse des cascades"), an image which appears in *Jean le Fleuve*:

Sur l'autre rive il voit les amazones
Se baignant librement dans ses vagues astucieuses
Leurs grands yeux francs, nourris de belladone
Percent l'ancien secret des eaux incestueuses [120]

Chant XIV "Roche aux Trésors" [121] deals with the inner composition of the Rock. The structure of the Rock resembles that of the human body, "mains de craie, front d'anhydrite, poumons à pétrole, rate de barium", and so forth. The poet entreats the Rock to reveal its secret treasures:

---

[116] *Der Mythus*, p. 36.
[117] This appears in the poem *Tristesse Penthésiléenne* in *Multiple Femme**, p. 25.
[118] This appears in the unpublished *Roche-Lilith* cycle, poem 10.
[119] Ibid., poem 8.
[120] *Jean sans Terre*, p. 98.
[121] *Der Mythus*, p. 38.

Cède à ma sonde cède à mon oeil cède à mon petit doigt qui devine l'Essence

The "Essence" is undoubtedly the life-force within the Rock. The poet desires to descend into the very heart of the Rock and to sound its innermost depths:

Descendre descendre
Dans tes poumons à pétrole
Dans ta rate de barium . . .
Il me faut trouver le chemin des carnotites

By means of this descent, which is analogous to that of the alchemists, Goll is seeking not for gold, but for the presence of uranium in the Rock ("chemin des carnotites"). By holding his ear against the Rock, the poet becomes aware of the ceaseless activity within it:

Posant l'oreille à ta conque fossile
J'entends l'effondrement de tes églises
J'assiste à la fonte des plombs au désespoir des dolomies

Significantly the activity within the Rock reaches its climax at the height of day, "Il est midi au cadran de l'encope". This climax resembles the alchemical process of intensification.

The cycle closes with the poem "Roche Atome" [122] in which animism and atomism are synthesized. In contrast to the previous chant, this appears to take place at midnight ("Est-il minuit au cadran de l'encope"), for the poet states that everything has slackened speed, including the elemental forces of the universe; the metamorphosis of the Rock has begun:

Les matrices de l'univers ralentissent
La spirale de l'aigle s'amincit l'oeil de la lionne se rétrécit
Le serpent se métamorphose . . .

There is an atmosphere of tense expectation preceding the moment of union, comparable in some respects to the alchemical "coniunctio":

Le Coeur de roche se met à battre
Fruit plus mâle que le citron plus femelle que la mangue
Mûrit aux vergers de pitchblende
L'atome fraternise avec Saturne exténué

An idea similar to that expressed in the final line quoted above can be found in Goll's *Ars Poetica 1945*, [123] in which he recalls the great period during which alchemy flourished:

[122] Ibid., p. 42.

Dieu science nature: c'était la Trinité du 13e siècle
Dieu qui n'exista pas encore mais qui résultera
De l'alliance de l'atome et de Saturne
Dans la grande explosion de l'âme universelle [123]

The "alliance de l'atome et de Saturne" obviously represents that of "science" and "nature", and if by the latter one understands cosmos, or the power that creates and regulates the universe, then the equation of "nature" with Saturn becomes a little clearer. In old cosmology, Saturn was the ruler of life and lord of death. Moreover, "La figure de Chronos-Saturne symbolise le Grand Destructeur qu'est le Temps, donc aussi bien la mort (= Putrefactio) que la nouvelle naissance. Saturne, symbole du Temps ...". [124] It is in this capacity that an explanation of Saturn's significance must be sought (both in these poems and in *Fruit from Saturn*). Saturn (ancient cosmology) has been superseded by the atom (symbolizing the new era) and is therefore "exténué".

The synthesis of animism and atomism ("Oh noce des noces") is seen by Goll as the only means of revealing the secrets of the Rock, for although the Rock has existed for thousands of years, it has always been isolated and remained mute. This alliance means the destruction of the Rock itself, but also a "new means of perception of universal unity". [125] Thus the revelation brought about by atomic fission resembles the final revelation of the Great Work of alchemy:

Les chiffres microbiens envahissent la chair de roche
Un levain d'équinoxe fait lever le pain de pierre
Et une joie d'uranium jaune
Emplit la terre longtemps morte de patience
Vierge enchaînée parmi les couvaisons les migrations ...
Explose!
Roche Percée! Roche Fendue!
En ton cœur d'atome!

The preceding discussion of the subject-matter of Le Mythe de la Roche Percée has illustrated the wide range of esoteric associations attracted by the "archetypal image" of the Rock. However, the individual poems remain difficult to interpret, primarily because the dividing lines between the various ideas expressed in them are so indistinct. Inevitably such questions are raised as to what is myth, what magic, what science and what occultism

[123] Yvan Goll, Ars Poetica 1945 in Quatre Études, p. 205.
[124] Cf. Eliade: Forgerons, p. 166.
[125] Carmody, pp. 125—126.

in these poems. The truth of Richard Exner's statement that "die Objekt-grenzen gehen ineinander über" is all too clear. But at the same time, such uncertainty undoubtedly constitutes part of the attraction of Goll's poetry.

Starting from the basic "Urbild", Goll then progresses to the realm of metaphysics and touches upon problems concerning the origins of the universe, the nature of matter, and the fundamental beliefs of man himself. As such, no more apposite description of this cycle of poems can be given than Helmut Uhlig's characterization of it as "angewandte Kosmologie". [126] Nevertheless, the final account of Goll's material in *Le Mythe de la Roche Percée* is well rendered by F. J. Carmody: "Tous ces thèmes de la préhistoire, de la composition chimique et du mouvement circulaire se rapportent à la connaissance du microcosme. L'ensemble des sujets, la synthèse de toutes les manifestations de la réalité, dépasse le cadre scientifique et remonte vers une métaphysique des causes. C'est très exactement le domaine de la poésie, car dans ce domaine, la physique nucléaire aboutit aussi à des images. C'est encore un domaine qu'on peut appeler 'occulte'." [127]

[126] HELMUT UHLIG, loc. cit., p. 202.
[127] See CARMODY's article "L'Oeuvre d'Yvan Goll" in *Quatre Études*, p. 53.

Chapter IV

MASQUES DE CENDRE

In 1944 Yvan Goll discovered that he was suffering from leukemia. As far as his poetry was concerned, this discovery resulted in two distinct modes of expression. The one was a purely subjective, the second a more objective type of poetry, aimed at alleviating the poet's emotional and intellectual suffering. The former consisted of meditations on the implications of leukemia, on the futility and transience of life and the imminence of death. The latter consisted of metaphysical speculations on similar problems, relieved of their immediacy, however, by their transference into esoteric symbols.

Masques de Cendre, [1] a cycle of seven poems [2] written in 1944 or 1945, represents a synthesis of these two types of poetry, a synthesis of personal and esoteric elements. Goll's awareness of the fatal implications of his illness is reflected in the title: the "masques de cendre" represent his own death-mask.

In some cases the titles of the poems recall familiar themes, but these are given a new treatment in this cycle. In the opening poem, *Le Chant de Raziel,* for example, the material is not presented in purely descriptive terms as in previously discussed cycles, but takes the form of an enumeration of various aspects of the Word, or of a succint apostrophe to the Word itself. The change in subject-matter, from a description of the cabbalist's task to a consideration of the basic material used by him, and of his relation to this material, is indicated by the title *Le Chant de Raziel,* which now illustrates Raziel's personal involvement with his material.

In this poem the vital aspect of the Word is emphasized, for example, in mineral terms:

---

[1] For information on the edition in which *Masques de Cendre* appears, refer to Ch. III, note 69.

[2] Claire Goll's German translations of the poems in *Masques de Cendre* are given in *Dicht.,* pp. 396—404. However, no translation of the poem *Mon Père le Feu* appears, and the translations given for *Le Chant de Raziel* and *Tête de Plâtre* are exceedingly liberal.

> Dans le marbre de mon Verbe
> Battent les veines du sang

and in animal terms:

> Alouette Verbe fais ton nid . . .
> Chassons le Verbe de proie
> Plus rapide que le tigre
>
> Les hénissements du Verbe

The occult attributes of the Word are indicated by the lines:

> Et dans l'oreille du Verbe
> Roulent les dés du hasard

and the alchemical attributes by the lines:

> Dans la cage de mon Verbe
> L'oiseau noir devient mercure

The Word's active power of transformation is further emphasized by references to its inflammatory quality:

> "Sois mon bûcher!" dis-je au Verbe
> "Sois mon armure de flammes!
>
> Verbe sanglant! Dynamite!
> Conquiers le bastion de Dieu!"

This particular aspect of the Word is frequently alluded to by Goll, as for example in certain versions of *Raziel*: [3]

> Mais la dynamite d'un seul mot
> Mettra la mèche de soufre
> A la crevasse du siècle stérile

and likewise: [3]

> Il caressa le Verbe . . .
> Fit exploser la cheddite du Verbe . . .

It is of interest in this connection to note that as far back as 1921 Goll had written: "Das Wort ist der brennende Reiter durch die Landschaft der stillen Gedanken. Das funkende Signal . . . Und nur Worte können so rasch wie Streichhölzer die Nacht anflackern". [4]

The basic idea of gaining knowledge of God is common to all the poems on the theme of Raziel. In this poem Goll alludes to all the ruses employed

---

[3] Quoted from the unpublished versions of *Raziel*, versions 5 and 2 respectively.

[4] From GOLL's article "Das Wort an Sich" published in *Die Neue Rundschau*, 1921, Bd. 2, pp. 1082—1085.

by the Word to open the "oyster-shell of night" which will reveal the "pearl" of ultimate knowledge.

It is clear in the context of this poem that the Word has a double significance — on the one hand, for Raziel the cabbalist, on the other hand, for Goll the poet. With regard to the latter aspect, the final line of the poem, "A la fin était le Verbe", foreshadows Goll's idea expressed in *Le Réisme*: " 'Au commencement était le Verbe?' Le Réiste dira plutôt: 'A la fin était le Verbe', après une longue et patiente métamorphose qui, dans le poète, transforme l'objet en Verbe". [5]

A technique of enumeration similar to that used in *Le Chant de Raziel* appears again in the second poem of the cycle, *Oeil*. This poem also deals with familiar material in an unfamiliar way, thus providing an interesting contrast to the poem *Oeil* in *Les Cercles Magiques**. [6] It is concise and abstract and composed mainly of nouns, in contrast to the latter which is based on more natural description and normal sentence construction. A comparison of the opening stanzas serves to illustrate this point:

> Te regardant me regarder
> Oeil de ma nuit Oeil de mon dé
> Oeil de ma face Oeil de terreur
> Surgi de quel profondeur
> Oeil-soleil Oeil de l'œuf fécond . . . (*Masques de Cendre*)

> Je te regarde me regarder: mon œil
> Monté je ne sais d'où
> A la surface de mon visage
> Avec l'impertinent regard des lacs . . . [7]

The synthesis of personal and familiar esoteric elements is forcibly illustrated in *Oeil* of *Masques de Cendre*. In *Oeil* of *Les Cercles Magiques**, the eye is given a cosmic significance: it is considered to be the moving principle of the universe. In *Masques de Cendre*, however, the eye is seen more as the illustration of the poet's condition than as the illustration of a universal principle keeping the cosmos in motion. The description of the eye in *Masques de Cendre* has a double significance. On the one hand the various images may be interpreted as factual descriptions of the poet's own condition, reflected in, and affecting the appearance of his eye. The eye in this poem is "effroyablement humain" since, like a mirror, it reflects the poet's deteriorating condition:

---

[5] From GOLL's manifesto *Le Réisme* in *Quatre Études*, p. 206.
[6] *Les Cercles Magiques**, pp. 45—47.
[7] Ibid., p. 45.

> Oeil de volcan Oeil d'une rose
> Méditant ma métamorphose

On the other hand, however, the images refer to broader esoteric concepts such as the condition of man, caught in a world of perpetually rotating circles.

This dual aspect appears throughout the entire poem. Thus the lines "Oeil de mon dé" and "Oeil à lots", for example, may be regarded as simply describing the poet's own conclusions about his fate, which he sees reflected in his eye, or alternatively the concepts can be interpreted as Goll's idea of the general condition of man who is a prey to the workings of chance. Similarly the lines

> Oeil dépoli des nouveaux-nés
> Roue éternelle des damnées

contain the idea of the glassiness of the poet's eye, due to his illness, and also the extension of this to the eyes of new-born creatures. The two are finally fused with the idea of the iron wheel of fate which, like the eye, cannot be avoided by man. A similar process of cosmic extension is to be found in the play between the microcosm and the macrocosm, as in the lines:

> Mauvais œil de ma vieille lune
> Oeil irascible de Saturne

> Oeil suppurant sous ma paupière
> Mer trouble de quelle hémisphère

The poet's conviction that the cessation of the eye's rotation (implied here by the command "Tourne, œil!") would signify death, both on a personal and a cosmic level, [8] is indicated in the final lines of *Oeil*:

> Mon œil crevé cachet de sang
> Au bas du Dernier Jugement

In this poem, unlike in *Oeil (Les Cercles Magiques*)*, Goll proposes no action in relation to the eye (i.e. descent into it), but regards the disintegration of his world, as reflected in the eye, in a purely resigned and passive manner.

The poem *Mon Père le Feu*, dealing as it does with the symbol of fire, anticipates in various ways the imagery of several poems in *Traumkraut*. The symbol of fire, already encountered in *La Fille Chaste d'Héraclite*

---

[8] Ibid., p. 61: "Qui tout s'arrêtera au repos de mon œil."

also forms the basis of the poem *Jean le Feu*,[9] which is undoubtedly the preliminary version of yet another poem utilizing the same symbol, the *Élégie sur le Feu*.[10] This particular symbol raises the problem of a possible source. During his stay in New York, Goll read *Das Buch Bahir*[11] and noted the following quotation from it in his diary: "Da fiel ein Feuer Gottes und verzehrte das Opfer, das Holz, die Steine und die Erde" (I. Reg, 18:38). Possibly Goll took from here merely the general idea of himself as a sacrifice. During the same period Goll read books on Zoroastrianism and the ancient Iranians[12] (in whose rites fire symbolism played a dominant part), although there is no account in them of any legend explicitly involving a "Père le Feu" or a "Mère la Folie", to whom Goll refers in the opening lines of *Mon Père le Feu*:

> Mon Père le Feu
> Ma Mère la Folie
> Par vous je suis Famine et Flamme

However, the possibility of the concepts of "fire" and "madness" being respectively purely personal symbols for pain and a potential outcome of leukemia — and thus unrelated to any usage in ancient rites and religions — cannot be overlooked. One critic sees in the "flame" concept a possible link with either alchemy or with a legend of the "Hiawatha" type, but once again this claim has not been substantiated.[13] Nevertheless, the claim of a link with alchemy does appear to be justified to a certain extent, particularly in those cases where the concept of heat/fire is identical with that of coldness/ice, both of which are synonymous according to the tenets of alchemy. This usage is particularly apparent in *Traumkraut*.

In the opening stanza of *Mon Père le Feu*, Goll speaks of the fiery pain raging through his body, and of his madness, as being a legacy from his parents. The intense pain and suffering caused by his illness are expressed in images of fire consuming the poet's body and gradually bringing him nearer to death:

---

[9] *Jean sans Terre*, pp. 104—105.
[10] Unpublished MS. in the possession of Mme. Goll.
[11] For further information see Chapter I, note 8.
[12] Goll read, for example, A. CHRISTENSEN, *L'Iran sous les Sassanides*, Copenhagen 1944, and FIRDUSI, *Le Livre des Rois*, Paris 1878.
[13] See *Jean sans Terre*, p. 181 for the editor Carmody's brief discussion of this problem.

Brûle! Brûle! Feu de mon oeil
Coq de mon sang
Fleur d'huile lourde

Ma chair à feu
Ma faim ma transfiguration

As in the cycle *Les Géorgiques Parisiennes* the cock, in conjunction with
fire, appears as a symbol of imminent death:

O coq de flamme! O feu de coq
Brûle nos rêves arbitraires
Dans les cendres du souvenir [14]

By his reference in *Mon Père le Feu* to "ma faim", Goll may wish to
suggest that, by allowing the fire to feed off him, he is in reality consuming his own life-blood and thus contributing towards his own death.
The same idea recurs later in the poem — "Je te nourris mon enfant-feu"
— and again the implication is that by not resisting the fire, the poet is
nourishing it.

As in various poems of *Traumkraut* (and as in *Chien de ma Mort* in
this cycle), animals and birds of prey symbolize the ravaging and consuming aspects of leukemia:

Renard à fourrure roussie
Traverse mes forêts ardentes
Dévore ô corbeau rouge
Les restes de l'oubli

Scorpion de Feu dans mon poumon

Paradoxically, the animals consuming his body are usually red in colour,
whereas in reality it is the white corpuscles which are responsible for
the disintegration of the poet's body. This idea may have been suggested
to Goll by the synonymity of the colours red and white in alchemy. Again,
an affinity with alchemical ideas is indicated by the allusion to the
"corbeau rouge". The raven or crow is a variant of the phoenix, which
consumes itself in the final stages of the Great Work, just as Goll's illness,
in the form of a red raven, finally devours "les restes de l'oubli". Likewise,
Goll's allusion to the "mandoline de feu",

Quand la mandoline de feu
Allume sa douleur précoce

[14] From a poem entitled *Le Coq*, p. 34 of Yvan Goll, *Die Pariser Georgika*, Darmstadt 1956. In the text the original French title *Les Géorgiques Parisiennes* is used; in
the notes, however, the abbreviated title of the above edition — (*Die Pariser Georgika*)
— is used.

recalls the vast fiery statue in *La Fille Chaste d'Héraclite*. It could indicate a similarity between the process of "transfiguration" taking place within the poet, and some sort of alchemical transmutation effected by fire.

The illness racking the poet's body is frequently described in vegetative terms: "fleur d'huile lourde, figue de lave, le chant des feuilles mortes, raisin de feu", while his arteries are described in similar terms as "mes forêts ardentes". The poet's body resembles a funeral pyre ("mon bûcher de tous les jours"), and the successive stages of his combustion are described in almost parodic terms:

Raisin de feu mange ma bouche
Amour de feu mange ma chair
Chair de feu mange ma montagne
Montagne mangera mon dieu

The poem closes on a note recalling the opening verse:

Mon Fils le Feu
Ma Fille la Folie
Je vous ferai Famine et Flamme

In this final instance, however, the poet is nourishing the "fire" and "madness" acquired from his parents as if they were his own children. They have become his "Fils" and "Fille", and since he cannot resist them, they have become an integral part of him.

Basically the poem *Tête de Plâtre* echoes ideas expressed in *Le Moulin de la Mort* [15] (cf. "Sous le plâtre de ma présence" etc.) in its emphasis on pallor, on the ravaging effects of leukemia and the poet's imminent death. The emphasis on pallor and whiteness, relating to the lymphocytes in his body, predominates throughout the poem and is illustrated mainly by images from the physical or organic world: "aurores blanches, givre, cèdre blanc, arbre de feu blanc, hermines, naphtaline de la lune, le badigeon, masque de cendre, raffineries des sucres" etc. The poet's realisation that he is reaching the end of his life is indicated by such images as "vieux soleils, hivers, masque de cendre, soleils couchants", not forgetting the "tête de plâtre" of the title. The brittleness of his bones and the gradual disintegration of his body are illustrated by the verb "craquer" and by the allusion to the whitewash falling from his temples ("N'empêche plus le badigeon/De tomber de mes tempes"). Death itself is symbolized by the owl:

[15] Cf. *Les Cercles Magiques**, pp. 32—35.

Mais quel hibou en robe de ténèbres
Me couve de son oeil?

Goll's concept of circularity reappears in the image of the turbines of the setting suns, together with yet another "technical" idea — that of the poet being ground up and refined like sugar, a process which is nourishing his madness:

Roulez tambours de l'heure blanche
Tournez turbines des soleils couchants
Raffineries des sucres de la mort
Nourissez ma folie

In this poem Goll has combined elements relating to personal circumstances with alchemical concepts; thus his fear is alluded to in alchemical images:

L'alembic de ma peur
Distille un marc impur

Goll's fear resembles an alchemical still which is producing an unhealthy distillation. Furthermore, the seemingly paradoxical ideas suggested by "feu blanc" are undoubtedly based on alchemical concepts.

The more unpleasant aspects of his illness are indicated by the image of the "mothballs of the moon" ("La naphtaline de la lune") and by the implication that these are giving off a foul and fatal odour; and further, by the horrific reference to Goll's "rire d'ibis" — ironical, too, since the bird once worshipped by the ancient Egyptians as the herald of dawn, here symbolizes the dawn of death itself. [16]

The poem *Lilith* again marks a new method of approach towards familiar subject-matter, and the various aspects of Lilith encountered in single poems are here synthesized by Goll. Thus Lilith is portrayed as the traditional demon of Jewish folklore, who entices men to their death (Goll speaks of her "panier plein d'yeux de tes victimes"), and who descends into their graves to seduce them ("Oh toi qui couchais dans les tombes ..."). She is also the equestrian of *Les Cercles Magiques** and of *Fruit from Saturn* ("J'attends que les sabots de ta monture ..."). Lilith is both a vast stone statue ("le silex en ton front ... tes os de statue") with fathomless eyes which indicate her antiquity ("les années de lumière/Qui gisent au fond de tes yeux"), and a source of occult wisdom

---

[16] Cf. H. BAYLEY, *The Lost Language of Symbolism*, London 1912, vol. 1, p. 68 for a discussion of the symbolic significance of the ibis.

("la pierre occulte où tu habites"). Lilith is able to initiate the poet into occult secrets:

> Que le silex en ton front inusable
> Dessine mon triangle

She is the embodiment of the forces of nature ("Lilith au tremblement de feuille ... dans tes jaspes, dans tes seins perce-neige ..."), and the external world of nature is projected into her ("Par tous les vents qui chantent dans ta tête/Par les soleils semés dans tes rousseurs"). This final quotation reveals a new element in the subject-matter, for the reference to "rousseurs" indicates that Lilith has become identified with Claire. Thus the poet is able to exhort Lilith-Claire:

> Par ton sang purificateur
> Annule le forfait des siècles

That part of Lilith which is identifiable with Goll's wife appears in direct contrast to the demonic aspect of Lilith, since the poet implies that the former is capable of exerting a beneficial and propitiatory effect on him. This identification of Lilith with Claire is substantiated by the fact that a poem from the cycle *Neila*, entitled *Lilith-Neila* [17] (Goll frequently called Claire Neila or Liane — adaptations of her second name Liliane), incorporates similar ideas and in some instances, almost identical images:

> In deinem Asphodelenfleisch
> In der Schneeglöckchen deiner Lenden
> In deiner Statuengestalt ...
> Nicht im Winde den deine Mähne roch
> Nicht in der Sonne deiner Sommersprossen
> Nicht im Dreieck der Stirn

The poet's ventures into the occult in his attempt to penetrate the mystery of Lilith,

> J'ai bu l'esprit du blé pour te connaître
> J'ai soupesé la pierre occulte où tu habites

appear to have been successful. The final indication is that the poet has discovered the secret of Lilith's demonic power, a discovery which will result in her death:

> Oh toi qui couchais dans les tombes
> De tes amants plus nombreux que tes nuits
> Serai-je seul à coucher dans la tienne?

[17] *Dicht.*, p. 576.

The last two poems of the cycle return in their subject-matter to the essentially personal theme of Goll's illness, which was accompanied not only by excruciating pain, but also by various hallucinations. *Hôpital* presents a vivid and horrific picture — reminiscent in many ways of Expressionist poems on similar themes — of Goll's hospitalization, which is seen by him in terms of a gradual process of combustion in the "blast-furnace" of the hospital:

> Hôpital haut-fourneau où brûlent pêle-mêle
> Les chairs de l'homme et les charbons de la souffrance
> Afin que mûrisse la figue du cancer

Here, fire becomes both a symbol of Goll's pain and suffering, and at the same time a symbol of the ravaging effects of leukemia. The heat of the furnace is seen by the poet as a necessary condition for the maturation of the "fig of cancer". The visible effects of Goll's illness take the form of gaping wounds, so crimson that a rose-garden could be made from them:

> Tant de pourpre entassée dans une plaie
> Pour en faire une roseraie
> Que viendront cultiver les nèpes

Similarly, the hospital itself is described in vegetative images:

> O forêts de la Charité! Jardins de la Salpêtrière!
> Aux mille variétés de chairs
> Aux chatoiements de fleurs septiques

In these terms the decomposing flesh of the patients resembles the hallucinatory shimmer of septic flowers. Similarly, Goll's feverish condition is described in terms of a hallucinatory landscape. The dangerous imminence of death is illustrated by the allusion to wolves:

> J'entends le frôlement des loups
> La fièvre des marais aux libellules rouges . . .

In his moments of delirium Goll's senses are blurred. The doctors and nurses at his bedside resemble rapacious harpies, "Harpyes", although in reality they are attempting to help him. Goll sees them as "démons guérisseurs". They take on an unreal, dreamlike aspect, and appear to be moving in slow-motion:

> Au fond d'un aquarium de quartz
> Vaquent les démons guérisseurs
> Avec une lenteur vertigineuse
> A curer l'amarante au coeur pourri d'un ange

Ironically Goll visualizes them as extracting the last vestiges of life from his decaying body in the form of the amaranth, an everlasting flower. The coldness of the state of death itself is implied in Goll's reflections,

> Éther substance des ice-bergs
> Éther au rire de glaciers

and also by the extremely unpleasant image (undoubtedly a reference to Goll's personal appearance):

> Givre ivre aux commissures de la mort

The poet's suffering and approaching death are concretized in visions of an exotic nature, in bursts of tropical vegetation:

> Ah l'agonie approche sur des béquilles de banians
> Une orchidée plus vieille que moi-même
> Ouvre ses mandibules
> L'échafaud de l'aurore est dressé sur mon lit

The final image of the scaffold erected on his bed reminds the poet of the nature of his death, and he recalls the fatal excess of white corpuscles in his body, "funérailles blanches, fourmis blanches, orties, globules blancs et blancs soleils", causing its inevitable disintegration. Goll's periodic declines into unconsciousness, in some cases induced by the administration of sedatives to ease his pain, are expressed in terms of his entry into a vague and vaporous garden. External reality has become imperceptible:

> Dans le mur à murmure
> Une porte invisible
> S'ouvre sur un jardin d'iode et d'améthyste
> J'entre dans la montagne au soleil de bromure

Goll then imagines his bones being reclaimed by the earth in the same way as slag is thrown back by the forge:

> La forge rend ses mâchefers
> Et la terre réclame mes calcaires

His final hallucination, the symbolic prelude to death itself, is that of the host being offered to him in the eyes of lynx and bombyx:

> Lynx et bombyx
> Dans vos yeux X
> Tendez-moi l'hostie au mercure

Hôpital is a preliminary and less concise version of the poem *Die Hochöfen des Schmerzes* [18] (*Traumkraut*). The vague alchemical overtones of

---

[18] Ibid., p. 448.

the former (provided by the symbols of fire, furnace, etc.) are more explicit in the German poem and will be considered more closely in the second part of this chapter.

The final poem *Chien de ma Mort*, dealing basically with the same subject-matter as *Hôpital*, provides in the image of the "red dog" an allegory of the decomposing red corpuscles in Goll's body. The friendly domestic animal portrayed in *Chien de Joie* [19] is here portrayed as a wild devouring beast. The significance of the dog is twofold. Firstly it symbolizes the poet's blood; and secondly, it symbolizes his fatal illness:

> Chien rouge assis devant ma porte et veillant sur mes feux
> Mangeur de coeurs et de rognons dans les faubourgs de ma détresse
> Ta langue chaude une flamme mouillée
> Lèche le sel de ma sueur le soufre de ma mort

It is evident from the final line quoted above that Goll views the changes taking place in his body in terms of an alchemical transmutation, (cf. "soufre, sel"); the description of the dog's tongue ("flamme mouillée") embodies the idea of the opposing alchemical elements of fire and water. Goll then entreats the dog, as a symbol of his blood, to ward off the consuming lymphocytes and the delusions which accompany the process of disintegration:

> Chien rouge de ma chair
> Happe les rêves qui m'échappent
> Aboie à mes fantômes blancs
> Ramène à leur bercail
> Toutes mes gazelles voleuses
> Et mords l'osselet de l'Ange en déroute

The dog must bring back the disappearing blood-cells ("gazelles voleuses") and at the same time prevent Goll's guardian spirit, or perhaps his consciousness, ("l'Ange") from escaping.

The red dog is described by Goll in images connected with esotericism, in many respects recalling the imagery of certain poems in *Les Cercles Magiques**:

> Chien roux venu d'on ne sait d'où devant ma porte
> Avec le signe du Voyant entre les yeux
> Et cette obéissance aux cercles
> Plus ronds que ceux de mon vautour

---

[19] *Die Pariser Georgika*, p. 20.

Here the dog appears to fulfil a third function. It seems to represent some sort of occult messenger, possibly a prophet of doom ("Voyant"), whose obedience to the circles indicates its comprehension of, and close contact with the underlying principles of the universe, the laws which govern life and death. The symbol of circularity is of course reminiscent of *Les Cercles Magiques**, as is the image of the wheeling vultures waiting for the poet to die.

In Goll's hallucinations, the blood trickling from his wounds is transformed into horrific images:

> Mais quel est ce vin de groseille jailli de mon corps
> Quelle est cette morsure bienfaitrice
> Qui se transforme en tulipe parlante
> En bulbe enceinte de la parabole
> D'où montera l'Arbre transfiguré?

His physical disintegration is projected into paranoiac visions of vegetative proliferation, foreshadowing the imagery of *Traumkraut*. The "Arbre transfiguré" conjures up associations with cabbalism, for Goll goes on to speak of the appearance of the Sephiroth and the ten rotating fruits of the cabbalistic tree:

> Des marais pétrolifères de l'oeil
> S'élèvent les sphères du séphiroth
> Tournent les dix fruits de lumière

In an almost surrealistic setting, the spheres of the Sephiroth are visualized by Goll as rising from the murky depths of the eye.

In its capacity as a prophet, the dog had warned the poet of his impending death, having recognised the occult symbol of the broken triangle upon the poet's brow. In occult terms the triangle signifies life; broken, it therefore signifies death:

> Le chien m'a prévenu
> Il a vu de ses yeux chiffrés
> Le triangle brisé
> Dans mon front d'accusé
> Il a vu se fermer les paupières d'Hélène et les roses de Rhoswita [20]
> Et le dégel des neiges dans les faubourgs de ma face

[20] *Helen:* according to Greek mythology was the daughter of Zeus and Leda, wife of Menelaus, renowned for her great beauty. Her seduction by Paris led to the Trojan War, but after the conquest of Troy, she was taken back to Sparta by Menelaus.

Roswitha: Hrotsvitha von Gandersheim. Medieval poetess of Lower Saxony nobility. Born around 935, died probably sometime after 975.

The poet refers to himself as "accusé" since he is condemned to die, and the signs of disintegration are beginning to appear in his face. In stating that the dog has witnessed both the death of Helen and that of Roswitha, Goll implies that it is a timeless and universal guardian of the dead. As such, it hastens the final stages of Goll's life by drinking the remainder of his blood:

> Et c'est alors qu'il a mordu
> Et qu'il a bu mes cinq litres de sang

The dog's disregard for the poet's life is implied from the use of vegetative images:

> Langue plus râpeuse que l'ortie blanche
> Et sans fraternité pour les cressons

The white nettle is an obvious symbol of decay, while the nasturtiums, being red or orange in colour, represent the poet's blood.

Finally Goll states that he hates the dog's fidelity, "J'ai haï sa fidélité", and its connections with the world of the dead (inferred from "son rire orcain", which brings to mind the myth of Cerberus, the monster who guarded the entrance to Hades).

In the concluding lines of the poem Goll mentions familiar symbols of disintegration and decay:

> L'oiseau de cendre chantait dans le soir
> Tandis que sous ses crocs craquait l'os de ma Croix

The image of the dust-bird, already noted in *Élégie de la Liberté* [21], is particularly significant since it foreshadows an important aspect of the *Traumkraut* cycle.

Masques de Cendre is a difficult cycle, but significant since it marks a period of transition both in Goll's subject-matter and in his poetic technique. In many ways it makes use of themes encountered in *Les Cercles Magiques** (eg. *Le Chant de Raziel, Oeil, Lilith*), but is generally characterized by the theme of the transience of existence. It is, however, much more personal than the cycles already discussed, and the entire cycle is overshadowed by Goll's awareness that he is suffering from a fatal illness. In its esoteric adaptation of personal themes (eg. the theme of illness viewed in terms of an alchemical or vegetative process of growth and decay) *Masques de Cendre* closely resembles, indeed, anticipates many of the *Traumkraut* poems.

[21] *Les Cercles Magiques**, pp. 30—31.

Finally, in such poems as *Le Chant de Raziel* and *Oeil, Masques de Cendre* gives evidence of new techniques which in turn anticipate the more abstract techniques adopted by Goll in *Traumkraut*.

TRAUMKRAUT

The poems of *Traumkraut* [22] offer a wealth of remarkable material for the critic, not only from the point of view of imagery, but also from a linguistic or technical standpoint. The latter aspect warrants a study in itself, but such a study is to a large extent beyond the scope of the present investigation, which is primarily concerned with Goll's iconography.

The significance of Goll's return to the German language in his last poems, however, must not be overlooked. Various explanations for this return have been forwarded by critics such as F. J. Carmody and Richard Exner. The former states that "in returning to his second language, Goll perhaps meant to isolate his last poems; or German may have seemed the necessary medium for expressing his thoughts. Tere is nothing in *Traum-kraut* which could not have been expressed successfully in French or which, if translated into that language, differs from his earlier imagery, except in intensity". But as Carmody so rightly points out, "the rich noun-compounding loses greatly in French use of the connective 'de', and English compounds, even if pushed beyond standard possibilities, retain only a part of the effect of the German originals". [23] Richard Exner raises the following question: "Faut-il y voir, dans l'oeuvre du poète, une suprématie finale et définitive de l'allemand sur le français, qu'il avait parlé dans la maison de ses parents? Ce serait méconnaître totalement quelle bénédiction est le bilinguisme dont l'éclat singulier inonde l'oeuvre de Goll ... Il ne 'possédait' pas ces langues, c'étaient elles qui le 'possédaient' ... Il fut 'possédé' par l'allemand dans les grandes 'Odes' par lesquelles il se jalonna à lui-même son espace poétique, ... dans les poèmes du bien-heureux et du malheureux Job — et dans les grands chants d'adieu qui jaillirent de lui, si inoubliablement, pendant ses derniers mois". [24] In

---

[22] *Dicht.*, pp. 437—477.
[23] CARMODY, p. 161.
[24] RICHARD EXNER, article entitled "La Poésie allemande d'Yvan Goll" in *Quatre Études*, p. 66.

another article, Richard Exner points out the technical innovations effected by Goll in his change from the French to the German language: "Es kommt mir darauf an zu zeigen, dass hier Golls eigenes surrealistisches 'Können' ins Deutsche übertragen wurde und zwar in dieser Weise zum erstenmal. Der deutsche Expressionismus trotz aller programmatischen Neuerungen und sprachlichen Entdeckungen in den Gedichten Trakls, Heyms und der Lasker-Schüler kennt diese aus dem Französischen stammenden Züge nicht". [25]

The significance of Goll's final return to the German language is explained by yet another critic — Eva Kushner — in the following terms: "l'allemand semble représenter un refuge, surtout lors des grandes crises existentielles et plus particulièrement devant la mort. C'est en allemand que Goll écrira son hallucinant adieu à la vie, Traumkraut". [26]

Traumkraut consists of fifty-two poems chosen for publication after Goll's death from a group of over a hundred poems. The remaining poems were incorporated in the volume Abendgesang* (Neila) of 1954. [27] Not all the poems can be dated, but those which bear specific dates were composed mainly during the last two or three years of Goll's life, for the most part during his various hospitalizations. One poem, Ozeanlied, however, dates back to the year 1941. [28]

The poems of Traumkraut present a significant and fascinating synthesis of Goll's earlier poetry, ranging from the early Expressionist poems written in German, to his love poetry (mainly composed in French), and culminating in the more esoteric type of poetry which has been studied in this thesis. While incorporating such diverse elements, however, Traumkraut remains an essentially personal expression of the poet's reaction to death.

Possibly the most significant new feature of Traumkraut is indicated initially by the title itself. According to F. J. Carmody, Goll's use of the title Traumkraut was suggested to him by his reading in Heine of the

[25] RICHARD EXNER, from "Yvan Golls Werk seit 1930", essay in Dicht., p. 823. This is stated with particular reference to the poem Tochter der Tiefe.

[26] EVA KUSHNER, "Yvan Goll deux langues une âme", Proceedings of the IVth Congress of the International Comparative Literature Association, ed. F. Jost, Netherlands 1966, vol. 1, p. 579.

[27] YVAN GOLL, Abendgesang*, Heidelberg 1954. The title of this cycle should have been Neila, not Abendgesang* as published. However, references used in these notes are taken from Neila in Dicht., pp. 554—588.

[28] Dates for the various Traumkraut poems are given in unpublished notes and diaries.

word 'Unkraut', [29] but this theory is invalidated not only by the fact that 'Unkraut' is a fairly commonplace German word, but further by the fact that Goll uses it many years before the supposed influence on him of Heine's works:

Wiesen lagerten um sein Kinn
Und Blumen und Unkraut [30]

The title "dream-plant" anticipates to a large extent the imagery of the cycle. "Dream" indicates the oneiric aspect of the poems, while "plant" refers to Goll's projection of his bodily decay into images of plants and trees. His fear of insanity leads to hallucinatory images of vegetative proliferation. Such hallucinations were induced by the poet as a safeguard against their potential reality. At the same time, however, these induced visions raise the problem of the extent to which Goll was using them as a foil, or the extent to which he had been influenced by similar "experiments" or "techniques" on the part of the Surrealists. [31]

Once again, as was the case with Les Cercles Magiques*, the choice of poems for this volume (a choice made by Claire Goll) seems quite arbitrary, for in some cases equally good poems have been rejected from this main cycle and included in Abendgesang*. The first twenty-three poems [32] appear to be the poet's meditations on death, pain, fear, transience, etc. Several of them are based on adaptations of alchemical concepts and bear affinities with Les Cercles Magiques*, but in those instances in which the symbols of masks, ashes, fire and chemical changes predominate, the cycle Masques de Cendre is indicated as a point of departure. The poem Hiob, [33] besides emphasizing Goll's interest in biblical themes, is a picture of the poet himself and has no parallel among Goll's French poems. The Drei Oden an Claire constitute a second section; [34] a group of ten poems dedicated to Claire, An Claire, constitutes a further section, [35] which is followed by a final group of sixteen poems dedicated to Claire, of which only the final seven bear titles. [36]

[29] Cf. Jean sans Terre, p. 203.
[30] Genesis in Dicht., p. 12.
[31] In this connection see CARROUGES, particularly "Dérèglement des sens et hallucination volontaire", pp. 107—118.
[32] Dicht., pp. 440—458.
[33] Ibid., pp. 452—453.
[34] Ibid., pp. 459—460.
[35] Ibid., pp. 461—465.
[36] Ibid., pp. 466—477.

The interweaving of themes and images has already been shown to be a major feature of Goll's poetry, and in this, *Traumkraut* is no exception. Since the poems of this cycle were not selected by Goll himself, the necessity of discussing all of them does not arise. Moreover, many of the poems are so similar to each other, or so similar to poems encountered elsewhere, that any discussion of them would be superfluous. A selection of poems will be discussed which best provides an illustration of Goll's tendency to combine the esoteric imagery of previous cycles with imagery relating to his personal situation.

A number of poems deal with Goll's fatal illness expressed in adapted alchemical images or in hallucinatory visions of plants and trees. A poem such as *Sprengung der Dotterblume* [37] provides a good example of the fusion of autobiographical and esoteric elements, in its evocation of hallucinatory objects and its adaptation of alchemical concepts. The central vision is the explosion of the buttercup, a burst of brilliant yellow, a dynamic diffusion of energy and destructive power:

> Gewittergelb
> Wie Blick von Amazonen
> Voll Lüsternheit des Chroms
> Entsteigt die schwangere Dotterblume
> Dem Ahnenteich

The visual impression of the flower is achieved by references to "Gewittergelb ... Voll Lüsternheit des Chroms", while the harsh dynamic aspect of the buttercup is indicated by "Gewitter-, Blick von Amazonen, Lüsternheit des Chroms". The growth-potential of the flower is indicated by its characterisation as "schwanger". The buttercup represents a fantastic "objet végétatif en action". The "ancestor-pond" establishes a definite spatial aspect, and it is from the depths of the water, as the primeval element — the "materia prima" — that life is generated in the form of this flower, itself a dream-plant. In many ways the bursting forth of the flower resembles an alchemical emanation.

Goll's own emotions seem to be indicated in the allusion to "Der Götter Einsamkeit", and also in the final line of the poem:

> Der Lerchen Lachen macht mich schaudern

It is almost as though his personal emotions are concretized in the physical world.

[37] Ibid., p. 440.

136

The poem *Alasam* [38] constitutes a similar "hallucination in yellow". [39] In this case the "dream-plant" of the title is described as having grown from an unshed tear with the magic name of Alasam:

Alasam
Die ungeweinte Träne
In der Mulde meines Schädels

Ein Traumkraut wuchs
Nachtgelb mordfahl
Lange lange Menschenalter
Später daraus empor

Significantly, the dream-plant is yellow, like the buttercup of the previous poem. Again it rises in the poet's consciousness as his perception diminishes. Once again the personal aspect makes itself felt in the words 'ungeweinte Träne, Schädel, nacht-, mord-". There is an apparent application of alchemical concepts: the poet's skull represents a sort of hermetic vessel in which the tear is transformed and from which it springs forth, metamorphosed, as the dream-plant. This metamorphosis occurs only after a long process of maturation ("wuchs ... Lange lange Menschenalter/Später daraus empor"). The strange, unique aspect of the flower is described by Goll:

Einmalige Blume
Unvermerkt von den Bienen

As a hallucinatory vision it is an "unnatural" flower, and for this reason it is incomprehensible to the bees. It is also unique in the sense that it is an object perceived only at the approach of death. Goll experiences a similar vision of a brilliant yellow flower in the poem *In den Äckern des Kampfers:* [40]

Die gelbe adelige Blume
Die alle tausend Jahre einmal blüht
Windet sich langsam aus deinem Brustkorb

and likewise in *Irrsal:* [41]

Eine adlige Blume friert
Im berstenden Brustkorb

---

[38] Ibid., p. 443.
[39] This is the description given to these visions of yellow flowers by CARMODY, p. 168.
[40] *Dicht.*, p. 458.
[41] Ibid., p. 442.

The use of vegetative images to describe the symptoms of Goll's illness and his reaction to it, is a notable feature of *Traumkraut*. In *Die inneren Bäume* [42] Goll visualizes trees growing out of his head, which again represents a kind of hermetic vessel:

> Die trunkenen
> Die todestrunkenen Bäume meiner Jahre
> Heiss wachsen sie aus meinem Haupt
> Mit Frucht und Wurzel
> Mit Händen und mit Sonnen
> Behenden und besonnenen Tieren

The personal significance of this grotesque vision is indicated by "todestrunken" and "heiss" (the latter referring to the fever accompanying Goll's illness). This horrific vegetative growth has both human and animal attributes ("Mit Händen ... Behenden und besonnenen Tieren"), while the allusion to "Sonnen" creates the impression of vivid yellow. In the final stanza,

> Im Aug des goldenen Frosches glüht
> Das Licht des Saturn
> Während auf den Wiesen
> Die Kometen blühen

the emphasis on bursts of yellow indicates Goll's violent pain and the chemical changes taking place in his body. These are given a cosmic significance by Goll's use of familiar images related to the concept of microcosm and macrocosm.

The poem *Rosentum*, [43] although connected with the preceding poems by virtue of its adaptation of organic images, nevertheless merits attention as an example of the synthesis of esoteric subject-matter encountered in earlier cycles and Goll's own view of leukemia.

Viewed in the light of Goll's entire work, the image of the rose may be seen to possess various meanings according to the context in which it is found. In *La Rose des Roses*, [44] for example, the word "rose" was used mainly for the purposes of illustrating a verbal technique ("rose-roue, rose-oeil, rose-astre", etc.). In *Les Cercles* it became an "absolute object", an "objet végétatif en action", designed to illustrate the relentless cyclic

---

[42] Ibid., p. 444.
[43] Ibid., p. 450.
[44] Ibid., p. 422.

aspect of fate ("Je suis le Fou ... attaché à la roue des roses"). [45] In *Lilith* (*Les Cercles Magiques**) the rose represented the sensual aspect of Lilith ("Ton sein est la rose des roses"). [46] In *Azoth* (*Le Char Triomphal*) it symbolized an alchemical process ("La rose naît du minerai"), [47] while in the poem *Les Cercles Magiques*, its significance as an emblem of the Tarot was implied ("Je jardine la roseraie magique ..."). [48] In the later poems, generally speaking, the rose is used by Goll to convey the idea of wounds and bodily decay (eg. "Meine Geschwüre blühen/Wie gelbe Teerosen"; "Meine Geschwüre/Goldrote Rosen/Wie sie gedeihen!" [49]; "Tant de pourpre entassée dans une plaie/Pour en faire une roseraie"; [50] "Dans les léproseries des roseraies/Revêtons la pourpre des fièvres .../Ah dans la pourriture de roses/Laver la face d'homme" [51]), and the ideas of madness ("les rosiers de ma frénésie") [52] and combustion, connected with the ravaging effects of leukemia ("Rosenbrände"; [53] "Blühn die Wunden und die Feuer/Wild ... in den heissen Rosenäckern"). [54] Because it blooms and fades so quickly (cf. the poem *Naissance* [55]), the rose becomes for Goll a pertinent symbol of the transience of man's existence and the fugacity of time.

In *Rosentum* [56] (as in the preliminary version of the poem, *Blaublütige Rose* [57]) Goll's bodily decay, centred in the brain, is transferred to the rose. The significance of the flower is by no means evident from a reading of this poem, but is only understandable by reference to similar passages in other poems, and by a knowledge of the autobiographical circumstances which prompted their composition. The poem consists of a description of events taking place simultaneously internally (i.e. chemical changes in the poet's body), and externally (i.e. in nature, which is characterized as essentially negative). Thus the microcosm-macrocosm situation of *Les Cercles Magiques** reappears:

[45] *Les Cercles* from *Les Cercles Magiques**, p. 58.
[46] Ibid., p. 23.
[47] *Dicht.*, p. 408.
[48] *Les Cercles Magiques**, p. 13.
[49] From *Hiobs Revolte*, *Dicht.*, pp. 377 & 378.
[50] *Hôpital* in *Masques de Cendre*.
[51] *Die Pariser Georgika*, p. 24, poem entitled *Nuit de Lave*.
[52] From *Le Moulin de la Mort* in *Les Cercles Magiques**, p. 32.
[53] *Feuerharfe*, *Dicht.*, p. 447.
[54] *Die Hochöfen des Schmerzes*, ibid., p. 448.
[55] *Die Pariser Georgika*, p. 26.
[56] *Dicht.*, p. 450.

Mondrose
Die in Tierköpfen brennt
Hirnrose
Aus Schädeln geschält
O jähes Rosentum

The opening lines reveal the destructive influence exerted by the "moon-rose". In *Jean sans Terre* the moon is described as having a similarly contaminating and burning effect ("En pleine lune un bain de chlore/Me brûle de son poison blanc");[58] a similar idea appears in *Südnordblau* ("Verbrennst dir die Hände im Mondchlor").[59] The planet ("Mondrose") exerts a destructive influence on life — embodied in the "Tierköpfe" — the connection being established by the signs of the Zodiac. A simultaneous process of destruction is taking place on a microcosmic level, within the poet's brain, which is decaying as a result of his illness. The phrase "Aus Schädeln geschält" conveys the idea of his festering sores leading ultimately to insanity and death. By the "sudden rose-realm" the poet would have us understand the sudden onslaught of pain (cf. "rose sadique" in *Le Char Triomphal*). [60]

In the second stanza, the rose is portrayed as the familiar spherical "absolute object" in motion, recalling poems of *Les Cercles Magiques**:

Solang das Rad der Rose
Schwingt und schwingt
Die Mittagsroserei
In Äckern fiebert
Bohrt sich das Rosenaug
In meinen wachen Schlaf

The entire stanza contains esoteric imagery encountered in earlier poems. The "Rad der Rose" recalls the perpetually rotating "roue des roses" of *Les Cercles* and symbolizes destiny or the cyclic process of birth and death to which man is condemned. Likewise, the repetition of "schwingt" reinforces the idea of perpetual motion and dynamic energy. With the mention of "Mittagsroserei" and "bohrt", the familiar idea of a process of manufacturing is introduced into the poem, while "Mittag" and "fiebert" convey the idea of a scorching midday heat, understandable too, in

---

[57] Ibid., p. 572.
[58] From *Jean sans Terre — mais non sans Mystère* in *Jean sans Terre*, p. 75.
[59] *Dicht.*, p. 578.
[60] Ibid., p. 422.

erms of the searing pain experienced by the poet. As long as the wheel of roses maintains the universe in motion, the "rose-eye" (representing a constantly rotating spherical object) will prevent the poet from sleeping, .e. from dying. Once again, as in *Les Cercles Magiques**, Goll is condemned to life and suffering, "zu ewigem Untod", [61] by the circles from which he cannot escape.

The third stanza contains a complexity of interconnected ideas:

Doch wehe wenn die Unrose
Aus den Metallen steigt
Und meine Rosenhand sich hebt
Gegen die Sonnenrose
Und die Sandrose welkt

Here the rose has an essentially negative significance, emphasized by the prefix "Un", indicating the invalidity of its existence. Its emergence from the metals recalls the alchemical idea in *Azoth*, "la rose naît du minerai", or could equally well indicate the rusting of metal, with obvious similarities between the colour and decaying effect of rust and wounds. The poet attempts to defend himself, possibly against the circles of fate (represented by "Sonnenrose"), but the weakness of his body is indicated by his "Rosenhand". In this context the word combination "Sonnenrose" implies both the destructive force of the sun and the idea of bodily decay represented by the flower. A similar idea is expressed in *Die Sonnen-Kantate*, [62]

O Sonne! Werde grausam mit deinem Korn!
Leg deine Todeseier in unser Ohr!
Auf dass aus jeder Schädelspalte
Kupfern die Blume des Wahnsinns blühe!

linking the destructive aspect of the sun with the process of vegetative proliferation in the brain.

As the end result of the process of disintegration in *Rosentum*, the rose turns to sand and this sand-rose finally fades. "Sand" implies disintegration, emptiness and barrenness, while the "rose" (here a symbol of man's existence) fades and dies, epitomizing the fate of the poet himself. In the final lines of the poem,

O Rose Rose der Rosen
Die nur dem Rosenlosen loht

[61] Ibid., p. 572.

the rose has no significance as such, but is merely a word successfully used for linguistic effect (cf. "Wo noch immer die Rose/Des Rosenloser loht" [61]).

The use of adapted alchemical images is again apparent in the poem *Die Hochöfen des Schmerzes*, [63] but even more explicit in an earlier draf of the poem entitled *Totenchemie*. [64] The furnace, besides being a well-known alchemical symbol, is also a symbol of the poet's pain and physica disintegration, which is viewed in terms of an alchemical procedure:

> In den Hochöfen des Schmerzes
> Welches Erz wird da geschmolzen
> Die Eiterknechte
> Die Fieberschwestern
> Wissen es nicht

The horror of this poem recalls that of Gottfried Benn's *Krebsbaracke*, [6] indeed, is reminiscent of several Expressionist poems. The blast-furnace in which the ore is being melted — in other words, the poet's body is which chemical changes are taking place — resembles that of a factory where the workers ("Eiterknechte" and "Fieberschwestern") toil nigh and day:

> Tagschicht
> Nachtschicht allen Fleisches
> Blühn die Wunden und die Feuer
> Wild in den Salpetergärten
> Und den heissen Rosenäckern

In this instance, the nurses and doctors attending Goll have become in-distinguishable from his inner suffering. The wounds and fire are the equivalent of alchemical agents effecting a metamorphosis within the poet's body. Here Goll may be thinking of those primitive societies in which the act of fusing metal in the furnace required a human sacrifice — he himself would naturally be that sacrifice. [66]

Once again the process of disintegration is projected into vegetative images — "Salpetergärten, Rosenäckern". Similarly, the poet's intense

---

[62] Ibid., pp. 456—457.

[63] Ibid., p. 448.

[64] Ibid., p. 561.

[65] Cf. GOTTFRIED BENN's poem in *The Harrap Anthology of German Poetry*, eds. A Closs and T. P. Williams, 2nd. ed., London 1961, pp. 517—518.

[66] See ELIADE: *Forgerons*, "Sacrifices humains aux fourneaux", pp. 68—74, fo: examples of this.

motions of horror and fear are projected into flowers blooming on the
slopes of night (i.e. death). Significantly, the flowers are again yellow:

Asphodelen meiner Angst
An den Abhängen der Nacht
Ach was braut der Herr der Erze
In den Herzen? Den Schrei
Den Menschenschrei aus dunklem Leib . . .

In alchemical terms the adept, "Herr der Erze", (probably the surgeon
attending Goll) is undertaking the distillation of a new substance, which
in human terms represents "Den Schrei/Den Menschenschrei". As in
alchemy, this is generated from the darkness of the matrix, "aus dunklem
Leib".

The earlier version of the poem, *Totenchemie*, [64] is important since it
shows more explicitly that the point of departure for this poem is to be
found in alchemical procedures. It also resembles many of the *Traumkraut*
poems in its description of the hallucinatory vision of a flower:

In den Retorten des Traums
Wächst gelb rot gelb
Die Fieberblume
Und Tollkirsche der Angst
An den Abhängen der Finsternis

The use of "retort" immediately links the procedure with one of an alchemical nature, while the allusion to "dream" illustrates that the procedure is taking place in a vague realm of diminished consciousness, which
is of course the poet's personal state. The flower, bursting on the borders
of consciousness, is in this case the product of chemical transmutations in
the retort, but the use of "Fieber" links it directly with the poet's traumatic
condition. The yellow-red flower is identified with the deadly nightshade
("Tollkirsche") and like the "Asphodelen", grows on the slopes of darkness (cf. *Nuit de Lave*, "Tout en sachant que l'asphodèle croîtra toujours/
Au bord des sommeils"). [67] As in *Die Hochöfen des Schmerzes*, Goll's
emotions concerning the fatal effect of his illness (cf. poems *Die Angst*
and *Die Angst-Tänzerin*) [68] are projected into a flower. His fever and fear
are mirrored in the rapid change "gelb rot gelb". Thus the process of
bodily decay is projected into the growth of a poisonous flower, and
visualized as an alchemical procedure (cf. "Nächtliche Chemie des Blutes"

[67] *Die Pariser Georgika*, p. 24.
[68] *Die Angst* in *Dicht.*, p. 555; *Die Angst-Tänzerin*, ibid., p. 471.

in the second verse). In *Totenchemie* the idea of disintegration, symbolized by the "Vögel aus Asche", is more pronounced:

Vögel aus Asche setzen sich euch auf die Hände
In den brüchigen Fingern
Bröckelt der letzte Tag

The poem *Salz und Phosphor* [69] provides yet another variation on the theme of Goll's illness, but at the same time incorporates vague alchemical allusions connected with the symbolism of fire and water, together with an allusion to the occult properties of gems. Both salt and phosphorous can be used as purifying agents. In Goll's poem salt symbolizes the poet's mental suffering, phosphorous his physical suffering. In the opening verse salt alludes to the dried tears of the poet, themselves symbols of his pain and suffering:

Entkümmerte sich nur das Salz
In meinem Aug!
Wer wird das Eisen bergen
Aus meinem Herzbergwerk?

The poet's heart resembles a mine from which the iron, the force of his life, must be salvaged; but the metals of his body are disintegrating:

Alle meine Metalle
Zersetzen sich in der Erinnerung
Der reine Phosphor tobt sich aus
In meinem Gemüt

These have been destroyed by the fire of suffering, which destroys all slag. The final verse indicates that the poet's only hope of salvation lies with the agate stone on his finger, for the stone is in league with the stars:

Vom schwingenden Achat an meinem Finger
Erwarte ich die Hilfe der Gestirne

Goll, being aware of the reputed connection between planets and precious stones, probably also knew that the agate was credited in ancient times with curative powers and "was believed to have a cooling influence upon the body". [70]

The symbolism of fire and water appears again in adapted form in the poem *Morgue*, [71] in which the poet experiences as ice the approach of death,

[69] Ibid., p. 441.
[70] See KUNZ, p. 129.
[71] *Dicht.*, p. 449.

Im Eis des Schlafs
Wurzelbefreit
Wandert der Träumende

and as fire the searing pain in his flesh:

Doch im Abgrund seines Fleisches
Ein altes Feuer baumgeboren
Reift ruhig weiter

A similar use of imagery appears in *Irrsal*: "*Feuer* wedelt noch im südöst-
lichem Kopf/Eine adlige Blume *friert"*). [72]

In his moments of delirium, his journeying away from the "Gasthaus
der Erde", the poet experiences a feeling of detachment from his surroundings and speaks of being "wurzelbefreit". In contrast to this, the burning
fire of his pain is referred to as "baumgeboren", as an integral part of
an organic structure generated in the abyss of his body. However, the
effects of fire and ice (or water) are seen as identical, since both lead
ultimately to death.

As a final example of Goll's adaptation of alchemical concepts might
be noted part of a poem bearing no title, but dedicated to Claire, "Aus
Gräbern steigt aus Schattengenist das Ei ...". [73] In the opening stanza
Goll draws a parallel between the flight of Claire's crystal-clear voice
round his soul and the emergence of the bird-sun from the darkness:

Aus Gräbern steigt aus Schattengenist das Ei
Der Vogelsonne nach der verstaubten Nacht
Und deine diamantene Stimme
Wirft sich im Flugsturz um meine Seele

In imitation of alchemical procedures the egg of the bird-sun, symbolizing
new life, is described as emerging from the darkness of the "prima materia", from the darkness of death ("Gräbern") and putrefaction (indicated
by "Schatten" and "verstaubt"). In this instance the terms ("Gräber,
Schattengenist, verstaubte Nacht") are interchangeable, and all the more
closely related to each other by Goll's technique of compression — better
expressed by the German word "Verschränkung". The "prima materia"
is concretized by "Gräber, Schattengenist, Nacht", while the corresponding generation of life from the darkness is symbolized by "Ei, Vogel,
Sonne". The process is linked to the human sphere, to "Stimme", and
thence to "Flugsturz", so that the pure voice of Claire signifies the birth
of new hope for the poet, overshadowed as he is by the threat of death.

[72] Ibid., p. 442.

Likewise, a link with alchemical ideas can be seen in the second stanza of the poem:

Aus unsrem zwiegewundenen Rosenstock
Der schwarzen Winterwinde noch kaum entkeimt
Erstrahlt die einmalige Rose
Unserer Körper erlauchter Blutkuss

The unique rose ("einmalige Rose"), which could be a symbol of the alchemical work, is shown to be the product of a union similar to the alchemical "coniunctio" ("aus unsrem zwiegewundenen Rosenstock"). Thus new life in the form of a flower arises from the darkness of the "prima materia", from "der schwarzen Winterwinde". This flower is identified with the "Blutkuss", which is also the product of a union ("unserer Körper erlauchter Blutkuss"). The reference to "Blut", however, indicates that it is the kiss of death. In reality the birth of the flower and that of the blood-kiss presuppose the death of the poet, a process which shows distinct affinities with the cyclic nature of the Great Work.

A natural consequence of Goll's reflections on his illness is his pre-occupation with the concept of time and with the idea of the transience of existence. In *Traumkraut* the concept of time is expressed in images connected with water. The transience of existence is thrown into relief by Goll's attempts to erect lasting structures which will withstand the ravages of time.

Two poems in particular, namely *Stunden* [74] and *Ozeanlied* [75], employ the symbol of water as the concretion of time. The evaporation of water is therefore a symbol of the transience of existence. In *Stunden* [74] Goll again makes use of the technique of "Verschränkung", attempting to link disparate elements into a paradoxical unity:

Wasserträgerinnen
Hochgeschürzte Töchter
Schreiten schwer herab die Totenstrasse
Auf den Köpfen wiegend
Einen Krug voll Zeit
Eine Ernte ungepflückter Tropfen
Die schon reifen auf dem Weg hinab
Wasserfälle Flüsse Tränen Nebel Dampf
Immer geheimere Tropfen immer kargere Zeit
Schattenträgerinnen
Schon vergangen schon verhangen
Ewigkeit

[73] Ibid., p. 468.   [74] Ibid., p. 445.

Goll combines two elements: the mythological image of the hours as water-bearing goddesses, and water as the symbol of time. Water itself becomes an image of increasingly sparsely alloted time, and corresponding-ly the "Wasserträgerinnen" become "Schattenträgerinnen". Time repre-sents a process of becoming, culminating in completion, but it also re-presents a process of wasting-away. From fullness ("Einen Krug voll Zeit") it gradually evaporates ("Wasserfälle Flüsse Tränen Nebel Dampf") until it reaches the final state of eternity ("Ewigkeit"). The course of time is also represented as a descent of the street, ("Schreiten schwer herab die Totenstrasse"; cf. the poem *Strasse durchs Land* [76]). In *Stunden* the idea of water is combined with that of time so that the evaporation of water becomes the transience of existence ("Die schon reifen auf dem Weg hinab"). By his reference to "Eine Ernte ungepflückter Tropfen", Goll seems to imply that man does not make use of the little time he has. The poem *Wasser Zaubergesicht* provides similar ideas: [77]

> Über dir hängt die Zeit die weisse Zeit
> Und rundet sich und altert in deinem metallenen Spiegel . . .
> In den Wellen welkt die Zeit sie altert in der Frucht

Time ripens to fullness and perfection like a fruit, but this process of growth is inevitably followed by a process of decay.

In the poem *Stunden Goldgesalbte*, [78] the diminishing aspect of time is symbolized by the changing image of the hours from "Schwere König-ginnen eines Mittags" to "Magre Wandlerinnen gegen Abend". In this particular poem time, like man himself, is subject to the cyclic process of growth and decay, a process which the poet feels can only be halted by an act of force resembling the forceful breaking of the "magic circles":

> Doch wehe wenn ich euch von eurem Wagen
> Nicht in meine Nesseln niederzerre
> Eure Augen eure Räder
> Rasseln mich in dunklen Staub
> Stunden

In *Ozeanlied* [75] Goll again makes use of water symbolism. He desires to find refuge and protection by an act of reintegration with the primeval

---

[75] Ibid., p. 454.
[76] Ibid., p. 443.
[77] Ibid., p. 567.
[78] Ibid., p. 561.

element (cf. *Élégie d'Ihpétonga* VII [79]). Such an act is welcomed by the poet as positive. Since he is aware that the river is subject to the rapid flow of time towards death ("Salzwelle die nie sich versäult und versäumt"), and that he is powerless to halt this flow — which symbolizes his own fate — he desires to submit himself to the embrace of the water and to descend with it towards its origins, to return to the source from which it sprang:

> Und wir zusammen niedertaumelten
> Die todlose Treppe
> Des Zeit-Ozeans
> Dem Pole des Gehorsams zu

Goll's desire to return to a primal state is similar to that of the alchemists. According to Goll the course of the river is analogous to that of man's life. In the same way as the river flows between two banks, so man's life runs between extremes. In one of the *Traumkraut* poems [80] Goll adapts this idea, and as a result, Claire becomes the river, the concretion of time, and thus a symbol of Goll's own fate:

> Geliebte du mein Strom [81]
> An deinem rechten Ufer steht das Vergangene
> An deinem linken Ufer steht das Werdende
> Zusammenströmend singen wir die Gegenwart

Here Claire is represented as a synthesis of Goll's past, present and future.

Five poems of *Traumkraut* — *Der Regenpalast, Das Wüstenhaupt, Die Aschenhütte, Der Salzsee* and *Der Staubbaum* — represent a dream sequence and, with the exception of the last two, they all describe the poet's attempts to erect or inhabit constructions of a durable nature as a foil against impending death. The constructions are to provide a refuge for Yvan and Claire, a retreat for the preservation of their love, which represents the poet's only hope of overcoming the tragedy of his existence. The dream visions appear to rise from the poet's subconsciousness, and it is impossible to know whether they were perceived as hallucinations, or whether they were solely the product of Goll's poetic imagination. Hints of similar ideas appear in earlier cycles (cf. *Élégie de la Liberté*

---

[79] "Descendez mes anguilles vertes de la folie/L'escalier du Hudson/Descendez mes désirs/Vers l'orgie pourpre des Sargasses/Où guettent le mâle et la mort".
[80] *An Claire-Liliane* in *Dicht.*, p. 461.
[81] Should read "Strom" and not "Stern" as printed in *Dicht.*

in *Les Cercles Magiques** [82]), and also in earlier poems of *Abendgesang**/ *Neila* and *Traumkraut*. The former cycle includes the original version of *Das Wüstenhaupt* [83] and a poem entitled *Die Angst,* [84] which contains references to a castle constructed by the poet:

Ich hatte ein Schloss dir gebaut aus granitenen Quadern
War ein Festsaal darin aus schwingendem Kristall
Aus Kristall durchschauert von siebenschichtigem Licht
In dem kein Schatten verblieb

In the poem *In unsrer Zinne am Meer* [85] Goll speaks of being "In unsrem Haus am Berg", while in *Die Vogellieder werden alt,* [86] he refers to the "Trauertürme" which resemble the towers of *Der Staubbaum*. In the third Ode to Claire in *Traumkraut* [87] Goll perceives the ruins of his palaces reflected in Claire's eyes:

In deinem Aug sind unsre Paläste schon
Vom Salz verzehrt, ist bröckelndes Leuchtergold
Von alten Fischen angefressen

Later he perceives a lantern, the last sign of visibility, flickering in the tower:

Deine Trauerampel Geliebte
Scheint durch alle Fernen zu mir [88]

Der Regenpalast [89] presents a description of the palace Goll has built. He has made its interior as shining and splendid as possible in order to drive away the dark thoughts of death that haunt him:

Ich hab dir einen Regenpalast erbaut
Aus Alabastersäulen und Bergkristall
    Dass du in tausend Spiegeln
    Immer schöner dich für mich wandelst

The materials used in its construction have been chosen by Goll to reflect Claire's beauty and purity ("Alabastersäulen, Bergkristall, Perlensaal"). This "rain-palace" and its exotic surroundings ("Die Wasserpalme, trunk-

---

[82] *Les Cercles Magiques**, p. 30: "Nous construirons au sein de l'océan impassible/ ... Le palais de miroir aux cent portes ...".
[83] Cf. *Dicht.*, p. 566.
[84] Ibid., p. 555.
[85] Ibid., p. 560.
[86] Ibid., p. 570.
[87] Ibid., p. 460.
[88] Ibid., p. 468.
[89] Ibid., p. 472.

ne Libelle, Käfig der Lianen" etc.) recall the enchanted castles of fairy-tales. Thus secure against the outside world, Goll and Claire watch time pass by:

> Aus Regenfenstern blicken wir wie die Zeit
> Mit Regenfahnen über das Meer hinweht
> Und mit dem Schlachtheer fremder Stürme
> Elend in alten Morästen endet

The final line contains a hint of Goll's constant preoccupation with the fugacity of time, and his personal sentiments are indicated by the use of "elend". Thoughts of death recur in the final stanza, in which Goll visualizes Claire making a "rain-cloth" to protect them:

> Du aber strickst mir verstohlen im Perlensaal
> Durchwirkt von Hanf und Träne ein Regentuch
> Ein Leichentuch breit für uns beide
> Bis in die Ewigkeit warm und haltbar

The second poem presenting a picture of a gigantic construction is entitled *Das Wüstenhaupt*. [90] This particular poem is perhaps more interesting with regard to its esoteric imagery than *Der Regenpalast*, since in it Claire is immortalized as a vast statue, recalling Goll's earlier descriptions of statues and oracles (Memnon, Lilith, Vénus). The personal element embodied by Claire is fused with Goll's esoteric concept of stone and its function as an oracle. The personal reason for Goll's construction of the statue of Claire is indicated in the opening line of the poem:

> Ich baute mir dein Haupt über der Wüste des täglichen Todes

The vast statue will represent yet another durable construction in the face of impermanence. The poet goes on to evoke oriental scenes:

> Zahllose Sklaven brannten die Ziegel deiner Gestalt
> Aus dem Blut des Sonnenaufgangs
> Auf Regenleitern stiegen Maurer in deine Augen
> Legten die Kuppeln aus mit dem Goldstaub der Sterne
> Und die Pupillen mit Kohol und Smaragd
> Diese schwebten wie die ewige Waage
> Auf der sich Sonne und Mond messen

The reference to slaves and to kohol (a fine powder of antimony used in the East for staining the eyelids) reinforces the oriental aspect of the scene, recalling the construction of pyramids and sphinxes by slaves in ancient Egypt. The statue is constructed of actual building materials

---

[90] Ibid., p. 473.

("Ziegel"), of precious stones ("Smaragd, Gold"), but also of cosmic elements ("Blut des Sonnenaufgangs"). This latter aspect is important since it stresses the cosmic significance of the statue, which in fact represents a world figuration. The idea of light playing on the red stone recalls the rays of the rising sun striking the gigantic granite statue of Memnon. A personal element evoking the magical atmosphere present in these "dream-poems" appears in the allusion to "Regenleitern". The emphasis placed by Goll on the eyes of the gigantic statue recalls their significance in connection with Lilith and Vénus, and even with *La Fille Chaste d'Héraclite*. Like the eyes of Lilith and Vénus, those of Claire's statue are in constant motion ("schwebten wie die ewige Waage") and absorb and reflect the cosmos in their depths ("auf der sich Sonne und Mond messen"). The eyes are in fact replicas of the heavens (implied from "Kuppeln" and "Sterne"). The enormity of the statue is further emphasized in the second stanza:

> Bald stieg aus dem Tor deines granitenen Mundes
> Der wahr- und irrsprach
> Die Zauberlehre deines alten Volkes

The vast statue, constructed of granite like Memnon, is envisaged as an oracle (cf. Memnon and Lilith), but an oracle no longer capable of answering questions or making predictions.

Goll's personal desire to immortalize Claire and her love, in an attempt to minimize the tragic implications of transience, is revealed in the third stanza:

> Ich glaubte dein Herz für immer geborgen
> In der tiefsten Wohnung der Wüste
> Dein Seherinnenauge die Zeit überstrahlend

But his inability to achieve this is also revealed. Despite the fact that Claire's heart is hidden away in the depths of the desert, it is nonetheless ephemeral. Goll has deluded himself into thinking of the statue as a timeless sibyl, but even a statue is not free from the ravages of time:

> Doch ach wie bald erblindetest du
> Im Sandwind und Nebel der Geister
> Die Ziegel verwesten schneller als alles Fleisch
> Die Karawanen die am Salzsee deiner Augen lagerten
> Erkannten dein verwehendes Haupt nicht mehr
> Und deiner bröckelnden Lippen Gesang
> Verschallte im blauen Gewölbe des Mondes

The vast eyes of the statue can no longer see, its huge lips no longer prophesy, and its bricks are corroded by desert storms. It is nothing but a crumbling mass of stone, whose disintegration is indicated throughout the final stanza ("erblindetest, Sandwind und Nebel, verwesten, Salzsee deiner Augen, verwehendes Haupt, bröckelnde Lippen") culminating in the final vision of desolation ("Und deiner bröckelnden Lippen Gesang/ Verschallte im blauen Gewölbe des Mondes").

At this stage, Goll abandons his visions of palaces and statues, and sets off with Claire on a dream adventure, recorded in the final three poems of *Traumkraut*.

The imagery of the first of these poems, *Die Aschenhütte*,[91] anticipates that of the two final poems *Der Salzsee*[92] and *Der Staubbaum*[93]. Ashes, snow, dust and salt are to be interpreted in personal terms as symbols of Goll's physical disintegration. In *Die Aschenhütte* Goll describes a landscape of extreme desolation in which he and Claire are wandering, exiled and homeless:

> Wir hatten kein Haus wie die andern an sicherem Berghang
> Wir mussten immer weiterwandern
> Im Schnee der weder Salz noch Zucker war
> An runden Kegeln des Mondes entlang

The setting is that of a surrealistic lunar landscape in which there is no semblance of reality, and in which even the snow has lost its substance ("Schnee der weder Salz noch Zucker war"). Goll and Claire are totally abandoned, for the birds accompanying them have flown away and no flowers grow by the wayside:

> Du riefst nach deinen Schutzvögeln
> Die hoch im Äther zu den Gräbern Afrikas flogen
> Die Strasse des Vergessens machte grosse Schleifen
> Und keine blasse Blume sann am Weg

Soon, however, they discover the "Aschenhütte", which represents a refuge for them in their loneliness and homelessness:

> Gen Mitternacht fand sich eine Aschenhütte
> Man hört das lachende Bellen der Wölfe
> Mit Fackeln hielt ich sie fern
> Und fing im Nesselbach einen Ölfisch
> Der uns lange erwärmte
> Breit war das Bett aus geschnitztem Schnee

---

[91] Ibid., p. 475.   [92] Ibid., p. 476.   [93] Ibid., p. 477.

It also represents a refuge against the hostile forces of the outside world, embodied by the wolves. The fact that the hut is constructed of ashes indicates the unreality of the situation, as do the allusions to "Nesselbach, Ölfisch, Bett aus geschnitzem Schnee".

The final stanza, in which love is shown to provide an escape from hopelessness and despair, is magnificently simple:

Und da geschah das Wunder:
Dein goldener Leib erstrahlte als nächtliche Sonne

As the embodiment of love, Claire provides light and warmth and a haven for the poet in the midst of a depersonalized and desolate world. In the darkness her body nourishes, sustains and spreads warmth like the sun, thus bringing a last vestige of joy and hope to the poet.

In the last two poems of this "dream" group, Der Salzsee and Der Staubbaum, the diversity of the physical world is reduced to a salty, chalky, amorphous mass of dust, indicating the barrenness and futility of the poet's final visions. Interestingly enough, the titles of the five "dream" poems correspond to the gradual reduction of the poet's vision of the world, from the enormity of the "rain-palace" down to the smallest particles of dust in the "dust-tree". In Der Salzsee, [92] after a somewhat surrealistic opening stanza, Claire and Yvan are portrayed as arriving at their destination:

Da steht für uns erbaut die gesuchte Traumstadt
In der die Strassen alle schwarz und weiss sind

They seem to have found the "dream-city" they were looking for. It is an unreal city, however, in which everything is reduced to extremes of black and white. The houses of the city are constructed of chalk, and within them burn yellow candles, last symbols of Goll's fading consciousness:

Die Häuser sind mit Kreide gegen den Himmel gezeichnet . . .
Nur oben unter Giebeln wachsen gelbe Kerzen
Wie Nägel zu zahllosen Särgen

Thus it is evident that Goll's thoughts are never far from death. In the final verse, when they reach the "salt-lake", Yvan fights to protect himself and Claire against the predatory birds lying in wait for them:

Doch bald gelangen wir hinaus zum Salzsee
Da lauern uns die langgeschnäbelten Eisvögel auf,
Die ich die ganze Nacht mit nackten Händen bekämpfe,
Bevor uns ihre warmen Daunen zum Lager dienen

He finally manages to ward off the long-beaked ice-birds (symbols of death) and finds temporary respite with Claire on a bed made of the birds' warm down.

Der Staubbaum [93] recounts the end of Yvan and Claire's dream adventure. The icy desert of *Der Salzsee* has now become a colourless dust-forest, dust representing the final symbol of dissolution:

> Ein Staubbaum wächst
> Ein Staubwald überall wo wir gegangen
> Und diese Staubhand, weh! rühr sie nicht an!

The physical world is transformed under the influence of transience into a realm of dust, and the poet himself is not exempt from the process of dissolution (symbolized by his "Staubhand"). Everywhere towers crumble into ruins and are replaced by towers of oblivion:

> Rings um uns steigen Türme des Vergessens
> Türme die nach innen fallen
> Aber noch bestrahlt von deinem orangenen Licht!
> Ein Staubvogel fliegt auf

The poet's last glimmer of consciousness in a rapidly disintegrating universe is indicated by the orange glow ("orangenes Licht"). Eventually however, the final sign of life disappears with the flight of the dust-bird. Even at the very end Goll still desires to immortalize his love for Claire and preserve the dreams they have shared:

> Die Sage unsrer Liebe lass ich in Quarz verwahren
> Das Gold unsrer Träume in einer Wüste vergraben
> Der Staubwald wird immer dunkler
> Weh! Rühr diese Staubrose nicht an!

Darkness falls on the dust-forest in which the dust-tree stands, a tragic symbol of the dissolution of life and hope. Even the rose, symbolizing life and love, becomes so fragile ("Staubrose") that the slightest touch will destroy it.

Many of the poems in *Traumkraut* are basically love poems and present almost surrealistic adaptations of Goll's portrayal of Claire in the *Poèmes d'Amour*. [94] This fundamental theme of love can by no means be considered as essentially esoteric, but Goll's adaptation of it is frequently coloured by his interest in occultisms, and thus elements of esotericism occur throughout these poems. The threat of death hanging over Goll,

---

[94] YVAN GOLL and CLAIRE GOLL, *Poèmes d'Amour*, Paris 1925.

the transience of his existence, are in a sense neutralized by his love for Claire. She becomes his refuge, his sustenance and his oracle (cf. "Ich war der Fragende und du die Magierin ..."; [95] and "In deiner zauberischen Stirneninschrift ..." [96]). At one point, in *Tochter der Tiefe*, [97] she even represents for him a figure similar to that of Lilith. This poem provides a further example of Goll's esoteric application and adaptation of previously discussed material. As Richard Exner points out, this poem constitutes the counterpart of *Lilith (Les Cercles Magiques**) both in concept and technique. [98] Lilith doubtless provided the point of departure for *Tochter der Tiefe*, in which Claire has become an extension of Lilith and is consequently vested with mysterious attributes and powers in keeping with the occult associations enjoyed by the latter:

> Du Tochter der Tiefe, wie halt ich dich im Glashaus des Mondes
> Wie verbind ich dein magisches Aug mit den Wolken des schnellen Ver-
> Wie gewöhn ich dich an die Rundheit der Erde?   [gessens
>
> Vom Neumond Besessene
> Wie bändige ich dein Binnenmeer
> Das über die Ufer des Menschlichen wogt?
> Wie fang ich die Feuerfische in meinen ungläubigen Netzen?
>
> Und wenn der Vollmond dich schwängert mit Samen des Mohns
> Wie kühl ich das Fieber der schlaflosen Berge
> Wie blend ich ab die Todesstrahlen deiner Rubine?
>
> Ach nur im abnehmenden Mond
> Da magern die Flüsse ab und erlischt
> Das Ginster-Irrlicht deiner Augen
> Dein rauher Ruf wie der der heiligen Tiere
> Ergibt sich meinem jagenden Herzen

Throughout the entire poem, the so-called "realistic" background is established by allusions to the interdependence of moon and tides: "Tochter der Tiefe, Glashaus des Mondes, Vom Neumond Besessene, dein Binnenmeer, Ufer des Menschlichen, Vollmond, im abnehmenden Mond/Da magern die Flüsse ab". In the opening line of the poem Claire is addressed

---

[95] *Dicht.*, p. 469.
[96] Ibid., p. 467.
[97] Ibid., p. 474.
[98] This aspect is discussed by RICHARD EXNER in his article "Surrealist Elements in Yvan Goll's Franco-German Poetry", in *Symposium*, Vol. XI, no. 1, New York 1957, pp. 92—99.

as "Tochter der Tiefe" and is thus immediately associated with the idea of water. At the same time, however, she is associated with the realm of magic or the supernatural ("magisches Aug, über die Ufer des Menschlichen" etc.). As such, she is incompatible with earth ("Wie gewöhn ich dich an die Rundheit der Erde?") and consequently with man, with the poet himself. Her associations with death and with the waters of oblivion are hinted at throughout the poem: "schnelles Vergessen, Mohn, Todesstrahlen deiner Rubine, erlischt, Ginster-Irrlicht". As in the French poem *Lilith* [99] a chain of associations is released by the "Urbild", the "œil rond", so here "magisches Aug" performs a similar function. The affinities of the "Tochter der Tiefe" with Lilith are further enhanced by the allusions to eyes: "magisches Aug, Todesstrahlen deiner Rubine, das Ginster-Irrlicht deiner Augen", all of which link the eyes with the realm of the mysterious, magical and dangerous unknown. The connection between eyes, water and death is perhaps even more evident in the French poem: "Tes yeux innombrables emplis d'eau noire/Hublots à jamais fermés du chaland de Charon ... Tes yeux Lilith qui me perforent à mort tous les jours". [100] In *Tochter der Tiefe* the "oeil rond" of Lilith is indicated in a series of images connected with circularity: "Mond, Auge, Rundheit, Vollmond, Samen, Rubine".

The third and fourth verses are open to a double interpretation. Firstly, they could be interpreted sexually, in which case the eroticism connected with Lilith in various French poems is here transferred to the "daughter of the deep", and the sexual aspect further emphasized by "schwängert" and "Samen", by the sensual connotations of the colour red implied by "Mohn" and "Rubine", and the implications of desire indicated by "das Fieber der schlaflosen Berge". As the tide recedes under the influence of the waning moon, so the danger threatened by the "Tochter der Tiefe" diminishes with the fulfilment of her sexual desire ("Ach nur im abnehmenden Mond/Da magern die Flüsse ab und erlischt/Das Ginster-Irrlicht deiner Augen").

Secondly, however, the stanzas could be interpreted as an illustration of the cosmic significance of the "Tochter der Tiefe", indicated by her subjugation to the phases of the moon. Thus her supernatural powers are at their highest point when the moon is full, and only in periods of the

---

[99] *Les Cercles Magiques**, pp. 18—20, in particular.
[100] Ibid., p. 20.

waning moon does the diminution of these powers make her accessible to man ("Dein rauher Ruf . . . ergibt sich meinem jagenden Herzen").

The poem *Hiob* [101] presents material not found in any of Goll's French cycles, although there exist various versions in German, namely, *Hiob* (erste Fassung) [102] and *Hiobs Revolte,* [103] both of 1947—1948, and a further poem entitled *Hiob* included in a different cycle. [104] These versions, which are longer and less abstract than the poem in *Traumkraut,* serve to elucidate the subject-matter of the latter. They all present a combination of personal and biblical elements. Goll follows the biblical story of Job only in as far as the latter's love for God is put to the test, but the poet's personal interest in the theme makes itself felt in the great emphasis he places on Job's suffering and his subsequent acts of penitence. It becomes clear from the use of familiar imagery that the physical suffering portrayed in the opening section of the poem is both that of Job and that of Goll himself:

> Alte Löwen meines Bluts
> Rufen umsonst nach Gazellen
> Es morschen in meinem Kopf
> Wurmstichige Knochen
>
> Phosphoreszent
> Hängt mir im Brustkorb
> Das fremde Herz

One verse in particular from the Book of Job provides a point of comparison, namely, Job 7, v. 5: "My flesh is clothed with worms and clods of dust: my skin is broken and become loathsome".

It is clear from the other versions of *Hiob* that Job's act of penitence must firstly be accomplished by the surrendering of his body to the earth. In some cases he becomes like the earth itself and thus participates in the state of permanence symbolized by the stones ("Mir aber bleibt der Stein . . ." [105]). This idea is not present in *Traumkraut,* but partially explains Job's desire to become part of the earth, to accept death with joy:

> Verzehre mich, greiser Kalk
> Zerlauge mich, junges Salz
> Tod ist Freude

[101] *Dicht.,* pp. 452—453.
[102] Ibid., pp. 372—375.
[103] Ibid., pp. 376—379.
[104] Ibid., p. 588.
[105] Ibid., p. 375.

Once again the physical suffering involved in this act of sacrifice is indicated:

> In meinen Geschwüren
> Pfleg ich die Rosen
> Des Todesfrühlings

Similarly in *Hiobs Revolte,*

> Auf meine Hände tropft Öl der Sonne
> Und ätzt meine schwärenden Wunden
> Lässt sie purpurn verblühn ... [106]

and elsewhere:

> Meine Geschwüre
> Goldrote Rosen
> Wie sie gedeihen! [106]

These are of course allusions to Goll's wounds which, as elsewhere, are projected into the familiar image of the rose. The allusions are also biblical, cf. Job 2, v. 7: "So went Satan forth from the presence of the Lord, and smote Job with sore boils from the sole of his foot unto his crown". The final humility of the biblical Job in the face of overwhelming physical and mental suffering is indicated in the lines:

> Siebzig Scheunen verbrannt!
> Sieben Söhne verwest!
> Grösse der Armut!

Job has been faced with a series of misfortunes in order to test his love for God but, reduced almost to death ("mein Gerippe") by his suffering, he nevertheless accepts his fate and sees himself as the "letzter Ölbaum/ Aus Asiens Wüste". He is only just alive and has undergone tremendous suffering purely in order to prove God's might to Him:

> Wieso ich noch lebe?
> Unsicherer Gott
> Dich dir zu beweisen

In the final stanza Job sees himself as the last olive-tree, but a tree with golden oil flowing from its branches:

> Letzter Ölbaum, sagst du?
> Doch goldenes Öl
> Enttrieft meinen Zweigen
> Die segnen lernten

---

[106] Ibid., pp. 376 & 377.

Job has learnt to endure and accept his fate, and has been sustained after each misfortune by his ability to bless and proclaim God's greatness. He has become the tree, and as such, is an integral part of the cosmos. His integration with the forces of nature is apparent from his statement:

Mein Wurzelfuss ist im Marmor gerammt

In a different version of *Hiob*, this process of integration is expressed in more straightforward terms: "Mein Sein wird wieder Element". [107]

In *Traumkraut* Job is part of the earth and reflects the rest of creation:

Im Glashaus meiner Augen
Reift die tropische Sonne

The first version of *Hiob* provides an interesting variation on the above lines:

Und im Glashaus des Auges
— Brennend vom Namen Gottes —
Der 72 farbene Blick [108]

There Goll is making use of cabbalistic material, with his reference to the seventy-two names of God, which indicates more clearly that the spirit of God is manifest within Job himself. In *Traumkraut* this idea is finally taken a step further, and Job is portrayed as having become the symbols of his faith:

Höre Israel
Ich bin der Zehnbrotebaum
Ich bin das Feuerbuch
Mit den brennenden Buchstaben

Ich bin der dreiarmige Leuchter
Von wissenden Vögeln bewohnt
Mit dem siebenfarbenen Blick

The imagery of the penultimate verse is straightforward, but that of the final verse is somewhat obscure. It appears to refer to the Menorah, a seven-armed candelabrum wrought of fine gold, and one of the favourite symbols of Judaism (cf. Exodus 25, v. 31 f.). In this instance Goll visualizes it as inhabited by birds, frequently alluded to by the poet as symbols of spirituality, since they are in contact with the world above. Thus Job has

---

[107] Ibid., p. 588.
[108] Ibid., p. 375.

finally become a significant symbol of the faith for which he has suffered so much. This conclusion is to be understood in biblical terms, rather than in terms of Goll's personal attitude.

It is clear from the preceding discussion that *Traumkraut* represents a synthesis of Goll's entire work. Autobiographical and esoteric elements are fused in the final tragic vision of a man and a poet on the threshold of death. Bearing in mind that the cycle is dominated — and understandably so — by Goll's preoccupation with his fatal illness, the poems dealt with in this chapter may be grouped generally in the following manner:

(a) Poems dealing with the theme of Goll's illness presented in adapted alchemical images, and/or as hallucinatory visions of vegetative growth, the former representing an extension of ideas encountered in *Le Char Triomphal de l'Antimoine* and *Les Cercles Magiques**, the latter representing a new departure (except for sporadic references in *Masques de Cendre*). In this instance the nature poems of Goll's Expressionist years have turned into horrific visions of organic proliferation, in many ways resembling the surrealist visions of Salvador Dali and Max Ernst. [109]

(b) Poems concerned with the rose, which besides being a symbol for Goll's illness, is also an esoteric symbol taken from earlier cycles. Moreover, it is an example of Goll's "absolute object" and of his "objet végétatif en action", connected in its sphericity with the cyclic process of fate. It is also a symbol of the alchemical Work and therefore related to the Tarot emblems.

(c) Poems concerned with the transience of existence encountered (i) in the concretion of time as water and (ii) in the statues and "dream" constructions unsuccessfully erected as a foil against impermanence.

(d) The love poems of earlier years have become expressions of Goll's own emotions reflected in the person of Claire. These poems have not been considered, since their imagery is straightforward. They cannot be classified as esoteric, unlike those poems expressing Goll's vision of Claire as his last oracle, or as an extension of Lilith.

(e) Poetry centred on the figure of Job, incorporating both autobiographical and biblical elements. Job is a symbol of Goll's personal suffering, but also a general symbol of the suffering of the Jewish race. Although the

---

[109] See DALI's painting "Début automatique des portraits de Gala" of 1932; also ERNST's painting "Human Figure" of 1931.

poem *Hiob* introduces elements not encountered in Goll's French poems, it is nevertheless a variation on biblical themes encountered in his earlier German poetry.

(f) A final group of poems dealing with Goll's physical decay (eg. *Bluthund, Die Kastanienhand, Der heilige Leib, Feuerharfe,* etc.). These have been excluded from the discussion because of their similarity to poems already considered.

The contribution made by Goll in *Traumkraut* is accurately assessed by Marcel Brion: " 'Herbe du songe' ... me paraît être une sorte de conclusion, à la fois de sa vie et de son oeuvre, avec de nostalgiques regards, jetés en arrière sur des images anciennes, et une entrevision de plus en plus claire, de plus en plus sublimée par la résignation, de ce qui l'attendait. Moissonnant l'herbe du songe, sur le seuil de cette porte au-delà de laquelle on ne revient pas ... il a enfermé dans ce livre, le plus pur et le plus vibrant écho de son âme de poète". [110]

[110] From MARCEL BRION's article in *Quatre Études*, p. 22.

Chapter V

ESOTERICISM IN POETRY: GOLL AND YEATS.

The use of esotericism in poetry demands not only a reappraisal of traditional attitudes on the part of the critic, but a more complex method of investigation than is generally employed. With these factors in mind, this thesis has attempted to examine the iconography of Goll's later poetry. Goll's particular attitude towards esoteric material can best be illustrated by a comparison with that of one of the most significant modern poets who used similar material, W. B. Yeats. Yeats's subject-matter, embracing what he termed his "heterodox mysticism" (which included alchemy, cabbalism, neo-Platonism, Rosicrucianism etc.) may be viewed as one example of the new complexity in poetry, and this complexity is reflected in the critics' tendency to replace the terms "symbol" and "image" by the term "iconography" when dealing with his poetry. Thus Thomas Parkinson states, "I use the term 'iconography' which is becoming the normal term in the vocabulary of Yeats's critics, because it has a wider connotation than either symbol or image and can be used to include both." [1]

In some respects Yeats's preoccupation with esoteric subject-matter is similar to that of Goll, and the reason why Yeats — unlike Goll — is generally regarded as a major poet (almost, as most critics would have it, despite the obscurity of his poetry) would provide an interesting subject for discussion.

On one level, Yeats's greater popularity may well arise from his work's concordance with the traditionally accepted function of lyric poetry; in other words, it is emotive in a way that Goll's is not. On a deeper level, its appeal to the educated reader is perhaps greater than Goll's because the symbolism, although complex, is nevertheless fixed and constant: it is "traditional". Furthermore, Yeats's faithful adherence to the "traditional"

---

[1] THOMAS PARKINSON, W. B. Yeats, the Later Poetry, Berkeley and Los Angeles, 1964, pp. viii—ix.

significance of his symbols offers the interested reader the possibility of tracing them back to their archetypal origins. This does not mean that Yeats's poetry is merely a translation of various hermetic doctrines into poetic language, for even readily identifiable, i. e. traditional symbols take on a new identity in the work of individual poets. This change from the general to the individual aspect of each symbol within the context of each poet's work has been noted by Wilhelm Emrich in his *Protest und Verheissung*: " . . . eine solche rein historische Topoiforschung durchbricht und sprengt gerade den Kunstcharakter, die künstlerische Einheit des Werkes; sie schafft nämlich einen Verweisungszusammenhang, der ausserhalb des Kunstwerkes selbst liegt. Mögen in ein Kunstwerk noch so viele tradierte, konventionelle bildungsgeschichtlich bestimmte Elemente eingehen, das Werk selbst kann nicht in seiner künstlerischen Sinnstruktur von diesen tradierten Elementen aus restlos aufgeschlossen und 'erklärt' werden, da sie in jedem neuen Werk auch eine neue Funktion und Sinnstruktur erhalten". [2]

Even allowing for the correctness of this view, it is obvious that Yeats's work is more accessible to an explanation based on a knowledge of the traditional meaning of the symbols used than is the poetry of Goll. For in contrast to Yeats's symbolism, that of Goll tends to be rather more arbitrary and fluid, and an understanding of it in one context by no means guarantees an understanding of it in another. His symbolism is not characterized by the cohesive, systematic structure and the imaginative ordering of experience which is the hall-mark of Yeats's work. [3]

In both cases, however, the complexity of the symbols surely warrants an investigation of the intentional "meaning" of the poets. The critic F. A. C. Wilson feels justified in attempting an iconographical study of Yeats's poetry:

> It has been maintained that the poet in the act of creation intends no 'meaning' but simply to express sequences of images flowing up from his subconscious; and this seems to me an unsafe generalisation, bound up with the rather prevalent hope that all poets may be made to seem primitives. Some poets surely are more self-conscious than others, and Yeats, as his laborious revisions show, was one of the most highly conscious craftsmen in our language. At least by the time he began to revise, he knew very well what effects a poem needed to achieve, and the

---

[2] EMRICH, pp. 53—54.
[3] In connection with this aspect of Yeats's work see especially, W. B. YEATS, *A Vision*, Revised ed., London 1937.

finished poems are directed towards achieving them ... if we do not like to think of the poet manipulating his symbols to given ends, we are left to suppose that, towards the same ends, his symbols manipulated *him* ... if we think of Yeats as a highly sophisticated, highly conscious, symbolist, we shall be most likely to understand why he revised so methodically, and why he gave his finished works the inflections they have. [4]

Although Goll cannot be said to be a "highly sophisticated, highly conscious, symbolist" in the way that Yeats was, he was undeniably aiming self-consciously at particular effects, which in their turn necessitated a constant reworking and revision of his poetry. His countless manuscripts bear testimony to this.

The fundamental difference between the poetry of Yeats and the later poetry of Goll lies in the poets' differing views of the function of esotericism in poetry. For Yeats the function of the symbols drawn from esoteric doctrines was to move the reader or the spectator by tapping the latent World Memory present in man's subconscious. Goll's interest in such doctrines, however, was largely intellectual, and for him the function of their symbolism was descriptive rather than emotive. That is to say, these doctrines offered him new and striking imagery relevant both to his poetic and personal preoccupations.

Yeats's critics have always been faced with the difficulty of coming to terms with Yeats's apparent belief in much of his source material. For many critics the sources are not only absurd, but worse still, academically disreputable. Platonism, in their view, at least had the advantage of beginning with Plato, whereas Hermes Trismegistus was in all probability an academic fraud. The reaction of such critics is to wonder how Yeats could have believed in such dubious notions. Thus, for instance, W. H. Auden remarks of Yeats's religious ideas, "*How* embarrassing!" [5] In studies on Yeats, therefore, attention is largely focussed on the validity or otherwise of the occult sources.

In the case of Goll, a poet of a different generation, the problem of the validity of the sources is largely irrelevant. The assumption that these doctrines were largely a source of images, icons which could serve to illustrate his own ideas, is corroborated by Goll's statements concerning his poetry — e. g. "J'avoue que je ne me suis pas imposé des règles fixes

---

[4] F. A. C. WILSON, *Yeats's Iconography*, London 1960, pp. 14—15.
[5] W. H. AUDEN, an essay in *The Permanence of Yeats*, Selected Criticism, eds. J. Hall and M. Steinmann, New York 1950, p. 344.

en écrivant moi-même ... la géologie m'a soufflé de belles images ... J'ai utilisé la géologie pour créer de la poésie ... De même j'ai utilisé de nombreux préceptes de la Magie ... et j'en ai extrait l'essence poétique, sans m'arrêter véritablement aux lois et aux théories de pseudo-sciences: alchimie, occultisme, etc. J'ai trouvé des gisements de pierres précieuses poétiques dans les mots et dans les images des Kabbalistes ... La Kabbale contient des trésors de matière poétique". [6]

Attention is thus directed not so much at whether, for instance, the doctrine of the cabbala is plausible, but rather at the great fund of images provided by the principles of cabbalism (the lonely search for truth, the manipulation of matter, and so on). Goll's search for new images suitable to his own ideas did not necessarily involve respect for the traditional meaning or structure of such doctrines, although this does not mean that Goll entirely rejected these traditional meanings. Since for Goll it was not a question of believing in these esoteric doctrines, his liberty with regard to their poetic application was much greater than that of Yeats. Whereas Yeats, as a believer, in many cases accepted their basic tenets into his poetry without modification, Goll had more freedom to appropriate and adapt those aspects which appealed to him, and furthermore, to reject whatever did not suit his purpose.

THE APPEAL OF ESOTERIC DOCTRINES

Goll's explicit reasons for his use of esoteric material are to be found only in his discussions on the nature of poetry and of poetic creativity. Following this lead, Goll's few critics have been content with an interpretation of the alchemical images, etc., solely as illustrations of Goll's conception of poetry, totally ignoring the wider connotations of alchemical images and their possible attraction for Goll. Thus F. J. Carmody, talking of alchemy in Goll's work, thinks that the sonnets in Le Char Triomphal de l'Antimoine show "what can be done toward the transmutation of words", and that they are "model experiments devoted to the manipulation of techniques (sic). They reveal no hidden secrets and offer no initiation into the possible scientific applications of language". He sees Goll as "the antipodes of a man like Blake" since Blake's "prophetic intuition has

[6] Cf. CARMODY, p. 127.

no relationship to Goll's world of living men; his belief in souls is countered by Goll's scientific exercises on sybils, his system of key words, as a kind of magic of correspondences, his circle for example as the everlasting round of Nature, cannot be related to Goll's symbolism".[7] This "scientific" or materialistic view of alchemical imagery does not, however, prevent Carmody from talking of the circles in Goll's work as "manifestations of physical laws, including chance". [8] What is omitted here is an examination of the symbolic nature of alchemy, cabbalism, etc., and thus any consideration of the possible correspondences between the fundamental experiences symbolized in these doctrines and Goll's own experiences and beliefs, i.e. those concerned not only with poetry. This has led to an evaluation of Goll's use of such material solely in terms of the correspondence between the laboratory-technique which is thought to be common to both.

It is evident from the manifestoes that Goll shared many nineteenth and twentieth century poets' preoccupation with the nature of poetry and its function, and it is equally obvious that he uses images taken from alchemy and cabbalism because they provide suitable analogies with the task of creating poetry. Alchemy provides the idea of the manipulation of basic material in an attempt to effect a transmutation and extract its essence. Cabbalism furnishes Goll with the concept of the primacy of the Word and its power to reveal the mysteries of the universe. The Word and its significance for Goll have already been touched upon in this thesis. Indeed, the Word forms the foundation upon which Goll erects his theories of poetic technique. It represents for Goll not only the basic material from which he desires to extract the essence, but the end-product of this process, achieved only after a "long patient metamorphosis". [9] Viewed thus, the task of the poet is seen as comparable to that of the alchemist seeking to transmute base metals into gold and thus attain the Philosophers' Stone. One of the main tenets of alchemy is metamorphosis, and when Rimbaud talked of the "alchimie du verbe", [10] he too had in mind the power of words to effect such a transformation.

Mallarmé had a similar belief in the magical properties of words. In an article entitled "Magie" he discusses the Great Work of the alchemists

---

[7] Ibid., pp. 133 & 130.
[8] Ibid., p. 141.
[9] Cf. *Quatre Études*, p. 206; "une longue et patiente métamorphose".
[10] Arthur Rimbaud, *Oeuvres*, ed. Garnier Frères, Paris 1960, pp. 228 f. (Rimbaud)

and indicates the similarity between magic itself and magical transmutations effected by poetry: "Je dis qu'existe entre les vieux procédés et le sortilège, que restera la poésie, une parité secrète". [11] Mallarmé's process of "transmutation" resembled that of Goll in that it was a long and arduous effort to transform baser substances into purer forms, but Mallarmé's was also an attempt to create what was known as "pure poetry".

For Goll the appropriation of the alchemistic view of life into the realm of poetry presupposed the unification of substance and essence, the integration of subject and object propounded by him in *Le Réisme*. The poet's task is therefore not to discover in the physical world the reflection of the spiritual world, but rather to penetrate the veil disguising earthly existence and to discover the realm beyond reality.

This view of poetry as conjuring up the spiritual realm out of, and yet beyond reality, has several points of contact with the principles of cabbalism, since cabbalism, too, was a search for the ultimate spiritual entity behind creation. More specifically, however, the very nature of the cabbalist's task was closely related in Goll's mind to the business of writing poetry. Goll's *Ars Poetica 1945* [12] explains his conception of the poet's task:

> Au poète désemparé qui patauge dans la neige fondue des songes
> Au poète trop épris de lui qui manie le revolver et la fronde
> Rendons le Verbe pour le Verbe
> A la fois matière et pensée
> A la fois granit et temple
>
> Il n'y a plus de châteaux dans les déserts de la réalité
> Mais il y a des laboratoires dans les grottes de l'étoile
> Et par les rayons de radar nous revient la magie de l'écho
> Extase et science
> Vieux attributs de la Kabbala
>
> Dieu science nature: c'était la Trinité du 13e siècle
> Dieu qui n'exista pas encore mais qui résultera
> De l'alliance de l'atome et de Saturne
> Dans la grande explosion de l'âme universelle
>
> Voici poète le château où tu résideras
> Comme au coeur d'un diamant aux 72 facettes lumineuses
> Château magique Diamant dialectique
> Que Raziel édifia et tailla

---

[11] Stéphane Mallarmé, *Oeuvres Complètes*, Gallimard, Paris 1945, p. 400.
[12] See *Quatre Études*, p. 205.

To the poet who is floundering amid his visions, or is too subjective ("trop épris de lui"), or to the poet who attempts to create poetry by revolutionary methods ("manie le revolver et la fronde"), Goll offers the advice "Rendons le Verbe pour le Verbe", in which context the "Verbe" is reasonably interpreted by one critic as the "poetic use of words". [13] It is again evident that Goll regards the "Verbe" both as the basis and the end-product of the poem ("A la fois matière et pensée"), an idea already encountered in his work. Goll's statement that "Il n'y a plus de châteaux dans les déserts de la réalité", signifies that the "Château du Verbe" erected by Raziel no longer exists — possibly to be interpreted as a reflection of the intellectual climate in which Goll found himself in the early decades of the century, when there was a general search for new techniques and modes of expression, and a complete rejection of former values in literature and in the plastic arts. Thus the literary world is visualized as a sterile waste-land ("les déserts de la réalité") and the poet's only hope, Goll implies, rests with his own creative faculties ("dans les grottes de l'étoile"), which alone offer the possibility of artistic or poetic regeneration. Significantly, aid is at hand in the form of modern scientific techniques ("les rayons de radar"), those high-powered wireless impulses which will enable the poet to locate the "magie de l'écho", and regain the fusion of "extase et science" so necessary in the search for spiritual regeneration.

When new linguistic techniques have been invented and mastered, the poet will once again inhabit the "Castle of the Word". As the equivalent of the cabbalist's hermetic castle or tower, this castle reflects the purity and spirituality of God Himself, and is like a diamond with seventy-two facets, the all-powerful number of the names of God. Interestingly enough, in Rimbaud's poem "O saisons, ô châteaux .." [14] the castle appears as a symbol of the perfection of the poet's experience and of his attainment of the Philosophers' Stone. The seventy-two faceted diamond is of course a variation of the Philosophers' Stone, the spiritual gold; from the dialectic diamond of the Word, a further activity of the poet is developed — the cutting of the precious stone. The Word is fashioned like a diamond, and by constant re-working it is precisely formed. Only by his constant work with language will the poet achieve the clarity and purity of the "dialectic

[13] CARMODY, p. 122.
[14] RIMBAUD, pp. 179—180.

diamond". Goll might well state with Gottfried Benn: "Ich bin Prismatiker, ich arbeite mit Gläsern". [15]

The entire poetic process is one of fabrication, a phenomenon seen by Hugo Friedrich (in his *Moderne Lyrik*) as peculiarly symptomatic of modern poetry: "Zeitgenössische Lyriker sprechen gerne von ihrem 'Laboratorium', von 'Operieren', von der 'Algebra', vom 'Calcul' des Verses ... Bezeichnend, dass Valéry die Poesie, unter Verwertung der griechischen Urbedeutung des Wortes, gerne umschreibt mit 'fabrication' (Herstellen, Machen) und damit weniger an das Werk denkt als an den Akt des Herstellens, mittels dessen sich der Geist selber steigert und vollendet". [16]

The purposeful manipulation of words as the cornerstone of poetic technique was further elaborated by Goll in his manifesto, *Le Réisme*. Here too the end of poetry, the purpose of the manipulation, is more explicitly defined. That Goll recognised the similarity between the aims of poetry (as he viewed them) and those of cabbalism, can be seen from a further statement: "C'est uniquement par le Verbe et par la Connaissance que les Kabbalistes espèrent parvenir à leur but suprême; celui de découvrir Dieu, à travers le nom de Dieu. Celui qui nommera Dieu le connaîtra". [17] More in line with modern European thought, Goll expresses this in his manifesto: "Pour exprimer l'essence de la vie, poésie et art doivent émaner de la Chose en Soi, le Ding an sich, le Res ... S'il est exact que le monde est créé par une énergie se renouvelant sans cesse, que les peuples ont appelée Dieu, le poète, armé du Verbe, a la mission d'enfanter de sa propre substance, res, le verbe au rayonnement total. Le Réisme, en opposition à l'art arbitrairement abstrait, à la poésie jouant avec l'idée ou l'image de l'objet, serre le Res d'aussi près que le croyant l'essence de Dieu". [18]

However, the Word which is born of the object is not the Word as raw material. First the raw material must be purified (a process resembling alchemical distillation) until a transmutation is effected: " 'Au commencement était le Verbe?' Établissons plutôt: 'A la fin était le Verbe, après une longue et patiente métamorphose qui, dans le poète, transforme l'objet en Verbe' ". [19]

[15] Quotation from HUGO FRIEDRICH, *Die Struktur der modernen Lyrik*, Rowohlts deutsche Enzyklopädie, Erweiterte Neuausgabe, Hamburg 1967, p. 163.
[16] Ibid., p. 163.
[17] Quoted in CARMODY, p. 127.
[18] YVAN GOLL, *Le Réisme* in *Quatre Études* pp. 206—207.
[19] Ibid., p. 206.

Since Goll's reasons for his use of esoteric material are to be found only in statements such as those above, his critics, as noted, have tended to look no further than this, and to accept unquestioningly that his motives were governed by purely technical considerations. Indeed, a further technical reason may be added — that of the appeal for Goll of the highly visual aspect of the esoteric symbolism. To a poet interested in imagery as the basis of poetry — "Das Bild ist heute der Prüfstein guter Dichtung. Seit 20 Jahren triumphiert das Auge. Wir sind im Jahrhundert des Films. Mehr und mehr machen wir uns durch visuelle Zeichen verständlich" [20] — these doctrines would have recommended themselves by their systematic use of explanatory diagrams. Moreover, this visual aspect fulfilled a function denied to conceptual thought: "symbolical images belong to the very essence of the alchemist's mentality. What the written word could express only imperfectly, or not at all, the alchemist compressed into his images; and strange as these are, they often speak a more intelligible language than is found in his clumsy philosophical concepts". [21] This expressive potential of the symbols was, however, only one side of their appeal for Goll. They had, in addition, the value of still retaining a richness and complexity lacking in more "conventional" symbols. One of the central preoccupations of twentieth-century poets has been the search for new imagery; in this Goll was no exception.

With the above considerations, however, one enters the dangerous realm of speculation. In refusing to consider reasons other than those explicitly stated, Goll's previous critics have not laid themselves open to attack on the grounds of reading too much into his poetry. But such a narrow approach, although "safe" is nevertheless highly unsatisfactory. A consideration of the implicit attractions of these doctrines, even if it yields no positive results, is surely preferable to what constitutes either (a) an acceptance of Goll's attitude as being that of "art for art's sake" (which it is not), or (b) a total dismissal of any metaphysical preoccupations on the part of Goll (which is unjust).

When attempting to find reasons for Goll's choice of images and themes, the only possible method of investigation is the conjectural, governed at all times by conscientious checking with the facts. It is therefore proposed to examine some of Goll's fundamental preoccupations, and to indicate

[20] YVAN GOLL, *Manifest des Surrealismus* in *Dicht.*, p. 186; trans. Claire Goll.
[21] JUNG, p. vii.

how these preoccupations were themselves reason for the use of esotericism. From this investigation will perhaps emerge a better-proportioned portrait of Goll the poet, for whom man and man's condition were of fundamental importance. In the first place, this investigation entails a renewed consideration of alchemy and cabbalism as systems of symbolism, as the outward representation of certain cosmological and ontological experiences.

Because of its nature, an examination of the alchemists' cosmos and its symbolism presents great difficulties. The easiest way to begin is to state that the alchemists held the belief that the universe was originally a totality. Naturally, therefore, the central concept was that of macrocosm and microcosm. Not only man, but everything in the natural world was governed by the same divine laws or principles of creation. The symbol which the alchemists used to illustrate their concept of totality was the circle. Since they regarded the centre of the circle as the point of perfect harmony and equilibrium, their aim was correspondingly the recuperation of that "central point". "Le Grand Oeuvre, c'est la conquête du point central où réside la force équilibrante". [22] In contrast to this, man's chaotic condition was symbolized in terms of his situation on the circumference of the circle, which, like a rotating wheel, was in constant motion.

It is often thought that the belief that the universe is a totality arises out of a sense of loss; in other words, only when man feels that he is lost or that he is missing something, does the concept of totality impress itself upon his consciousness. Mircea Eliade has characterized this aspect of man's belief in essential unities: "Man often feels himself torn and separate. He often finds it difficult properly to explain to himself the nature of this separation, for sometimes he feels himself to be cut off from 'something' powerful, 'something' utterly *other* than himself, and at times from an indefinable, timeless 'state', of which he has no precise memory ... a primordial state ...". This realisation of loss and the subsequent wish to recover the lost unity, Eliade continues, "has caused man to think of the opposites as complementary aspects of a single reality. It is as a result of such existential experiences, caused by the need to transcend the opposites, that the first theological and philosophical speculations were elaborated". [23] While it is here not the intention to identify

---

[22] Quoted from E. LÉVI in CARROUGES, p. 32.
[23] MIRCEA ELIADE, *The Two and the One*, trans. J. M. Cohen, London 1965, p. 122.

such doctrines as alchemy with mysticism or philosophy, it is evident that alchemy shares the same preoccupations to a large degree. In alchemy, man's conception of the underlying unity finds expression in an elaborate theory of polarity. The dissatisfaction with the human awareness of totality, and the sense of loss, are illustrated by a complex wealth of symbols, the most significant of which is the hermaphrodite or androgyne.

Here the paradoxical nature of alchemical symbolism makes itself clear. Not only does the androgyne illustrate the concept of polarity, it symbolizes the overcoming of this polarity and the perfect fusion of opposites in the Whole. Furthermore, the object of the alchemists' quest, the Philosophers' Stone, the essence of the universe, is often illustrated as an androgynous figure. Thus the search itself is also a way of overcoming duality.

Viewed in this light, the alchemists' search is intimately related to the fundamental concept of unity. The escape from duality, from disharmony, which is attempted in the Great Work, is universally thought to be possible only by a process of destruction. Destruction, however, is not to be viewed negatively, for it means a return to the matrix, the primordial level at which totality and unity exist. From this "death", life on a higher essential plane is born. Once again the concept of totality is apparent and is exemplified in the most common symbol for the nature of the Great Work, the Ouroboros: Jung has characterized this perfect symbol: "Time and again the alchemists reiterate that the opus proceeds from the one and leads back to the one, that it is a sort of circle like a dragon biting its own tail. For this reason the opus was often called 'circulare' or else 'rota.' Mercurius stands at the beginning and end of the work; as dragon he devours himself and as dragon he dies, to rise again as the lapis ... He is the hermaphrodite that was in the beginning, that splits into the traditional brother-sister duality and is reunited in the coniunctio, to appear once again at the end in the radiant form of the lumen novum—the stone". [24] With Jung it is possible to interpret this in the sense of a harmonious and unified beginning, the primordial state, followed by the sense of loss expressed in duality and the subsequent achievement of balance at the end of the search. The "religious" connotations of this scheme are at once apparent.

[24] JUNG, pp. 281 f.; cf. also note 12(b), p. 281.

The spiritual significance of alchemy has become apparent mainly as a result of Jung's writings. Starting from the celebrated quotation in the *Rosarium*, "Aurum nostrum non est aurum vulgi", Jung considers the significance of the alchemists' search for those with "subtler minds", for those not obsessed by the greed for gold. For these at least, the search was a symbol of the soul's inner journey, an outward sign of inner transformation. In this case the Work and its symbolism stand for man's search for salvation, but in a sense far removed from the Christian. As Jung remarks, with Christianity "man attributes to himself the need of redemption and leaves the work of redemption, the actual opus, to the autonomous divine figure"; in alchemy, however, "man takes upon himself the duty of carrying out the redeeming opus". [25] This particular aspect of alchemy he finds is supported by the actual methods of work. The accent on individual effort is attested not only by the vast number of widely differing accounts of the Work, but also by numerous exhortations to alchemists not to collaborate. "Alchemists are, in fact, decided solitaries ... Each worked in the laboratory for himself and suffered from loneliness". [26]

Cabbalism, although it shares alchemy's aim of illumination, is essentially a commentary on the sacred books of the Jews. The expositions of the teachers are in a sense the "deciphering" of the old texts, and they are intended to provide not only a moral guide, but an explanation of the principles upon which God created the universe. The cabbalists' cosmos bears a close resemblance to that of the alchemists, especially in its fundamental concepts. The most notable similarities are the belief in the microcosm and the macrocosm, the belief in the system of polarity, and in the role of the individual. However, it must be borne in mind that, in contrast to alchemy, cabbalism is essentially a body of religious beliefs. The idea of a mighty and vengeful God, and of the submission of man to His "deciphered" Will, play a role unknown in alchemy, where the sense of equality between man and the Creator is particularly evident. Indeed, it might be said that the alchemists' concern with the liberation of spirit from matter constitutes man's attempt to redeem God, rather than vice-versa. [27]

The Jewish origin of cabbalism is evident from the outset. The fundamental concept of unity expressed in the belief in the congruence of micro-

---

[25] Ibid., pp. 293—294.
[26] Ibid., 301.
[27] Ibid., pp. 294 f.

cosm and macrocosm is tempered by the insistence that in both God and His Creation there is an evil side. On the other hand, there is the belief that the natural world and man are necessary for the activation of the spiritual world. This is expressed as follows in the *Zohar*: "All that is on earth is formed in the likeness of the world above ... By setting in motion the objects here below, the forces on high, which govern, are made to act. Thus every object in this world below is the image of a heavenly force which is set in motion by moving the object here below". [28]

As in alchemy, the awareness of this unity finds expression in the complex symbol of the hermaphrodite. The original paradise was a fusion of opposites, and according to the *Zohar*, Adam was born both as male and female. There followed the loss of this unity and the subsequent desire to regain it. Thus the hermaphrodite is not only a symbol of perfection, but also the symbol of the principle of creation. God created the world from a union with the Matrona, His female side, and what was created originally was the hermaphrodite.

The cabbalist's search for his twin-soul, his female counterpart, has affinities with the alchemist's search for the Philosophers' Stone. Indeed, the Stone was often referred to as the Heavenly Virgin, the female half of the perfect androgyne. Although it is evident that this aspect of alchemy has sexual implications, these are by no means as strong as in cabbalism. Here it must be remembered that according to the Jewish commentators, sexual union was not only a necessary, but a holy duty. It served primarily to propagate images of God, but it also enabled God to unite with His other self, and thus create. According to the cabbalists, sexual union was a question of balance. It had to be performed within a certain mental framework in which man was conscious of the symbolic nature of the act. Imbalance, the prime evil, was often symbolized by the figure of Lilith, the night-demon who inflamed passion and destroyed man's reason. Thus, although woman is necessary, she should never be allowed to dominate man. The symbol of the hermaphrodite is one of perfect balance, not only of the two desires, but of the two natures (male and female).

Recapitulating, it is evident that the cabbala and alchemy, in their belief in the essential unity of creation and in their manner of expressing their awareness of this unity, have certain affinities. Both are concerned with man's experience of the world. This view of alchemical symbolism is, of

---

[28] Quotation in SAURAT, p. 87.

course, open to debate. It is perfectly possible to consider alchemy as a "science" alone. However, here the difficulty arises of understanding why, in a "science" like this, the alchemists resorted to mystical and fantastic symbols to describe their work. It may be suggested that, since the alchemist was ignorant of the real nature of matter, and since he did not possess our present terminology for describing physical change, he was forced to record his observations in the only language possible — analogy. However, this view does not explain the type of image used in alchemy. Jung, as noted previously, has attempted a different estimation. In his view, these symbols refer as much to the alchemists' own experiences, as to the explanation of the Work itself. He states: "The alchemist does not practise his art because he believes on theoretical grounds in correspondence; the point is that he has a theory of correspondence because he experiences the presence of the idea, or of spirit, in physical matter". [29] It is this aspect of alchemical symbolism which is under discussion here and, it might be added, which has been fruitfully studied by literary historians. Ronald Gray, starting from Jung's theories, remarks on the fascination of alchemy for imaginative writers: "The reason for this fascination is to be found in the alchemist's preoccupation with processes deep down in the mind. At some time in the past, one feels, these must have been examined and described in some detail by men who felt that the knowledge thus acquired could be handed on only in a symbolical form". [30]

It is now possible to turn from this short survey of esoteric doctrines and their symbols, to a consideration of their attraction for Goll. Here it is hoped to show that many of Goll's own experiences, specifically those connected with the problem of man's consciousness of himself and his surroundings, led to an intellectual interest in the alchemists' and cabbalists' attempts to order experience and to make sense of the universe. The following discussion is not an attempt to state unequivocally why Goll used this material, but rather to offer possible suggestions.

Apparent from the beginning of his poetic career — and determined no doubt by his Expressionist connections — was Goll's concern with "humanistic" themes, his concern with man's nature and man's attitude in the face of an often bewildering universe. Helmut Uhlig has character-

[29] JUNG, p. 234.
[30] GRAY, p. 254.

ized this: "Vom Menschen her erweiterte Goll seine Thematik. Der Zeit-
bezug wurde zum Ewigkeitsbezug, der Wortbezug zum Weltbezug, Zeit-
bewegte Ausdruckskunst füllte sich mit antiker Symbolik, mythischen
Bildern, magischer Beschwörung, und kosmischen Träumen". [31]

Goll's concern with man's place in the universe is evident even in his
poetry which is not centred on occult doctrines, as for example in the
Élégie d'Ihpétonga. [32] There man's need to belong, to be situated in a
system of reciprocal relationships, is apparent. The totemic society symbolized by the Indian civilisation is in one respect a civilisation at a primordial
level. Here man has no need of thought, since the concept of totality is
silently assumed and felt. Consequently there is no system of duality, not
even between man and creator. The equality is felt to be a mutual necessity. In contrast to this Goll places "modern" civilisation, which he considers to be barren and sterile in the sense of lacking communication with
God and with creation as a whole. The technical advances have split
civilisation from creation, establishing an advanced but clinical system in
which man has no place. The sense of loss is for Goll a sense of being
totally divorced from the centre. The idea of lost unity finds expression in
his poetry as the incompatibility between man's spiritual nature and his
physical drives, in the polarities of time and eternity, etc.

Goll's statement that he used esoteric material "sans (s)'arrêter véritablement aux lois et aux théories de pseudo-sciences: alchimie, occultisme,
etc." [33] is of course quite literally true. He did not adopt, for example, the
theory of alchemy. What he did adopt, subject to modifications, were the
images in which were expressed the alchemists' experiences of the world
and of man's situation. The image of the androgyne in alchemical literature
is scarcely exhausted by an interpretation of it as a description of a certain
phase of the alchemists' work. Goll was undoubtedly aware of, and
fascinated by the wider implications of the image. Here was expressed an
experience of harmony and one of duality, of perfection and impotence,
and it is in this framework that Goll has employed it in his poetry.

The alchemists' symbolic cosmos therefore probably appealed to Goll
because it was an attempt to order and interpret experience. This is not
to say that Goll's own poetic cosmos was a translation of the alchemical.

---

[31] HELMUT UHLIG, "Yvan Golls Werk bis 1930", essay in *Dicht.*, p. 805.
[32] For information on the edition in which this appears, see Chapter III, note 69.
[33] Quotation in CARMODY, p. 127.

This thesis has been in part an attempt to show how Goll in fact adapted the alchemical images to his own ends. Goll's poetry cannot be easily or totally explained by references to such doctrines, for although the "traditional" meaning will be present, the image itself will consist of elements both "traditional" and personal.

The majority of poetry studied in this thesis was written after Goll had learned that he was suffering from leukemia. Although it is impossible to ascertain fully the effects on Goll of this knowledge, his poetry gives clear indication of the reorientation of his thought following this discovery. To the average person, thoughts of death, or of what might be termed the "direction of life" seldom occur, not only because they are traditionally unpleasant, but also because the fundamental attitude seems to be that man is on earth to live. The effect of realising that one is suffering from a fatal illness therefore focusses attention on problems normally left "in abeyance". What is brought home by such a revelation is that one is here to die; the direction of life is made brutally plain. The way in which Goll attempted to lessen the emotional implications of his illness was to engage his mind in purely intellectual speculations on the problems of existence. Moreover, the imminence of death forced Goll to consider the meaning of his own life. It is here perhaps that the source of Goll's intellectual interest in occult doctrines is to be found. Not only did the images provide him with a means of externalising his own experience and thus of objectifying it, they also attracted him because they were attempts to interpret the facts of experience. The alchemists' search, for example, was as much the search for the meaning of life, for inner comprehension, as it was the quest for gold. The meaning the alchemists gave to the chemical changes they observed in the laboratory was an existential rather than a scientific meaning. Moreover, in equating death with spiritual regeneration, they gave direction to their lives.

It is at this point, however, that Goll and the alchemists part company. Goll could not possibly share the alchemists' sense of optimism. For the latter there existed no clear distinction between mind and matter, and like most "mystics" the elements given in their own experience were projected as an eternal order of being or reality. The macrocosm-microcosm was firstly felt and only secondly justified. Moreover, the Creator was still a credible entity and the soul a unified substance. Thus the experience of unity was supported by a knowledge or a "tradition" of unity. For Goll, of course, this framework did not exist. Mind and matter were clearly distinguished and matter had been "atomised" and explained. In Goll's estimation, the possibility of a life-after-death had been shattered by modern scientific discoveries, and the remnants of his faith were symbolized by "God's corpse". [34] Atomic fission had given the lie both to the idea of spirit in matter and to that of man as the possessor of an immortal soul.

In one sense therefore, modern scientific research forced Goll to view such doctrines as alchemy purely as efforts of comprehension on the part of man. Goll saw what the alchemists, according to Jung, [35] never clearly realized, namely, that it was their own thoughts and feelings which were projected into the material. Thus alchemy was a work of the mind, an interpretation of the universe. Goll's attitude, therefore, could never have been one of belief. He was interested in esoteric doctrines because they were examples of man's effort to make sense of the world. They were positive efforts in so far as they attempted salvation of one sort or another. The alchemical notion of "insight" or "recuperation of the centre" through renunciation must be viewed in this light, as the earlier discussion of alchemical symbolism has shown.

In this context it could be said that Goll's main preoccupation was very similar to that of the alchemists. The idea of time as the most pressing problem for man is central to both. The wheel of time, on whose outer rim man is bound, is constrasted in alchemy and in Goll's poetry with a restful centre. Both have made use of a common symbol for time, gained from the facts immediately given in experience, e.g. the seasons, organic life etc. In alchemy, however, this inexorable process is interpreted positively, since time provides the raw material on which the alchemist works. As he works he approaches the centre of the circle, until at last he is united with the centre, a timeless region from which man can view the world with tranquillity and understanding. In this way, positive direction is given to the alchemists' life. In its conception this view is similar to the eschatological systems of the various religious orders.

Although Goll has adopted similar imagery to illustrate his own conception of time and of man's suffering caused by time, there are crucial differences between his view of the centre and that of the alchemists. Goll's illness gave him visible evidence of the cyclic process of time, since

[34] *Fruit from Saturn*, p. 19.
[35] JUNG, pp. 234 f.

he was being consumed in a literal sense. The imminence of death focussed his attention on the purpose of life, but he was unable to find a purpose as the alchemists had done. Although Goll, like the alchemists, sought to get outside time, and although he was ready to attempt the jump through the circle, he believed that there was nothing at the centre but a void, "le zéro central". [36] He was aware that the "ideal centre" was posited by man in an attempt to give meaning to life. In fact, all that was real was life and death, a universal process whose single historical manifestations could be highly individual, but whose principle was eternal and never varying.

Goll's later poetry must be viewed in the light of these ideas. Although it is full of speculation on the meaning of life, on the nature and structure of the universe, it does not offer a statement of metaphysical beliefs. Goll is always aware that esoteric doctrines are of value only to the mind seeking that type of reassurance. Hence the significance of his rhetorical question in Les Cercles Magiques*: "Rouleriez-vous sans ma pensée centrale?" [37] For the man of ruthless vision, existence is governed solely by the cycle of life and death. Having realized the futility of metaphysical speculations, man is compelled to come to terms with the conditions of his existence, and seek in this life any consolations he may find. In this context, therefore, Goll's remark that "Das Leben ist wahrer als der Gedanke" [38] may be regarded as a fitting summary of his attitude towards both esoteric doctrines and the poetry which makes use of them.

---

[36] Les Cercles Magiques*, p. 42.
[37] Ibid., p. 61.
[38] From the Manifest des Surrealismus in Dicht., p. 187.

CONCLUSION

The implications of the use of esotericism in poetry are widespread. Bearing in mind the distrust with which obscure poetry is frequently viewed, it is not surprising that Yvan Goll's work is known only to a limited circle of admirers. Furthermore, his later poetry requires a certain amount of specialized knowledge, of which the majority of readers, either through lack of time or inclination, are unwilling to avail themselves.

To those who do avail themselves of that knowledge, however, Goll's poetry offers a restricted but original fund of imagery for interpretation. In this study, an examination of six cycles of poems revealed that Goll's imagery, although repetitive, nevertheless admits of a wide variety of interpretations. Indeed, only its multivalency prevents the charge of monotony from being levelled too vehemently against it.

It was thought that Goll's general attitude towards his material could best be assessed by a comparative method of enquiry, since attempts to estimate it in isolation had proved unrewarding. By comparing Goll's view of the function of esotericism with that of Yeats, it was possible to conclude that Goll's attitude was largely intellectual, and that since he did not believe in esoteric doctrines, his freedom to modify their concepts and symbols was correspondingly greater than that of Yeats.

A subsequent investigation of Goll's statements of theory indicated that his use of esoteric material was governed, consciously at least, by purely poetic considerations. However, since explicit reasons by no means preclude the possibility of implicit reasons — a factor overlooked by Goll critics — the enquiry was extended to include a consideration of further reasons for Goll's interest in, and use of esoteric doctrines. It was suggested that Goll was attracted to certain fundamental concepts of alchemy and cabbalism, firstly because of their correspondence with his own beliefs and secondly, because of these doctrines' symbolic and highly visual method of illustrating such concepts. The symbols were appropriated by Goll because, being relatively unusual, they still retained a richness and complexity lacking in more "conventional" symbols. In addition, it was suggested that the use of such symbols enabled Goll to objectify in some measure his personal emotions and thus alleviate the suffering caused by his awareness of approaching death. Finally, the view was advanced that the imminence of death, bringing home to Goll the futility of all metaphysical speculation, led to his rejection of esoteric doctrines in favour of a more practical approach to the problems of existence.

BIBLIOGRAPHY

PRIMARY MATERIAL

Works by YVAN GOLL *used in this thesis*

Collected Works:

Yvan Goll, *Quatre Études*, Poètes d'Aujourd'hui series, Paris 1956. (*Quatre Études*)

Yvan Goll, *Dichtungen*, ed. by Claire Goll, Darmstadt 1960. (*Dicht.*)

Novels:

Die Eurokokke, first published Berlin 1927; quotations for this thesis from *Dicht.*, pp. 201—252.

Gala, Paris 1930.

Lucifer Vieillissant, Paris 1934. (*Lucifer Vieillisant*)

Poetry:

*Le Nouvel Orphée**, Paris 1923.

Poèmes d'Amour, with Cl. Goll, Paris 1925.

*Die Siebente Rose**, Paris 1928; quotations from *Dicht.*, p. 319.

Métro de la Mort, Brussels 1936. (*Métro*)

Fruit from Saturn, New York 1946. (*Fruit from Saturn*)

Le Mythe de la Roche Percée, first published New York 1947; quotations for this thesis from the bilingual edition, *Der Mythus vom Durchbrochenen Felsen*, Darmstadt 1956. (*Der Mythus*)

Le Char Triomphal de l'Antimoine, first published Paris 1949; quotations for this thesis from *Dicht.*, pp. 405—435.

Élégie d'Ihpétonga suivie de Masques de Cendre, Paris 1949. (*Masques de Cendre*)

Les Géorgiques Parisiennes, first published Paris 1951; quotations for this thesis from the bilingual edition *Die Pariser Georgika*, Darmstadt 1956. *(Die Pariser Georgika)*

Traumkraut, first published Wiesbaden 1951; quotations for this thesis from *Dicht.*, pp. 437—477.

Les Cercles Magiques*, Paris 1951. *(Les Cercles Magiques***)*

Abendgesang* / *Neila*, first published Heidelberg 1954; quotations for this thesis from *Dicht.*, pp. 554—588.

Multiple Femme*, Paris 1956. *(Multiple Femme***)*

Jean sans Terre, first published 1936—1939; edition used for this thesis was *Jean sans Terre*, critical ed., by F. J. Carmody, Univ. of California Publications in Modern Philology, Vol. 65, Berkeley and Los Angeles 1962. *(Jean sans Terre)*

Manifestos:

Das Wort an sich, in *Die neue Rundschau*, 1921, Bd. 2, pp. 1082—1085.

Manifeste du Surréalisme, originally published in Goll's magazine *Surréalisme*, no. 1, 1924. Quoted from Claire Goll's translation in *Dicht.*, pp. 186—187.

Ars Poetica 1945, quoted from *Quatre Études*, p. 205.

Le Réisme, published in *Combat*, Feb. 1950. Quoted from *Quatre Études*, pp. 206—207.

Journal:

Hémisphères, ed. Yvan Goll, 6 issues, New York 1943—1946.

Letters:

Yvan Goll, Claire Goll; Briefe, Mainz 1966. *(Briefe)*

Primary sources relating to alchemy, cabbalism, etc.

Das Buch Bahir, trans. G. G. Scholem, Leipzig 1923. *(Bahir)*

The Holy Bible.

HERACLITUS, *The Cosmic Fragments*, ed. G. S. Kirk. Cambridge 1954.

MAIMONIDES, *Guide for the Perplexed*, trans. M. Friedländer, London 1919.

PARACELSUS, *The Hermetic and Alchemical Writings of Paracelsus the Great*, ed. A. E. Waite, 2 vols., 2nd ed., New York 1967.

The Upanisads, ed. F. Max Müller, 2 vols., New York 1962.

VALENTINE, BASIL, *The Triumphal Chariot of Antimony*, trans., A. E. Waite, London 1893.

The Zohar, Basic Readings from the Kabbalah, ed. 3, G. G. Scholem, New York 1966. (*Zohar: Basic Readings*)

Works by poets other than Goll, statements by artists, anthologies, etc.

BRETON, ANDRÉ, *Les Manifests du Surréalisme*, Paris 1947.

ELIOT, T. S., *The Waste Land*, Faber ed., London 1965.

von GOETHE, J. W., "Die Entstehung der Erde" in J. W. von G., Gedenkausgabe der Werke, Briefe und Gespräche, ed. E. Beutler, Zürich 1952, Bd. 17.

The Harrap Anthology of German Poetry, eds. A. Closs and T. P. Williams, 2nd ed., London 1961.

HESS, W, ed., *Dokumente zum Verständnis der modernen Malerei*, Hamburg 1956.

KANDINSKY, WASSILY, *Concerning the Spiritual in Art*, Vol. 5 in the series "Documents of Modern Art", Geo. Wittenborn, New York 1966.

MALLARMÉ, STÉPHANE, "Magie" in S. M., *Oeuvres Complètes*, Gallimard, Paris 1945.

—, *Un coup de dés n'abolira jamais le hasard*, Paris 1914.

Modern German Poetry, 1910—1960, eds. C. Middleton and M. Hamburger, London 1963.

DE NERVAL, GÉRARD, *Oeuvres*, Bibliothèque de la Pléiade, Paris 1956, vol. I. (NERVAL: I)

RILKE, RAINER MARIA, *Das Stunden=Buch*, Insel Verlag, Frankfurt am Main 1962.

RIMBAUD, ARTHUR, *Oeuvres*, ed. Garnier Frères, Paris 1960. (RIMBAUD)

YEATS, W. B., *A Vision*, revised ed., London 1937.

—, *Essays*, London 1924.

—, *Collected Poems of W. B. Yeats*, London 1950.

SECONDARY LITERATURE

Critical works and articles on Yvan Goll

BRION, MARCEL, "Yvan Goll" in *Quatre Études*, pp. 11—22.

CARMODY, F. J., *The Poetry of Yvan Goll*, Paris 1956. (CARMODY)

—, "L'Oeuvre d'Yvan Goll" in *Quatre Études*, pp. 23—61.

—, Critical Analysis in *Jean sans Terre*, pp. 123—188.

EXNER, RICHARD, "Yvan Golls Werk seit 1930", in *Dicht.*, pp. 814—828.

—, "Yvan Goll: zu seiner deutschen Lyrik" in *German Life and Letters*, VIII, 1955, pp. 252—263.

—, "Surrealist Elements in Yvan Goll's Franco-German Poetry" in *Symposium*, Vol. XI, no. 1, Syracuse University, New York 1957, pp. 92—99.

—, "La Poésie allemande d'Yvan Goll" in *Quatre Études*, pp. 63—79.

GROS, LÉON-GABRIEL, "Yvan Goll, ou la Parole est à la Matière" in *Cahiers du Sud*, 36, no. 298, 1949, pp. 478—485.

—, "Yvan Goll, l'alchimiste fraternel", *Cahiers du Sud*, 43, no. 337, 1956, pp. 427—431.

HAUCK, W., *Die Bildwelt bei Iwan Goll*, Diss. Munich 1965.

HESELHAUS, C., "Yvan Golls Symbol-Verschränkung" in C. H., *Deutsche Lyrik der Moderne; von Nietzsche bis Yvan Goll*, Düsseldorf 1961, pp. 420—430.

KUSHNER, EVA, "Yvan Goll, deux langues, une âme" in *Proceedings of the IVth Congress of the International Comparative Literature Association*, The Hague 1966, ed. F. Jost, vol. 1, pp. 576—587.

MÜLLER, JOACHIM, "Yvan Goll im deutschen Expressionismus" in *Forschungen und Fortschritte*, 35—36, Akademie-Verlag, Berlin 1961—1962, p. 300.

NOULET, ÉMILIE, "Le Char Triomphal d'Yvan Goll' in *Synthèses*, Brussels, Feb. 1951.

RAYMOND, LOUIS-MARCEL, *Yvan Goll: Choix de poèmes, précédé par la vie et l'œuvre*, Quebec 1948.

ROMAINS, JULES, "Yvan Goll" in *Quatre Études*, pp. 7—10.

SCHAEFER, DIETRICH, *Die frühe Lyrik Iwan Golls*, Diss. Kiel 1965.

UHLIG, HELMUT, "Yvan Golls Werk bis 1930" in *Dicht.*, pp. 803—813.

—, "Yvan Goll" in *Expressionismus: Gestalten einer literarischen Bewegung*, eds. H. Friedmann and Otto Mann, Heidelberg 1956, pp. 192—203.

General Secondary Literature: works relating to esoteric doctrines, etc.

ABELSON, J., *Jewish Mysticism,* London 1913 (ABELSON)

ABBOT, A. E., *The Secrets of Numbers,* London 1963.

BACHOFEN, J. J., *Der Mythus von Orient und Occident,* Munich 1926.

BAYLEY, H., *The Lost Language of Symbolism,* 2 vols., London 1912.

BERTHELOT, MARCELLIN, *Les Origines de l'Alchimie,* Paris 1885. (BERTHELOT)

CASE, P. F., *The Tarot: a Key to the Wisdom of the Ages,* New York 1947.

CHABOSEAU, JEAN, *Le Tarot — essai d'interprétation selon les principes de l'hermétisme,* Paris 1946. (CHABOSEAU)

CHRISTENSEN, A., *L'Iran sous les Sassanides,* Copenhagen 1944.

ELIADE, MIRCEA, *Méphistophélès et l'Androgyne,* Paris 1962.

—, *Forgerons et Alchimistes,* Paris 1956. (ELIADE: *Forgerons*)

—, *Images and Symbols,* trans. P. Mairet, London 1961.

—, *The Two and the One,* trans. J. M. Cohen, London 1965.

FRANCK, A. D., *La Kabbale ou la Philosophie Religieuse des Hébreux,* Paris 1892, 3rd ed. (FRANCK)

GRAY, RONALD, *Goethe the Alchemist,* Cambridge 1952. (GRAY)

HOLMYARD, E. T., *Alchemy,* Penguin Books, London 1957.

—, *Makers of Chemistry,* Oxford 1931.

The Jewish Encyclopedia, New York and London 1901, 12. vols.

JUNG, C. G., *Psychology and Alchemy,* Vol. 12 of the Collected Works, trans. R. F. C. Hull, London 1953. (JUNG)

KUNZ, G. F., *The Magic of Jewels and Charms,* Philadelphia 1915. (KUNZ)

LÉVI, ÉLIPHAS, *The History of Magic,* trans. A. E. Waite, London 1963, reprint of 1st ed. of 1913.

OESTERLEY, W. and ROBINSON, T., *Hebrew Religion — its Origin and Development,* London 1933, 3rd ed. (OESTERLEY)

PAGEL, W., *Paracelsus; an introduction to philosophical medicine in the era of the Renaissance,* Basel 1958.

REINACH, SALOMON, *Cultes, Mythes et Religions,* Vol. 3., Paris 1908; 5 vols.

DE ROUGEMONT, DENIS, "Présentation du Tarot" in *Hémisphères*, New York 1945 (ROUGEMONT)

SAURAT, DENIS, *Literature and Occult Tradition*, trans. D. Bolton, London, 1930 (SAURAT)

SCHOLEM, GERSHOLM G., *Alchemie und Kabbala*, Berlin 1927 (SCHOLEM)

SELIGMANN, KURT, *The Mirror of Magic*, New York 1948. (SELIGMANN)

TAYLOR, F. SHERWOOD, *The Alchemists*, London 1951; reissue of 1949.

THOMPSON, C. J. S., *The Mystic Mandrake*, London 1934.

TRACHTENBERG, JOSHUA, *Jewish and Superstition*, New York 1939. (TRACHTENBERG)

TYLOR, E., *Primitive Culture*, Vol. 1, London 1920, 6th ed.; 2 vols.

Vallentine's Jewish Encyclopedia, London 1938.

WAITE, A. E., *The Occult Sciences*, London 1891. (WAITE: O. S.)
—, *The Doctrine and Literature of the Kabalah*, London 1902. (WAITE: D. L. K.)

Works relating to symbolism, imagery, etc., in poetry

ADAMS, HAZARD, *The Contexts of Poetry*, London 1965.

BACHELARD, GASTON, *L'Eau et les Rêves*, Paris 1964.
—, *La Poétique de l'Espace*, Presses Universitaires de France, Paris 1961.
—, *La Terre et les rêveries de la volonté*, Paris 1948.

BALAKIAN, A., *The Literary Origins of Surrealism*, New York 1947.

BODKIN, MAUD, *Archetypal Patterns in Poetry*, O. U. P., 1934.
—, *Studies of Type-Imagery in Poetry, Religion and Philosophy*, O. U. P., 1951.

BOWRA, C. M., *The Heritage of Symbolism*, London 1947.

CARROUGES, MICHEL, *André Breton et les données fondamentales du surréalisme*, Paris 1950 (CARROUGES)

ELLMANN, RICHARD, *The Identity of Yeats*, London 1954.

EMRICH, WILHELM, "Das Problem der Symbolinterpretation im Hinblick auf Goethes *Wanderjahre*" in W. E., *Protest und Verheissung, Studien zur klassischen und modernen Dichtung*, 2nd ed., Frankfurt am Main and Bonn 1963. (EMRICH)

FRIEDRICH, HUGO, *Die Struktur der modernen Lyrik*, Rowohlts deutsche Enzyklopädie, erweiterte Neuausgabe, Reinbek bei Hamburg 1967.

HENN, T. R., *The Lonely Tower*, London 1950.

KERMODE, FRANK, *Romantic Image*, London 1957.

LANGER, SUSANNE K., *Philosophy in a New Key; a study in the symbolism of reason, rite and art*, Cambridge Mass. 1942.

LEAVIS, F. R., *New Bearings in English Poetry*, London 1932.

MAY, ROLLO, ed., *Symbolism in Religion and Literature*, 4th ed., New York 1966.

MELCHIORI, G., *The Whole Mystery of Art*, London 1960.

MOORE, VIRGINIA, *The Unicorn: W. B. Yeats's Search for Reality*, New York 1954.

NADEAU, MAURICE, *Histoire du Surréalisme*, 2nd ed., Paris 1946.

PARKINSON, T., *W. B. Yeats, the Later Poetry*, Berkeley and Los Angeles 1964.

PONGS, HERMANN, *Das Bild in der Dichtung*, Bd. 2, *Voruntersuchungen zum Symbol*, Marburg 1939.

STARKIE, ENID, *Arthur Rimbaud*, London 1947.

STAIGER, EMIL, *Grundbegriffe der Poetik*, Zürich 1946.

TATE, ALLEN, ed., *The Language of Poetry*, Princeton 1942.

WELLEK, R. and WARREN, A., *Theory of Literature*, Peregrine Books, London 1966; reprint.

WHEELWRIGHT, P., *The Burning Fountain, A study in the language of symbolism*, Bloomington Indiana 1954.
—, *Poetry, Myth and Reality* in Tate, ed., *The Language of Poetry*.

WILSON, EDMUND, *Axel's Castle*, New York 1931.

WILSON, F. A. C., *Yeats's Iconography*, London 1960.

Miscellaneous

CASSIRER, ERNST, *An Essay on Man*, Yale Univ. Press, 12th printing, 1964.

Chambers's Twentieth Century Dictionary, ed. W. Geddie, 4th ed., London 1960.

Encyclopedia Britannica, New ed. 1964, 24 vols.

JUNG, C. G., *Modern Man in Search of a Soul*, trans. W. S. Dell and Cary F. Baynes, London 1933.

van MELSEN, A. G., *From Atomos to Atom*, trans. Henry J. Koren, New York 1952.

MEYERHOFF, H., *Time in Literature*, Berkeley and Los Angeles 1960.

PANOFSKY, ERWIN, *Studies in Iconology*, 2nd ed., New York 1962.

INDEX

Index to works by Yvan Goll mentioned in this book

N. B. *For the purposes of this index only* the cycles of poems are given in capital letters. Abbreviations in brackets after individual poems indicate the cycle in which the poem is to be found.

Key to Abbreviations:

(A) ABENDGESANG/NEILA.
(CM) LES CERCLES MAGIQUES.
(CT) LE CHAR TRIOMPHAL DE L'ANTIMOINE.
(E) ÉLÉGIE D'IHPÉTONGA.
(F) FRUIT FROM SATURN.
(G) LES GÉORGIQUES PARISIENNES.
(JsT) JEAN SANS TERRE.
(L) LACKAWANNA ELEGY. (Unpublished).

(MC) MASQUES DE CENDRE.
(MM) MÉTRO DE LA MORT.
(MF) MULTIPLE FEMME.
(MRP) LE MYTHE DE LA ROCHE PERCÉE.
(NO) LE NOUVEL ORPHÉE.
(SR) DIE SIEBENTE ROSE.
(T) TRAUMKRAUT.

For details of the editions used see Bibliography.

196